SALMAN RUSHDIE AND THE THIRD WORLD

Salman Rushdie and the Third World

Myths of the Nation

TIMOTHY BRENNAN

Assistant Professor of English and Comparative Literature
Purdue University, West Lafayette, Indiana

St. Martin Press   New York

First published in the United States of America in 1989

Printed in Great Britain

ISBN 0–312–03308–7

Library of Congress Cataloging-in-Publication Data
Brennan, Timothy, 1953–
   Salman Rushdie and the Third World : myths of the nation / Timothy
Brennan.
      p.   cm.
   Bibliography: p.
   Includes index.
   ISBN 0–312–03308–7: $19.95
      1. Rushdie, Salman—Criticism and interpretation. 2. Developing
countries in literature.   3. Nationalism in Literature.   I. Title.
PR9499.3.R8Z59   1989
823—dc20   89–32822
                                                          CIP

For Za

Contents

Preface

Few of us who wrote about Rushdie's work in the mid-1980s predicted that his name would one day be on the steely lips of James Baker and Geoffrey Howe. Why would statesmen and philistines like them care about an intellectual like him? It was impossible also to foresee that Saudi Arabia would declare a *jihad* against literary modernism or that the British government would sever ties with Iran over a dispute about one of Rushdie's books. True, his reputation had been extensive already in 1981, with his books receiving prominent reviews in the best places. But there seemed very little to make him the lead story of the Six O'Clock News, as actually happened through the month of February 1989. So it is odd to see one's subject suddenly thrown into prominence after years of slogging through background sources, and then to realise that while the interest is now greater than ever, it is an interest already framed by the warping lens of the newsmakers.

Rushdie is obviously much more than *The Satanic Verses*, and I want to leave my comments on that novel to the closing chapter, which I originally wrote several months before the book-burnings in Bradford, the violent and fatal demonstrations in Pakistan and India, and the Imam's infamous bounty. Since Rushdie had for more than a decade been writing about the way books make real the chimeras of politics, he deserves to have written the very novel that would be that argument's case in point. For now, it is important to remember that he was already an author of international dimensions before *The Satanic Verses* was ever written.

I began this book by looking at a group of literary celebrities from the Third World who all seemed to share something. Originally, this included Mario Vargas Llosa, Derek Walcott, Salman Rushdie, Isabel Allende, Gabriel García Márquez, Bharati Mukherjee, and a few others – a group I would come to call 'Third-World cosmopolitans'. If there was any one of them who seemed to capture what they collectively represented, it was Rushdie.

By 'cosmopolitans' I meant those writers Western reviewers seemed to be choosing as the interpreters and authentic public voices of the Third World – writers who, in a sense, allowed a flirtation with change that ensured continuity, a familiar strangeness, a trauma by inches. Alien to the public that read them because they were black, spoke with accents or were not citizens, they were also like that public in tastes, training, repertoire of anecdotes, current habitation. Just as the 'discovery' of Third-World writers by mass-market publishing in recent decades has had very little to do with some sudden outbreak of artistic inspiration in the Third World (it was instead the result of the colonies shooting their way into our consciousness, of Palestinians rising up on the West Bank, South African miners striking against apartheid, and Nicaraguan loyalists battling the contras in a US-sponsored war), so there seemed to be a basically political motive in this rise of the Third-World 'celebrity'.

From the late 1940s, with a Europe weakened by war and decolonisation in full swing, the empowering image for many Third-World intellectuals had been, in fact, the 'nation', a term that referred to something long since out of favour in metropolitan circles for often very suspect reasons. There was, I came to feel, an everything-and-nothing quality to the concept that helped explain its questionable uses at just this moment, and that helped explain the mediation provided by cosmopolitan writers in taming and reinterpreting it for a public tired of talking about Empire.

As a discursive practice or imaginative projection, rather than as a static *thing*, the 'nation' seems to have eluded much of the heavy commentary on these issues in recent decades. As a kind of mental armature, it has separated the cosmopolitans from the frontline fighters, or (what is really the basis for the same thing) sympathetic First-World audiences from their Third-World author-entertainers. These conflicts amounted to an untold story, and a crucial element in what the Kenyan novelist and playwright, Ngugi wa Thiong'o, once called 'decolonizing the mind'. Of all the internal debates raised by the rise of the African, Caribbean and 'new' Latin-American novel in the postwar period – what language, what genre, which people, what state – there was another, which I took as my starting point: who was doing the writing? The writers I had grouped together in various ways all supplied sceptical readings of national liberation struggles from the comfort of the observation tower, making that scepticism authoritative. And yet, while mastering the language of the metropolitan tribe, they did not assimilate in any one-way process. Being invited to speak as 'Third-World' intellectuals, they took the opportunity to chastise too, and with the aid of their global awareness stated in clear accents that the world is one (not three) and that it is unequal.

Why, then, Rushdie? For one thing, India – the largest and most important single colony in a long history of European greed – had not been given its due in the West's renewed interest in 'Third-World' literature. Beyond that, no one in the remarkable history of Indo-English prose – a tradition that includes Nehru, Gandhi, Mulk Raj Anand, Kamala Markandaya and Raja Rao – had anything like Rushdie's success in popularising the subcontinent for a Western public, although many of them tried. And there was also the point that Rushdie's story had as much to do with England as with India and Pakistan. Thus, the 'in-betweenness' of the cosmopolitan – a creature, as Rushdie puts it, of 'translation' – was not only essentially there in his person but theoretically accounted for on every page of his work.

Empire, after all, is not something done to others: it is a relationship, and it is in Rushdie's Britain that the effects of that relationship on the First World are most striking. The imperial leaders of the West for over two centuries have been English-speaking countries whose sense of literary tradition has evaded the global realities Rushdie forces into view. About twenty years ago, in a very widely read essay, Perry Anderson wrote of England's 'nullity of native intellectual traditions', its 'secular, insular stultification', the 'absent center' of English intellectual life. Later, Anderson, E. P. Thompson, Raymond Williams and others provided an alternative view of British culture based on lost English popular traditions. While they and others were looking for the lost literary socialist tradition in twentieth-century Britain, settling for unconvincing middle-class renegades mouthing second-hand ideas in strained voices – people like Christopher Caudwell, W. H. Auden, Ralph Fox and Jessica Mitford – a definitive English literary socialism was there all along, not only in the Chartist and Protestant sectarian legacies unearthed by Thompson, Christopher Hill and others, but writers of ultimately much greater world importance, so pervasive that they were invisible – namely, the leaders of the anti-colonial independence movements.

In England, decolonisation had always had a favoured place, for here was the greatest concentration of Third-World intellectuals anywhere in the world. Here C. L. R. James, George Padmore, W. E. B. Du Bois, Kwame Nkrumah and others plotted African independence; Sylvester Williams founded the Pan-African Congress; at an earlier date, the ex-slaves Olaudah Equiano and Ottabah Cugoano worked for Abolition; and Asian reformers like Rajah Rammohun Roy, Shyamaji Krishnavarma and Cornelia Sorabji earned their degrees and wrote their tracts, leading to the founding, on British soil, of the Indian Congress itself. The fresh intellectual traditions Anderson longed for were forming in the minds of the artists walking the streets of Ladbroke Grove, Southall and Brixton. Sweeping to England after 1948 in the wake of a massive labour recruitment by British industry came Punjabi Sikhs, Gujarati Hindus, Pakistani refugees, West Indians, Africans and others, constituting a unique expression of the national question as a community within 'established' Britain. Critics like Stuart Hall, Paul Gilroy and others have pointed out these omissions and argued (correctly) that these communities are, if not the starting point, at least the most graphic occasion and opportunity for any theory of British alternative culture.

The spirit of Anderson's critique of the 'absent centre' can be applied to the postwar British novel as a whole. Despite the brilliant work of William Golding, John Berger, Pat Barker, Alan Sillitoe, Doris Lessing and others, English novelists have managed to ignore what is really the essence of England right now – its being a colonising spirit with little to colonise but itself, an industrial nation assuming the colours of its underdeveloped former dominions, a racial and ethnic cross-section of the former Empire that is officially white – like Orwell's 'English People'. If the old-school view has been attacked by the revisionist critics, who popularised the contributions of the working classes to a common British identity, and if novelists like Sillitoe, Barker and Williams give these traditions a vivid fictional place, none of them saw their way to challenging the mental (and, of course, actual) exclusion of the black communities. In fact, they have had very little to say about Empire at all – England's central reality for the last century and a half.

There are three other, and related, ways of describing this absence and, consequently, the present focus on Rushdie. The postwar English novel has produced almost nothing to suggest the seething energies of a specifically *post-imperial* England, much less the 'other regions' with their hybrid characters, flooding in and out of contact with the centre. In terms of form, there has been no appropriately sprawling 'Rabelaisian' novel that could affirm, even if it did not partake in, the counter-culture, and so raise up the English literary imagination from the kind of constipated cleverness one finds in, say, Martin Amis.

Secondly, no real 'cross-over' existed to document for the public at large the experience of the black communities – their importance, their endurance and their divided sense of place. In journals like *Race Today Review, Artrage, Black Music, Mukti* and others, Britain's 'immigrant' artists have been celebrating the South Asian and West Indian forms and themes that are, as over a century of domestically produced work shows, British too. But pushed to the side by the establishment, they flourished within a walled garden known only to the few who visited. Attempts to publicise this work (like Kwesi Owusu's recent *The Struggle for Black Arts in Britain*) have already mapped out some of the post-colonial territory in the British imagination. What they don't do, however, is show how 'black' writing flowers (or wilts) in the heavy atmosphere of 'high' English culture with all its imperial afterglow. One of the strengths of Rushdie's work is that it brings these two together. As an upper-middle-class British Asian, Rushdie is not exactly representative of the black communities of Brixton and Southall, but he has still helped bring them into public view in that ambiguous way characteristic of cosmopolitan literary production, particularly in his most recent novel, *The Satanic Verses*.

Finally, despite the fact that English is a world language, and despite the vast patchwork of former English colonies in Asia, Africa and the Caribbean, there has been no stylistic equivalent in English to 'magical realism' – the style popularly associated with García Márquez and Alejo Carpentier, but actually a more general and inevitable outcome of mature post-colonial fiction. On all three counts, Rushdie's novels from 1980 to the present have filled the gap.

In another sense, though, Rushdie is an important case. His novels – unthinkable before the age of Khomeini, Ortega and Mandela – have made modernist style a vehicle for news extravaganza, street barricade and coup. He has done what few writers in any tradition have done: recorded the *totality* of neo-colonialism as a world system, with its absurd combinations of satellite broadcasts and famine, popular uprisings and populist rant, forced migrations and tourism. One might say he brings British literature up to date. For he occupies more than any

other contemporary writer a special place at the crossroads of
the English literary scene: the old 'Novel of Empire', which he
transforms and which (as he points out) still exists as television
special, film and travelogue for the popular magazines; 'Commonwealth' literature — that fictional entity created by scholars in
the provinces and depending on the imaginary coherence of tea
time, the Cambridge Overseas Examinations and the pound note;
and the tradition of anti-colonial polemic, richly represented in
England for over two centuries by foreign intellectuals more or
less permanently based there.

Writing a long and involved book about an author only
halfway through his career has a certain polemical quality.
It challenges the way charges of 'trendiness' make the present
safe from judgement until it is too late to do anything about it. In
writing this, I had in mind certain models – particularly a work
of recent sociology, *Policing the Crisis*, collaboratively written by
Stuart Hall, Chas Critcher and others, which dedicates over four
hundred pages to recording and explaining the British media's
reaction to a single mugging incident. In this book I cover much
more ground more quickly, but I am just as interested in the
history and traditions buried in 'current events'.

In the late twentieth century, the universal reach of culture has
created a previously unimaginable sense of immediacy – a culture
of 'instant' heroes, 'instant' tragedy, 'instant' record-breaking,
'instant' classics. This is, first of all, a function of the technologies
that allow for 'instant' communication. But there is more to it than
that; as always, the specific social causes lie behind a façade of
impersonal technology. That is, 'immediacy' also points to the
changeable policies of the institutions in control of the dispersal
of images. At no time more than the present has it been possible
to see the triumph of elusive 'forms', and imaginative constructs
of colour, sound and words on celluloid, plastic and paper – a
triumph over the concrete acts these 'forms' resemble but cannot
replace. Studying contemporary fiction in its neocolonial contexts, and giving it all the scholarly armature of 'serious' study, is
a comment on the responsible practice of interpreting the images
of *today* – how to place them, how to give them perspective, how
to discuss the way they reflect a submerged history while turning
it into a contemporary, instantaneous shadow.

Let me make one final note on the term 'Third World' that
fills these pages. I share the view of Aijaz Ahmad and others who

argue that it has no theoretical content whatsoever. As he says, 'we do not live in three worlds but in one', mutually affected and affecting. Obviously, the term has less to do with what a country essentially *is* – what colour its natives' skin, what longitude or latitude it occupies, what size its GNP – than what it *does*. From the first meetings of Nehru and Nasser in the 1950s until the era of the 'Non-aligned Nations', 'Third World' has meant simply those countries decolonising from what E. P. Thompson once called 'Natopolis'. It has a political not a sociological meaning. To use the title *Salman Rushdie and the Third World* for this book is then not only to place Rushdie in it, but to suggest his antagonistic relationship to it.

Beginning as a dissertation in the often hostile environment of a graduate programme addicted to the 'great books', this study needed (and received) the contributions of many. My thanks, then, go to the following people: first, to Robin Lewis, whose attentions and advice carried me at every stage, and whose knowledge of South Asia made me fall in love with another culture; to Edward Said, who as project director, critic and friend, made it all seem worthwhile, and whose example for almost a decade (as well as that of Jean Franco) have made me see what writing about culture could be; to Bruce King, who at an early stage gave me important contacts and valuable sources, and convinced me to persevere; to fellow-graduate students at Columbia, who have since gone on to better things – especially Rob Nixon, Eric Lot, Ann McClintock, Wendy Graham, Rita Constabile and others whose standards were always so high; to Columbia's Union Square Reading Group, which taught me more than I have learned before or since; to the education I received one night in the Village talking to Bruce Robbins and Aijaz Ahmad; to the other generous readers, who took the time to read the manuscript in its entirety – Ainsley Embry, Jean Franco and especially Edward Mendelson, whose encouragements and proddings for years have kept me honest; to Frederic Jameson for inviting me to read sections at a Third-World culture conference at Duke University, letting me benefit from the comments and friendships made there – especially those of Barbara Harlow with her ongoing assistance and Mary Layoun in more indirect ways; to Lisa Bloom, Jim Clifford and Donna Haraway at the University of California at Santa Cruz's Group for the Critical Study of Colonial Discourse, who at an early stage invited me to read sections dealing with the problem of 'postmodernism' in the Third World; to the anonymous reader at Macmillan who put into clear words what I had been thinking, and contributed so much to the book's final structure; to Homi Bhabha, who helped me with suggestions for Chapter 1; to the graduate students at Duke University working on the journal *Polygraph*; to S. Soucek and Massoud Pourfarrokh at the New York Public Library's Oriental Division for a wealth of specialist detail and nuance; to Srimati Basu, Nalini Iyer, Karen Dwyer, Nada Elia, Sujala Singh, Syed Hassan, Suranjan Ganguly, Kanishka Chowdhury and other graduate students at Purdue University whose insights found their way into the finished product; to A. Sivanandan for wanting to 'announce' the book in the pages of *Race and Class*; to Routledge for allowing me to reprint parts of Chapter 1, to *Cultural Critique* for permitting me to use parts of Chapter 2, and to *The Journal of Indian Writing in English* for allowing me to use parts of Chapter 4; and finally to Elizabeth Ruf. Her solidarity, intelligence, integrity and love counted most, and she gave them over many years.

T. B.

1

National Fictions, Fictional Nations

Yo quiero mar y montaña
hablando mi propia lengua
Y a nadie pedir permiso
pa' construir las patria nueva
                    Cueca de la Confederación Unida de los
                    Trabajadores (Chile)

From the shimmering swirl of waters where many, many thoughts ago the slave-ship first saw the square tower of Jamestown, have flowed down to our day three streams of thinking. One swollen from the larger world here and overseas, saying, the multiplying of human wants in culture-lands calls for the worldwide cooperation of men in satisfying them. Hence arises a new human unity, pulling the ends of the earth nearer, and all men, black, yellow, and white.

                    W. E. B. du Bois

In Europe and the United States, for the most part, the triumphant literary depiction of nationalism is Romantic. It is part of an earlier period when the forming of nations was a European concern, and before the experience of colonialism, world war and Fascism had soured people on what Edward Said has called nationalism's 'heroic narratives'. But the nationalist mood is, aesthetically as socially, more strongly felt in the emergent societies of the world today, including those ethnic or regional breakaways on the European continent itself (Basque, Irish, Albanian, and so on).

The terms of the phrase 'Myths of the Nation' are confusing because of their multiple meanings, which multiply still further when considered together. Myth as distortion or lie; myth as

1

mythology, legend or oral tradition; myth as literature *per se*; myth
as shibboleth – all of these meanings are present at different times
in the writing of modern political culture. If one inclusive sense
can be given, it is Malinowski's, where

> myth acts as a charter for the present-day social order; it
> supplies a retrospective pattern of moral values, sociological
> order, and magical belief, the function of which is to strengthen
> tradition and endow it with a greater value and prestige by
> tracing it back to a higher, better, more supernatural reality
> of initial events.[1]

As for the 'nation', it is both historically determined and
general. As a term, it refers both to the modern nation-state
and to something more ancient and nebulous – the *natio* – a
local community, domicile, family, condition of belonging. The
distinction is often obscured by nationalists who seek to place
their own country in an 'immemorial past' where its arbitrariness
cannot be questioned. The British cultural historian, Raymond
Williams, has commented on the need to distinguish between
these senses:

> 'Nation' as a term is radically connected with 'native'. We
> are *born* into relationships which are typically settled in a
> place. This form of primary and 'placeable' bonding is of
> quite fundamental human and natural importance. Yet the
> jump from that to anything like the modern nation-state is
> entirely artificial.[2]

This impatience with the apparently divisive and warlike character of nationalism is very common among European critics in
the postwar period, who work either within a Marxist tradition
of 'internationalism' or a liberal tradition of sensible 'patriotism',
perhaps most of all in Britain and the United States where even
Left social critics (until very recently) have ritually denounced
'imperialism' while withdrawing their support from the oppositional forces that imperial legacy has inevitably unleashed.

For we often hear that nationalism is dead. Despite ex-
plosive independence struggles in the Philippines, El Salvador,
Sri Lanka and dozens of other places, many seem convinced of
this. Some point to global developments that cast nationalism in

the refractory light of heroic memory, where the invariable goals
of creating an administrative economy, a repressive apparatus
capable of waging war and a sense of belonging that glosses over
class conflicts, are being passed over in favour of local affiliations
and loyalties on the one hand, and on the other, are being rendered
obsolete by the international realities of multinational corporations
and the telecommunications industry.

With a puzzling insensitivity to the emotional response to
Empire, Tom Nairn in *The Break-up of Britain* was an early and
eloquent proponent of these views. He stresses what he calls
nationalism's 'Janus-face' – the fact that it is both communal
and authoritarian, friendly and bellicose, all at the same time. He
insists that the most vital thing about it is its chameleon content:
its ability to rouse unlike peoples in dramatically unlike conditions
in an impassioned chorus of voluntary co-operation and sacrifice,
in which nationalism's unviability is less an impersonal fact
of neo-colonialism-plus-technics, than a political wish, since
it is a reactionary throwback that impedes the solidarities of
'internationalism'.

On the other hand, operating as an analyst of what he
calls 'cultural industries', the Belgian communications scholar
Armand Mattelart revises this view somewhat by supporting
the one-world thesis without ignoring the value of the independence movements (he has, for example, actively endorsed
the national-political strategies of Allende's Chile and post-1979
Nicaragua). He recognises that the Utopian projections of Marx
and Engels in the *Manifesto*, which looked forward to the withering
away of 'national one-sidedness and narrowmindedness' and
the transformation of 'national and local literatures' into a
single 'world literature' has grown, dialectically, into its opposite:

> The idea that it is necessary to smash the nation-state, the
> last obstacle to the new phase of the world-wide expan-
> sion of transnational capital, and transform it into a simple
> management state in an 'interdependent' world, is becoming
> naturalized . . . [T]he transnationalization process creates an
> appeal for increasingly similar, ecumenical and universal
> values, or, to use the terms of Brzezinski, 'a new planetary
> consciousness', a new 'harmony', a 'new world unity' and a
> new 'consensus'.[3]

The value of these words is that Mattelart clearly states here an important ideological tendency that is often only implicit – namely, that on one level the 'nationalism-is-passé' school of thought is unable to account for the positive necessity of defensive nationalism, and in that way unwittingly joins forces with imperial ideologues like former United States National Security Adviser Zbigniew Brzezinski, a member of the notoriously interventionist Trilateral Commission.

In another and more sensitive version, it was Paul Ricoeur who already in 1965 spoke of the tension – characteristic of the postwar period – between 'universal civilisation' and 'national culture', between the involuntary mutual awareness and dependency of every people and region made possible (and inevitable) by 'civilisation', as well as the dogged persistence of defensive movements helping subject peoples carve out a bit of space on the earth's economic turf:

> Everywhere throughout the world one finds the same bad movies, the same slot machines, the same plastic or aluminum atrocities, the same twisting of language by propaganda, etc. . . . [O]n the one hand, [the developing world] has to root itself in the soil of its past, forge a national spirit, and unfurl this spiritual and cultural revindication before the colonialist's personality. But in order to take part in modern civilisation, it is necessary at the same time to take part in scientific, technical, and political rationality, something which very often requires the pure and simple abandonment of a whole cultural past.[4]

In fact, it is especially in Third-World fiction after the Second World War that the uses of 'nation' and 'nationalism' are most pronounced. The 'nation' is precisely what Foucault has called a 'discursive formation' – not simply an allegory or imaginative vision, but a gestative political structure which the Third-World artist is very often either consciously building or suffering the lack of. The literary act, and the institutions of literary production, are not only a part of the nation-forming process, but are its realisation: that nations are mental projections, or polyglot renderings of a single epic creation that is *in* the world rather than about it; that nation-forming is of the present, rather than the past; that nations are made out of citizens' councils and peasant armies physically enacting the words of the national literatures that once imagined them. 'Uses' here should be understood both in a personal, craftmanslike sense, or as the *institutional* uses of fiction in nationalist movements themselves. At the present time, it is often impossible to separate these senses. It does not refer only to the more or less unsurprising idea that nations are mythical – that, as Hugh Seton-Watson wrote in his massive study of nations and states as recently as 1976 – there is no 'scientific' means of establishing what all nations have in common.[5] The phrase is also not limited to the consequences of this artificiality in contemporary political life – namely, the way that various governments invent traditions to give permanence and solidity to a transient political form.

While the study of nationalism has been a minor industry in the disciplines of sociology and history since the Second World War, the premise here is that *cultural* study, and specifically the study of imaginative literature, is in many ways a profitable one for understanding the nation-centredness of the post-colonial world, although without reducing all literary form there to what Frederic Jameson has called 'national allegory'.[6] It is rare in English studies to see 'nation-ness' talked about as an imaginative vision – as a topic worthy of full fictional realisation.[7] It should be said that this neglect is not true of other literatures with a close and obvious relationship to the subject – for example, those of Latin America and (because of the experience of the war) Germany and Italy. Even in the under-represented branch of Third-World English studies, one is likely to find discussions of race and colonialism, but not the 'nation' as such, and if so, certainly not as discursive formation.

In fact, only a handful of critics (often themselves tied to the colonised by background or birth) have seen English fiction about the colonies as growing out of a comprehensive imperial system.[8] The universality of this system, and its effects on the imaginative life, are much clearer – even inescapable – in the literature not of the 'colonies' but of the 'colonised'. The recent interest in Third-World literature reflected in special issues of mainstream journals and new publishers' series, as well as new university programmes, is itself a mark of the recognition that imperialism is, culturally speaking, a two-way flow.

For, in the period following the Second World War, English society was transformed by its earlier imperial encounters. The wave of postwar immigration to the imperial 'centres' – including in England the influx of large numbers of non-white peoples from Africa, South Asia and the Caribbean, and in North America from Asia and Latin America – amounted to what Gordon Lewis ironically calls 'a colonisalism in reverse': a process that has led unavoidably to a new national culture – a new sense of what it means to be 'English'. To a lesser extent, the same has happened in France.[9]

The wave of successful anti-colonial struggles from China to Zimbabwe has contributed to the forced attention now being given to the point of view of the colonised – and yet, inasmuch as it deals with the British or American Empires, it is a point of view that must increasingly be seen as a part of English-speaking culture. It is a situation, as the Indo-English author Salman Rushdie points out, in which English, 'no longer an English language, now grows from many roots; and those whom it once colonised are carving out large territories within the language for themselves'.[10] The polycultural forces in domestic English life have given weight to the claims of the novelists and essayists abroad who speak more articulately and in larger crowds, about neo-colonialism. And in turn, such voices from afar give attention to the volatile cultural pluralism at home. The Chilean expatriate, Ariel Dorfman, has written that 'there may be no better way for a country to know itself than to examine the myths and popular symbols that it exports to its economic and military dominions'.[11] And this would be even truer when the myths come home. One of the most durable myths has certainly been the 'nation'.

Again, not the colonies, but the colonised. 'Novels of empire' in their classic modernist versions (*Heart of Darkness*, *Passage to India*, *The Plumed Serpent* and others) could see and even diagnose imperialism, but not finally stand against it, however much they involved themselves passionately, unevenly and contradictorily in some of its inhuman realities. For English criticism – even among politically minded critics after the war – has refused to place the fact of domination in a comprehensive approach to its literary material, and that becomes impossible when facing the work of those who have not merely visited but lived it.

THE COLLUSION OF CULTURE

The rising number of studies of nationalism in the past three decades reflects its lingering, almost atmospheric, insistence in our thinking.[12] In cultural studies, the 'nation' has often lurked behind terms like 'tradition', 'folklore' or 'community', obscuring their origins in what Benedict Anderson has called 'the most universally legitimate value in the political life of our time'.[13]

The rise of the modern nation-state in Europe in the late eighteenth and early nineteenth centuries is inseparable from the forms and subjects of imaginative literature. On the one hand, the political tasks of modern nationalism directed the course of literature, leading through the romantic concepts of 'folk character' and 'national language' to the (largely illusory) divisions of literature into distinct 'national literatures'.[14] On the other hand, and just as fundamentally, literature participated in the formation of nations through the creation of 'national print media' – the newspaper and the novel.[15] Flourishing alongside what Francesco de Sanctis has called 'the cult of nationality in the European nineteenth century', it was especially the novel as a composite but clearly bordered work of art that was crucial in defining the nation as an 'imagined community.'[16]

In tracing these ties between literature and nation, some have evoked the fictive quality of the political concept itself. For example, José Carlos Mariátegui, a publicist and organiser of Peru's Quechua-speaking population in the 1920s, outlined the claims of fiction on national thought, saying simply that 'The nation . . . is an abstraction, an allegory, a myth that does not correspond to a reality that can be scientifically defined'.[17] Race, geography, tradition, language, size or some combination of these seem finally insufficient for determining national essence, and yet people die for nations, fight wars for them and write fictions on their behalf. Others have emphasised the *creative* side of nation-forming, suggesting the cultural importance of what has often been treated as a dry, rancorous political fact: 'Nationalism is not the awakening of nations of self-consciousness; it *invents* nations where they do not exist.'[18]

The idea that nations are invented has become more widely recognised in the rush of research following the war.[19] To take only one recent example, the idea circuitously finds its way into Eric Hobsbawm's and Terence Ranger's recent work on 'the invention of tradition', which is really a synonym in their writing for the animus of any successful nation-state:

> It is clear that plenty of political institutions, ideological movements and groups – not least in nationalism – were so unprecedented that even historic continuity had to be invented, for example by creating an ancient past beyond effective historical continuity either by semi-fiction (Boadicea, Vercingetorix, Arminius the Cheruscan) or by forgery (Ossian, the Czech medieval manuscripts). It is also clear that entirely new symbols and devices came into existence . . . such as the national anthem, . . . the national flag, . . . or the personification of 'the nation' in symbol or image . . . [20]

Corresponding to Hobsbawm's and Ranger's examples, literary myth too has been complicit in the creation of nations – above all, through the genre that accompanied the rise of the European vernaculars, their institution as languages-of-state after 1820, and the separation of literature into various 'national' literatures by the German Romantics at the end of the eighteenth and the beginning of the nineteenth centuries. Nations, then, are imaginary constructs that depend for their existence on an apparatus of cultural fictions in which imaginative literature plays a decisive role. And the rise of European nationalism coincides especially with one form of literature – the novel.

NATION AND NOVEL

It was the *novel* that historically accompanied the rise of nations by objectifying the 'one, yet many' of national life, and by mimicking the structure of the nation, a clearly bordered jumble of languages and styles. Socially, the novel joined the newspaper as the major vehicle of the national print media, helping to standardise language, encourage literacy and remove mutual incomprehensibility. But it did much more than that. Its manner of presentation allowed people to imagine the special community that was the nation. In the words of Benedict Anderson, the novel depicts:

the movement of a solitary hero through a sociological land-scape of a fixity that fuses the world inside the novel with the world outside. The picaresque *tour d'horizon* – hospitals, prisons, remote villages, monasteries, Indians, Negroes – is nonetheless not a *tour du monde*. The horizon is clearly bounded.[21]

It was in the novel that previously foreign languages met each other on the same terrain, forming an unsettled mixture of ideas and styles, themselves representing previously distinct peoples now forced to create the rationale for a common life. Mikhail Bakhtin's work on the novel – usually discussed in terms of a purely textual understanding of his key terms 'heteroglossia' and 'dialogism' – describes this aspect of the novel more clearly than anyone.[22] But Bakhtin meant 'heteroglossia' to have a basis in actual social life. The period of the novel's rise is that in which:

> the world becomes polyglot, once and for all and irreversibly. The period of national languages, coexisting but closed and deaf to each other, comes to an end . . . . The naïve and stubborn co-existence of 'languages' within a given national language also comes to an end – that is, there is no more peaceful co-existence between territorial dialects, social and professional dialects and jargons, literary languages, generic languages within literary languages, epochs in language and so on.[23]

If the novel for Bakhtin tended to parody other genres, the epic was that genre the novel parodied in its nation-forming role. Hobsbawm's description of the rhetoric of nationhood can be found also in Bakhtin's description of epic, where '"beginning", "first", "founder", "ancestor", "that which occurred earlier" and so on, are . . . valorized temporal categories'.[24] But whereas it was a feature of epic never to be addressed to or for one's contemporaries, the novel (on the contrary) directed itself to an 'openended present'. In its hands, 'tradition' became what Hobsbawm calls a 'useable past',[25] and the evocation of deep, sacred origins – instead of furthering unquestioning, ritualistic reaffirmations of a people (as in epic) – becomes a contemporary, practical means of *creating* a people.

If the epic's 'ritual' view gives way to the novel's political one, the change is mirrored in the linguistic basis for the novel itself. The separation of literature into 'national literatures' at the outset of the novel's rise to prominence reflected the earlier victory of the European vernaculars over the sacred imperial 'truth-language' of Latin – only one instance that seems to justify Benedict Anderson's claim that the 'dawn of nationalism at the end of the eighteenth century coincide[d] with the dusk of religious modes of thought',[26] or, as he puts it in another place, that nationalism largely extended and modernised (although did not replace) 'religious imaginings', taking on religion's concern with death, continuity and the desire for origins.

The religious answers to questions of continuity and origins were not specific enough to deal with the fragmentation of Papal Empire and monarchical realm. If languages imply nations, how many nations would eventually sprout from the hopelessly polyglot entities following the decline of the mediaeval empires within Europe? If new collectives are formed on a basis other than papal or dynastic authority, on what basis? How prevent a continual chaotic splintering? The novel implicitly answers these questions in its very form by objectifying the nation's *composite* nature: a hodgepodge of the ostensibly separate 'levels of style' corresponding to class; a jumble of poetry, drama, newspaper report, memoir and speech; a mixture of the jargons of race and ethnicity.

One of the advantages of a broadly cultural approach to the dilemma of nationalist politics has been its illumination of nationalism's reliance on religious modes of thought. Regis Debray, for example, had assaulted the view that the nation, because historically specific in its late eighteenth-century form, was also transient. He chose to take up the other half of Williams's dichotomy:

> like language, the nation is an invariable which cuts across modes of production . . . . We should not become obsessed by the determinate historical form of the nation–state but try to see what that form is made out of. It is created from a natural organization proper to *homo sapiens*, one *through which life itself is rendered untouchable or sacred. This sacred character constitutes the real national question.*[27]

Debray's focus is relevant here as an explanation in *literary* terms of the nation's universal appeal, and so locates the symbolic background of national fiction. The nation is not only a recent and transitory political form, but also responds to the 'twin threats of disorder and death' confronting all societies. Against these, the nation sets two 'anti-death processes':

These are, first of all, a delimitation in time, or the assignation of origins, in the sense of an *Ark*. This means that society does not derive from an infinite regression of cause and effect. A point of origin is fixed, the mythic birth of the *Polis*, the birth of Civilization or of the Christian era, the Muslim Hegira and so on. This zero point or starting point is what allows ritual repetition, the ritualization of memory, celebration, commemoration – in short, all those forms of magical behaviour signifying defeat of the irreversibility of time.

The second founding gesture of any human society is its delimitation within an enclosed space. Here also there takes place an encounter with the sacred, in the sense of the *Temple*. What is the Temple, etymologically? It was what the ancient priest or diviner traced out, raising his wand heavenwards, the outline of a sacred space within which divination could be undertaken. This fundamental gesture is found at the birth of all societies, in their mythology at least. But the myth presence is an indication of something real.[28]

Debray, of course, witnessed the vitality of nationalism as a younger man in revolutionary Cuba, an experience (like that of Algeria and Vietnam for the generations of the 1950s and the 1960s) that sharply modified Marxist and liberal theories of nationalism, and gave way to what has been called 'Third Worldism': an endorsement of anti-imperialist liberation movements that amounted to a panacea.[29]

This background of spirituality and permanence is never lost, even in the historically specific cultural expressions of the national form. The Marxist mystic, Walter Benjamin, has pointed out that the novel is dependent upon the book, and was historically unique among literary genres by being developed in its modern form after the invention of printing. 'Print-capitalism', according to Anderson, meant ideological insemination on a large scale, and created the conditions where people could begin to think of themselves as a nation. The novel's created world allowed for multitudinous actions occurring simultaneously within a single, definable community, filled with 'calendrical coincidences' and what Anderson calls (after Benjamin) 'transverse, cross-time'. Read in isolation, the novel was nevertheless a mass ceremony; one could read alone with the conviction that millions of others were doing the same, at the same time.

The *composite* quality of the novel cannot be understood only ethnically or regionally. The novel's rise accompanied a changing concept of 'realism' itself, which acquired its present association with the lower classes only after the Enlightenment when, as Auerbach describes, realism came to involve 'the serious treatment of everybody reality, the rise of more extensive and socially inferior human groups to the position of subject matter for problematic-existential representation'.[30] In other words, the novel brought together the 'high' and the 'low' within a national framework – not fortuitously, but for specific national reasons.

The first appearance of incipient nationalist consciousness, according to Kohn, took place in the Cromwellian forces of the English Civil War. The ideas here were so tightly bound up with the aspirations of the middle classes for 'free expression', 'self-assertion' and freedom from the authority of a wilful and tyrannical monarchy, that 'individual liberty' became inseparable from the nationalist ethos. The incipient liberal nationalism of Milton and, later, Locke found its way through the French *philosophes* to North America, where it raised its head in the form of attacks on authoritarianism, censorship and the strangling of free trade.

On this North American terrain, the idea of oppression from *afar* appeared, although it was not exactly the 'foreign' oppression that would become so common in the period after the Second World War. In this case, the same religion, language and history were common to England and its North American colony. But the very tenuousness of the stated need for independence pushed the grounds for separation from specific middle-class 'liberties' to the much broader *inalienable rights* – the universality of which applied in principle also to the lower classes. All this gave expression to Rousseau's concept of the collective personality of the 'people', the unity and common destiny of a 'community' whose cohesiveness relied upon forces emanating from the ground up, and which, being natural, encompassed all. In Germany, Herder transformed Rousseau's 'people' into the *Volk*. The significance of this latter concept is its shift from Rousseau's Enlightenment emphasis on civic virtue to a woollier Romantic insistence on the primordial and ineluctable roots of nationhood as a *distinguishing feature* from other communites. Each people was now set off by the 'natural' characteristics of language and the intangible quality of a specific *Volksgeist*.

It was, in fact, the urge to give solidity to this particular and differentiating 'spirit of the people' that led in Germany to the first serious collections of folktales and folksongs, which according to Bakhtin are the prototypes of the novel form: 'The novel's roots must ultimately be sought in folklore.'[31] These collections provided an impetus to the study of modern philology, which separated the study of literature into various 'national' literatures on the basis of linguistic distinctions considered to be inviolable and absolute. Contemporary literary study is still based on these distinctions first made in the period of incipient European nation-forming. In short, nationalism is enmeshed in the particular history of Europe and its ideology of 'democracy'; it necessarily invokes the 'people', although this people becomes, increasingly after the late nineteenth century, inseparable from the modern working class, both in the Marxist sense and in that hybrid of Marxism and Third-World populism made famous by figures like Ho Chi Minh, Amilcar Cabral, Kwame Nkrumah, Frantz Fanon and many others.

The 'folk', the 'plebeians', the 'people', the 'working class' were now important components for any inclusive treatment of the nation in fiction, as Bruce King has pointed out:

> Nationalism is an urban movement which identifies with the rural areas as a source of authenticity, finding in the 'folk' the attitudes, beliefs, customs and language to create a sense of national unify among people who have other loyalties. Nationalism aims at ... rejection of cosmopolitan upper classes, intellectuals and others likely to be influenced by foreign ideas.[32]

Without this sense of rejection of the 'cosmopolitan upper classes', plebeian authenticity has been a feature of English literature throughout the rise of modern nationalism in Europe. In the English nineteenth century, for example, authors adopted the concepts of German Romanticism, expressing them most often in debates over the 'literary language' and its debt to a 'common language' – the poor people's idiom, sometimes referred to as 'native speech'. In Wordsworth's 'Preface to the Lyrical Ballads' or Hazlitt's 'On Familiar Style', the issue of common speech had even gone beyond a defence of the writer's departure from the proprieties of style and was associated with peasant virtue – an abstraction and an idealisation of the democratic ideology necessary for the rise of market capitalism. This association is even more pronounced and even less concerned with style *per se* in Morris's 'Art of the People'. In *Marius the Epicurean*, Pater attempted to define a 'proletariate of speech' in the stylistic concept of 'Euphuism' – a fertile mixture of high and low idioms. There are, of course, many other examples.

The populist undercurrents of national thought have been put forth clearly by the novel's better-known theorists, although not in the form of a 'national' concept *per se*. Both Lukács and (as we have said) Bakhtin, despite their differences in many other respects, explain the novel in terms of epic. In both, the two are inverted images of the other – the former supplanting the latter in a period of transition from one ruling class to another. In the early Lukács, this rupture is traced to the disintegration of organic community in antiquity, the breakdown of its naïvely authoritarian and religious hierarchies. When the bourgeois individual became the dominant myth, the external became the internal, the worldly became the textual.

In Bakhtin, as we shall see, the issues are discussed less as content analysis than as an attempt to explain the evolution (and breakdown) of generic distinctions as such, where literary forms are shown to carry the weight of new perceptions made possible by changes in society. The epic is for him, 'preserved and revealed only in the form of national tradition', which he describes as 'a commonly held evaluation and point of view'.[33] For Bakhtin, the upheaval is less between elements within a given society than between societies, and although, (unlike Lukács) he takes his examples of the novel from Hellenistic Romance, Latin mock-epic and mediaeval satire, like Lukács he concentrates on those periods when large, incorporating dynastic realms are in the process of decline. For the modern novel, this means precisely the period of market capitalism and the age of exploration, which was also the period of the transformation of the vernaculars into languages-of-state, the creation of national economies and the subsequent recognition of nationalism as the dominant political ideology of the bourgeoisie. Thus, for the late Lukács, the key event in the development of the modern or (as he calls it) 'historical' novel is the French Revolution; for Bakhtin, that period when 'the world becomes polyglot once and for all and irreversibly' (see above).

It is striking to realise that these still pivotal theorists of the novel exhaust their analyses at their starting points – the era of the still revolutionary middle classes. Not only are the national–political implications of their work on fiction left merely implicit, but the contemporary consequences of their findings have remained completely submerged. According to Bakhtin:

> The embryos of novelistic prose appear in the heteroglottic and heterological world of the Hellenistic era, in imperial Rome, in the process of disintegration and decadence of the verbal and ideological centralism of the medieval church. Similarly, in modern times the flourishing of the novel is always connected with the decomposition of stable verbal and ideological systems, and, on the other hand, to the reinforcement of linguistic heterology and to its impregnation by intentions, within the literary dialect as well as outside of it.[34]

Is it not natural to assume that the novel itself would take on new forms following the institution of another closed system with its accompanying universal language, whose disintegration (the system and the language) we are now witnessing? For of course, the triumph of European nationalism co-existed with the consolidation of Empire, and the world became Europe's 'little circle' – just as beleaguered and constrained as the ethnic and linguistic sub-communities had been under the rule of the imperial Church, and the monarchies of the late Middle Ages and Renaissance. What then of the period following the Second World War?

Another pivotal critic, who is not normally thought of as an analyst of the novel, realises much more than Lukács and Bakhtin the parameters of the contemporary novel. In 'The Storyteller', Walter Benjamin provides the most useful leads for understanding the form of the novel for the postmodern period, because he evokes the conflict between originally oral literature and that (like the novel) which has from the beginning been dependent on the book. This conflict of the oral and the written, of

course, suggest the conflicts now occurring between developed
and emergent societies, a conflict that begins more and more to
characterise the postwar political scene, as we shall see below.
But in Benjamin it leads to a more fundamental conflict between
communal and individual experience – something which we saw
above was contained contradictorily in nationalist ideology from
the start:

> What differentiates the novel from all other forms of prose
> literature – the fairy tale, the legend, even the novella – is
> that it neither comes from oral tradition nor goes into it. This
> distinguishes it from storytelling in particular. The storyteller
> takes what he tells from experience – his own or that reported
> by others . . . the novelist has isolated himself.[35]

Benjamin's thesis is that, in our time, 'experience has fallen
in value' as a result of the cultural development of printing,
especially in the form of the newspaper; and so (although he
comes at it from a different angle) he joins Anderson in coupling
novel and newspaper as the decisive print media of bourgeois
society:

> with the full control of the middle class, which has the press
> as one of its most important instruments in fully developed
> capitalism, there emerges a form of communication which,
> no matter how far back its origins may lie, never before
> influenced the epic form in a decisive way. But now it does
> exert such an influence. And it turns out that it confronts
> storytelling as no less of a stranger than did the novel, but
> in a more menacing way, and that it also brings about a
> crisis in the novel. This new form of communication is
> *information*.[36]

Although Benjamin has been more prescient in isolating the
relevant components of social communication, he is intriguing
above all as a failed questioner. To counterpose information to
epic (or folkloric) 'experience' is, as I hope to show below, a
deep misunderstanding of what the novel has become in at
least one trend of Third-World fiction. Nevertheless, writing as
a European between the Wars, Benjamin instinctively predicted
where the developments would occur. Benjamin belongs to that

strain of nostalgic modernism which revolts against the 'ready-made' quality of modern life made possible by the uprooting of communal, village life. In this sense he is very similar to the early Lukács. For Benjamin, information is contrasted to 'intelligence' or 'epic wisdom'.

> The intelligence that came from afar – whether the spatial kind from foreign countries or the temporal kind of tradition – possessed an authority which gave it validity, even when it was not subject to verification. Information, however, lays claim to prompt verifiability. The prime requirements is that it appear 'understandable in itself'.[37]

Clearly, as Benjamin uses it, information is inseparable from propaganda – it is that news which we receive from all parts of the globe that is already 'shot through with explanation'. There were three major areas where Benjamin's account seems contradicted by many novels of the contemporary Third World. As a negation of epic, he supposed the novel to stand against 'memory' – the 'epic faculty par excellence', whereas 'memory' – for example in the quasi-journalistic banana massacre episode of García Márquez's *One Hundred Years of Solitude* – is what many of these novels insist on preserving.[38] The novel was supposed to tend to substitute the story's moral with an abstract, philosophical investigation into the meaning of life, whereas novels as various as Khushwant Singh's *Train to Pakistan* or Vic Reid's *The Leopard* deliberately moralise recent local history, sketching out known political positions. And, finally, because information must always sound plausible, the novel was thought to oppose the inclination of the storyteller to borrow from the miraculous, which the wholesale success of so-called 'magical realism' (not only in Latin America) has shown to be wrong. The fact is that 'news', precisely because it has become the nemesis of national fiction by originating in the imperial centres (which largely control the images projected to and about the Third World) is thematically and formally incorporated into the postwar novel. A large body of postwar fiction is, in this sense, 'neo-colonial', composed of various novels of 'information', voices from the Third World seeking to project themselves into a European setting.

And yet it is precisely here that the greatest paradox of the new novel can be seen. For under conditions of illiteracy and shortages, and given simply the leisure-time necessary for reading one, the novel has been an élitist and minority form in developing countries when compared to poem, song, television and film. Almost inevitably, it has been the form through which a thin, foreign-educated stratum (however sensitive or committed to domestic political interests) has communicated to metropolitan reading publics, often in translation. It has been, in short, a naturally cosmopolitan form that empire has allowed to play a national role, as it were, only in an international arena.

PHASES OF THE NATION

Soaked in the contentious project of European nation-forming, literary study has from its origins been stamped by it. The anachronism of these founding principles can be seen in the semantic shift in the 'nation' itself. Elie Kedourie has read the phenomenon entirely through the development of German idealistic philosophy, noting ominously, for example, Fichte's retrospectively shocking view that 'conflict between strata promotes indirectly to the self-realisation of the whole human race'.[39]

Indeed, since the Second World War, in a conveniently European lapse of memory, studies of nationalism have not only increased; they have for the most part condemned the thing they studied. Kohn and Kedourie, for example, both define nationalism by suggesting it has a totalitarian edge: 'Nationalism is a state of mind in which the supreme loyalty of the individual is felt to be due to the nation-state.'[40] Both the interest and the negative judgement are the result of events directly bearing on the war – the rise of various 'imperial' nationalisms among those latecomers to Empire in the developed West: Italy, Germany and Japan. Here the witnessing of extreme group loyalties, manipulated by the repressive regimes of European Fascism, led to a search for the nationalist roots of a Western tradition previously thought to be civilised.[41]

The terms of nationalism have from the European perspective apparently reversed. Not freedom from tyranny, but the embodiment of tyranny. The question is: how much is this new perspective a result of owning, rather than suffering, an empire?

That is, can't it be said that the recoiling from nationalism is also partly due to the challenge of the rising national movements of the developing world?

A good deal of the depression surrounding the term cannot, however, be explained by European prejudice alone. For one of its sources is the wholesale exporting of authoritarian military regimes to the fledgling countries of the Third World, although the observation is usually made without sufficiently noting the part played in this by the imperial legacies of differentiating administrative structures, unequal development and 'foreign aid'. Lamenting the savagery of many states in what should have been the Third World's 'springtime' of nationalist idealism is not an activity limited to European sociologists. It forms a major subcategory of Third-World fiction itself, featured in such representative works as Augusto Roa Bastos's *I, the Supreme*, Ayi Kwei Armah's *The Beautiful Ones Are Not Yet Born*, Earl Lovelace's *The Wine of Astonishment*, Salman Rushdie's *Shame* and many others – novels that are really a necessary adjunct to the insurgent and liberationist rhetoric of Frantz Fanon, Amilcar Cabral and their cultural descendants, although in an inverted form: a pointed exposure of what Ariel Dorfman calls the 'Empire's old clothes' worn by a comprador élite who, like Chile's Pinochet, Egypt's Mubarak or Haiti's Namphy, take on the nationalist mantle only to cloak their people more fully with the old dependency. Actually, Fanon himself already diagnosed this same process in his chapter entitled 'The Pitfalls of National Consciousness' in *The Wretched of the Earth*.

Because the states which must transform the post-colonial territories into 'nations' are (unlike those in the creole nineteenth century) already bequeathed and sitting upon seething disparities of class and background, the problem for the neo-colonial writer has not only been to create the aura of national community eroded by the 'monopolisation of the forms of cultural expression' in dominant culture, but to expose the excesses which the *a priori* state, chasing a national identity after the fact, has created at home. If, as Horace Davis argues, 'any reasonable consideration tells us that state and nation build each other' then the problem of nation is also the problem of the influence of state policy on national literary production; the conflict between anti-colonial inspiration, on the one hand, and on the other, the commercial and governmental pre-forming of the imagination. And what we

really have now is merely a confusion of terms and a false
and merely nominal continuity. For today's is the first period
of nationalism where the state *predates* or precedes nationalist
sentiments, which are then called in after the fact, so to speak.

If European nationalism was a project of *unity* on the basis
of conquest and economic expediency, insurgent or popular
nationalism (not, that is, of the Pinochet variety) is for the
most part a project of consolidation following an act of *separation* from Europe.[42] It is a task of reclaiming community from
within boundaries defined by the very power whose presence
denied community. Sometimes supporting, sometimes rejecting
the political states in which they find themselves, the writers must
have a goal that can only be a collective political identity still
incapable of being realised – despite multinational corporations
and regional alliances like Contadora, OPEC and the Pan-African
Congress – in any other form than the nation-state. It is not that
people, or the artists who speak for them, can imagine no other
affiliations, but that the solutions to dependency are only collective, and the territorial legacies of the last two hundred years
provide the collectivity no other basis upon which to fight
dependency.

The crippling subaltern status implied by having to follow
an imaginative form of another and oppressing culture is not
fact, however, but myth. The constraints are real, but not their
purported origins. As elsewhere, the myth thrives on a selective and ethnocentric history. We imagine that the advanced
countries of Europe, under the pressures of Enlightenment ideals
and the commercial needs of the rising industrial classes, *invented*
the nation-state, and then exported it into Europe's dominions,
where it would play a ridiculously unsuitable role, postdating the
arbitrary division of the world into administrative and economic
zones of influence, already with their own state apparatuses, and
therefore having to project independence on the terms set down
by the former rulers.

This scenario is accurate except where it assigns origins.
The nation–state is not only the by-product of the conditions
created by European exploration; it was, more or less from the
start, begun in acts of separation from the European centres of
Madrid, Paris and London. If one discounts the civil wars of
England and France, the first nationalists are not Frenchmen,
Spaniards or Englishmen, but the creole middle classes of the

New World – people like Simon Bolívar, Toussaint L'Ouverture and Ben Franklin. Thus Europe was not able to formulate its own national aspirations until after the markets made possible by imperial penetration had motivated them. In short, European nationalism was possible only because of what Europe was doing in its far-flung dominions.

The 'national idea' flourished in the soil of foreign conquest. Imperial conquest created the conditions for the fall of Europe's universal Christian community, but resupplied Europe with a religious sense of mission and self-identity that becomes *universal* (both within and outside Europe) after the war – a universalising that today has led, dialectically, to a break-up and a splintering: 'The twentieth century since 1945 has become the first period in history in which the whole of mankind has accepted one and the same political attitude, that of nationalism.'[43]

In a sense then, nationalist doctrine takes over religion's social role, substituting for the imperial Church; the most successful early European nationalist was Napoleon, who decried the regal centralisation of power while marching across Europe in the name of France. In its European origins, nationalism was also messianic, modelled on patterns of Judeo-Christianity. According to Kohn, modern nationalism took three concepts from Old Testament mythology: 'the idea of a chosen people, the emphasis on a common stock of memory of the past and of hopes for the future, and finally national messianism'.[44] If the concept of superiority ('chosen people') characterises the outlook of the European adventurer, it is the Hebraic underdog, the sense of being an outcast people, that characterises the other:

> Not only oppressed nationalities took refuge in the hope of a messianic mission; ... it expressed also the struggle of heretical sects and oppressed classes for the realization of their dreams and aspirations, and as the secular idea of historical progress it still retains today some of its religious force.[45]

The point here is how the earlier impulse towards *individuation* gave way though conquest to a universally shared outlook; the national becomes international in the postwar, to the point that it becomes possible to speak of such things as 'Islamic nationalism' or 'Latin American nationalism' in reference to entire continents or regions. There are two imperial legacies that have contributed to this internationalist feeling of solidarity against Empire – the presence of vestigial 'world' languages (primarily Spanish, English and Arabic) and international communications. Thus, a recurrent motif of contemporary Third-World fiction is the bridge that exists between imaginative literature and other forms of cultural information and communication: the place of literature within what C. Wright Mills called 'the cultural apparatus'. As with so much else, the imperial relationship has made this apparatus more visible.

A well-known UNESCO document of 1980 on world information imbalances (whose authors include García Márquez and the British cultural historian Richard Hoggart) suggests the special problem:

> It has become increasingly clear that the effects of intellectual and cultural dependence are as serious as those of political subjection or economic dependence. There can be no genuine, effective independence without the communication resources needed to safeguard it. The argument has been made that a nation whose mass media are under foreign domination cannot claim to be a nation.[46]

It is obvious how different this kind of cry is from 'no taxation without representation'. How does the Third-World writer participate in national culture under the conditions of what Herbert Schiller calls 'the monopolization of culture' by ceaseless Western commercial and informational outpourings?[47] What chance does the *natio* have against this constant reminder of dependency? How does one establish community on the grounds of an erstwhile imperial administrative sector, when the present rulers often perform like hand-picked successors of the colonial regime? While, from an administrative and economic point of view, distinct nations are multiplying, the mutual awareness and interlocking influences of global culture begun by imperialism is still increasing, creating those conditions described by Bakhtin (but now applicable on a worldwide basis) in which 'languages cast light on one another' and 'the period of national languages coexisting but closed and deaf to one another, comes to an end'.

EXILE VS. NATIONALISM

How could the most universally legitimate political ideology of our time fail to become a *topos* in postwar fiction? And how could its existence be ignored, or replaced by the *topos* of 'exile', nationalism's opposite? In our thinking, 'exiles' have usually been those famous American and British artists seeking a change in creative surroundings. They have not referred usually to those displaced by World War and colonisation, in the sense suggested by Edward Said when he says,

> it is necessary to set aside Joyce and Nabokov and even Conrad, who wrote of exile with such pathos, but of exile without cause or rationale. Think instead of the uncountable masses for whom UN agencies have been created, or refugees without urbanity, with only ration cards and agency numbers.[48]

Exile and nationalism are conflicting poles of feeling that correspond to more traditional aesthetic conflicts: artistic iconoclasm and communal assent, the unique vision and the collective truth. In fact, many words in the exile family divide themselves between an archaic or literary sense and a modern, political one: for example, banishment vs. deportation; *émigré* vs. immigrant; wanderer vs. refugee; exodus vs. flight. The division between exile and nationalism, therefore, presents itself as one not only between individual and group, but between loser and winner, between a mood of rejection and a mood of celebration. Literarily, the division is suggested by the tensions between lyric and epic, tragedy and comedy, monologue and dialogue, confession and proclamation, and has led in some recent Third-World literature to what Barbara Harlow has called 'a full-scale counter-hegemonic aesthetics', with a striking absence of hostility toward 'modernity' and an attempt to preserve identity (if not traditional values) by acquiring the technologies, the diplomatic strategies and the 'worldliness' of the former rulers.[49] Many of the novels often attempt to assemble the fragments of a national life and give them a final shape. They become documents designed to prove national consciousness, with multiple, myriad components that display an active communal life.

The nation-centred origins of literary studies distorts the coverage of that vast realm of experience arising from imperial contacts. Thus, for the most part, the English criticism of Empire has been, until recently, almost all of one kind: the slightly ill-at-ease, slightly ashamed but enormously forgiving recognition of imperial themes in writers from 'the centre': Forster on the possibilities of inter-cultural communication, Conrad on the savagery of civilised man, Lawrence on the liberating chaos of primitive religion, Greene on the political intrigues of European governments in cultures they do not understand.

In *Fiction and the Colonial Experience*, Jeffrey Meyers illustrates the kind of criticism widely found in English studies of the 'colonial novel'. He recognises liberally that 'Europe [has] impose[d] its manners, customs, religious beliefs and moral values on an indigenous way of life', and that the reverberations from centuries of foreign domination constitute 'one of the most significant historical developments in our century'.[50] But the spirit is past tense. He explains that 'the colonial novel runs parallel to the rise and fall of western colonialism', as if the colonial cycle had run its course. By doing so, he separates himself sharply from the discourse of critics from the former colonies who, despite their innumerable divisions and outlooks, are unified in identifying a postwar structure of neo-colonial dependency.

In this framework of past transgression and present enlightenment, Meyers finds the pattern for his study of canonical 'colonial' literature. He sets the early Kipling short stories against the collective efforts of Conrad, Forster and the Kipling of *Kim*, allowing him to complain of the stereotyping of the native in the earlier work and, above all, its outlook in which 'all moral issues are seen from only one point of view'. On the other hand, the 'good' colonial novel offers what Meyers calls a 'humanistic' approach, which has the attraction of trading in firm moral conviction for 'a universal fascination with the savage and the imcomprehensible'. This fascination is supposed to lead us to a point where we can meditate upon the 'human lessons of previous colonial entanglements'.

It is assumed that 'deracinated white men' who venture into hostile regions for the purpose of self-questioning are paying tribute to the native; their vision is purer than the early Kipling sort of white, because they understand that bestial nature is preferable to technological civilisation. Modernism has redeemed white men from the modern world by teaching them (through the savage's mute example) that rationality, commitment and technology are swindles. Meyers's projection attributes to the 'savage' an incomprehensibility that conveniently obscures the inequality of the colonial relationship, while pretending to thank the 'native' for a quality that, under the conditions of a developing world, could only hinder him.

Similarly on the Left, Terry Eagleton's *Exiles and Emigrés* – a well-known work on the exile theme by a writer often sensitive to the undersides of English rule, is surprisingly reluctant to address the effects of colonialism on the concept of exile itself. He begins by referring to the absence of English writers among the century's best, and by pointing to 'certain central flaws and impoverishments in conventional English culture itself. That culture was unable, of its own impetus, to produce great literary art.'[51] Eagleton attributes these impoverishments to England's inwardness. On the contrary, the successful James and Conrad 'bring to bear on the culture a range of experience – of America, Europe, Africa, the East . . . It was out of this tension that James and Conrad created their major work; and it was a tension notably absent in the work of their contemporaries.'[52]

Despite this suggestive way of putting things – finding in the transplanted English gentlemen James and Conrad, a vital contact with the colonial world – Eagleton's book basically combats English insularity only by binding it more closely to European insularity. His efforts are unnecessarily modest. While Eagleton in other places attempts to revivify English culture with theories from Germany and France, he stops short of including in this work the thinking of colonial subjects, despite their screaming relevance to his theme. Once more the colonies are a passive fund of good writing material: Conrad brings back impressions from Africa and the East, whose noteworthiness lies in their contribution to the production of 'great literary art'.

Again, novels in the postwar period are unique because they operate in a world where the level of communications, the widespread politics of insurgent nationalism and the existence of large international cultural organisations have made the topics of nationalism and exile unavoidably aware of one another. The idea of nationhood is not only a political plea, but a formal binding together of disparate elements. And out of the multiplicities of culture, race and political structures grows also a repeated dialectic of uniformity and specificity: of world culture and national culture, of family and of people. One of many clear formulations of this can be found in Fanon's statement that '[i]t is at the heart of national consciousness that international consciousness lives and grows'.[53] These universalist tendencies – already implicit in the concept of 'inalienable rights' – is accentuated by the break-up of the English and Spanish imperial systems, with their unities of language, their common enemies and (in the case of Spanish America) their contiguous terrain. Examples of the persistence of this motif might be found, for instance, in the controversial role of the terms 'Africa' in the writing of the Nigerian author Chinua Achebe, or 'America' in the essays of the Cuban patriot Jose Martí.

Thus, of course, not all Third-World novels about nations are 'nationalistic'. The variations range from outright attacks on independence, often mixed with nostalgia for the previous European status quo (as in the work of V. S. Naipaul, Manohar Malgonkar and others), to vigorously anti-colonial works emphasising native culture (Ngugi wa Thiong'o, Tayeb Salih, Sipho Sepamla and others), to explanations of the 'lower depths' or the 'fantastic unknown' by writers acquainted with the tastes and interests of dominant culture.

As we shall see, in one strain of Third-World writing the contradictory topoi of exile and nation are fused in a lament for the necessary and regrettable insistence of nation-forming, in which the writer proclaims his identity with a country whose artificiality and exclusiveness have driven him into a kind of exile – a simultaneous recognition of nationhood and an alienation from it. As we have said, the cosmopolitan thrust of the novel form has tended to highlight this branch of well-publicised Third-World fiction. One result has been a trend of cosmopolitan commentators on the Third World, who offer an *inside view* of formerly submerged peoples for target reading publics in Europe and North America in novels that comply with metropolitan literary tastes.

Some of its better-known authors have been from Latin America, a region which, we shall see, has a special relevance to Rushdie's work; for example, García Márquez, Vargas Llosa, Alejo Carpentier, Isabel Allende and others. But there is also a related group of postwar satirists of nationalism and dependency – writers of encyclopaedic national narratives that dismember a recent and particularised history in order to expose the political dogma surrounding and choking it. Here one thinks especially of

Günter Grass, E. L. Doctorow, Milan Kundera, Nadine Gordimer and many others.

In the case of Salman Rushdie, for example, the examples of India and Pakistan are, above all, an opportunity to explore post-colonial *responsibility*. The story he tells is of an entire region slowly coming to think of itself as one, but a corollary of his story is disappointment. So little improvement has been made. In fact, the central irony of his novels is that independence has damaged Indian spirits by proving that 'India' can act as abominably as the British did. In a kind of metafictional extravaganza, he treats the heroism of nationalism bitterly and comically because it always seems to him to evolve into the nationalist demagogy of a caste of domestic sell-outs and power-brokers.

In this, Rushdie, although more publicised, is far from alone, even on the subcontinent. He captures what Aijaz Ahmad has called the 'nationalism of mourning':

> What we witnessed was not just the British policy of divide and rule, which surely was there, but our own willingness to break up our civilizational unity, to kill our neighbors. . . . A critique of others (anti-colonial nationalism) receded even further into the background, entirely overtaken now by an even harsher critique of ourselves. The major fictions of the '50s and '60s – the shorter fictions of Manto, Bedi, Intezar Hussein; the novels of Qurrat ul Ain, Khadija Mastoor, Abdullah Hussein – came out of that refusal to forgive what we ourselves had done and were still doing, in one way or another, to our own polity.[54]

This message is very familiar to us because it has been easier to embrace in our metropolitan circles than the explicit challenges of, say, the Salvadoran protest author Manlio Argueta, or the sparse and caustic satires of the Nigerian author, Obi Egbuna. However, it is perhaps the trend's overt cosmopolitanism – its Third-World thematics as seen through the elaborate fictional architecture of European high art – that perfectly imagines the novel's obsessive nation-centredness and its imperial (that is, universalising) origins. Distanced from the sacrifices and organisational drudgery of actual resistance movements, and yet horrified by the obliviousness of the West towards their own cultures, writers like Rushdie and Vargas Llosa have been well-poised to thematise the centrality of nation-forming while at the same time demythifying it from a European perch. Although Vargas Llosa's erudite and stylistically sumptuous *The War of the End of the World*, for example, is not at all characteristic of the 'counter-hegemonic aesthetics' of much Third-World writing, its very disengagement frees him to treat the ambivalence of the independence process as a totality, and although negatively, reassert its fundamental importance to the post-colonial imagination.[55] His treatment may be neither the most representative nor the most fair, but its very rootlessness brilliantly articulates the emotional life of decolonisation's various political contestants. It is 'in-between'. As Vargas Llosa himself notes:

> I don't know to what extent one can himself measure the type of influences he has received, but I believe that in my case, as is unfortunately the case of many Latin American writers, I have been formed as a result of foreign influences, and that is because of the poverty, fragmentation, and dislocation of my own national literary tradition.[56]

Based on the historical classic, *Rebellion in the Backlands* (1902) by Euclides da Cunha, the novel immortalises that notoriously elusive moment in the history of post-independence when, having declared itself a democratic republic, the country erupts into civil war and all factions scramble for power. With the same cosmic pessimism as his earlier treatment of failed republicanism in *Conversation in the Cathedral* (1969), which dealt with the sadism and corruption of the Odría dictatorship in his native Peru as seen through the conversations of two characters in a seedy Lima bar, *The War of the End of the World* is in a sense a companion piece to that earlier novel. In a much less experimental prose and with a straight chronological structure recalling the Lukácsian high bourgeois 'historical' novel, it dissects the failures not of Peru, but of neighbouring Brazil, whose epic dimensions amount, in Vargas Llosa's view, to a kind of Latin-American model of disappointed promise, self-serving domestic machinations and foreign interventions, which combine to ensure the continuity of military dictatorship.

If *Conversation in the Cathedral* followed the logic of his epigraph there from Balzac that 'the novel is the private history of nations', and was filled with Vargas Llosa's own personal reminiscences of Peruvian life under Odría in the 1950s, *The War of the End of the World*, precisely because of Brazil's relative cultural distance within a common Latin-American reality, allowed for a more reportorial stance, the country separated from him not only by language and geography, but by time, since the story's events take place in 1896–7. In a sense, its setting in Latin America, which (unlike Africa, Asia and the Caribbean) achieved formal independence in the nineteenth century, captures with extraordinary clarity the ongoing link between the era of European nation-forming and the quite different process of contemporary decolonisation, since the novel, published in 1981, can only be read backwards through those well-known events. An angry opponent of Latin American guerrilla movements, Vargas Llosa here chooses a setting that allows him to mull over the components of a domestic liberal democracy that has eluded his own land, and that is characteristic (in his view) of the nation-forming of a Europe that he emulates artistically, and knows and loves personally from several decades of travel.

The story deals with an actual history: the turn-of-the-century rise of a commune of religious fanatics in the Canudos backlands region of Bahia in northeastern Brazil. They thrive under the direction of an apocalyptic visionary named Antonio Conselheiro (Anthony the Counsellor), whose devoted followers are drawn from Brazil's *jaguncos* – an underclass of reformed criminals, landless peasants and lumpen outcasts. Speaking in parables and working miracles, the 'Counsellor' wins an immense following dedicated to chasing the Devil from the land and enraptured by his call to 'animate your collective memory in order to remember the future'. After a while, the rabble becomes a well-drilled, paramilitary cult defending the 'New Jerusalem' of Canudos, which has become, both in their own minds and in that of the government, a counter-base of power, fiercely Catholic (although they practice free love), and unwilling to recognise the new constitution, the national census or the concept of using money as a unit of exchange. The millenarian promise of communal happiness enrages the local landowners after a series of raiding operations on the neighbouring haciendas and the seizure of land.

As we watch the rise of Canudos, and follow the dreams of its inhabitants, the reaction of the outside world gets full play in the novel. In the on-the-spot reporting of a 'myopic journalist', the Brazilian public gradually learns of the cult but only through the distorting veil of the ruling party's newspapers. Eventually, the Bahian Progressive Republican Party tries to disgrace the ruling Conservatives by claiming that the cult is their creation, and by arguing that they have enrolled the aid of the English Crown, which is supposedly running guns to the rebels through a certain Galileo Gall. A red-haired Scottish phrenologist, Gall is comically portrayed in the book as a libertarian anarchist and believer in scientific progress, who has fled imprisonment in Spain, writes political dispatches for a French journal, argues that Satan rather than God is the true rebellious prince of freedom, and who sets out for Canudos to find the living proof of his ideals. In fact, it is the Liberals who are arming Canudos. After three unsuccessful military expeditions, the army, by then throughly bedraggled and demoralised, finally crushes the commune in a genocidal fury in the novel's closing chapter.

In the unspeakable hopelessness and desolation of Vargas Llosa's vision of politics, the mythmaking necessary for mobilising large social forces for change becomes nothing more than, on the one hand, the pitiful Utopian dreams of what Fanon called in a different context the 'wretched of the earth', and on the other, the quite deliberate lies of the old guard. Nevertheless, even if in a series of ironic reversals it documents all the necessary components of nation-forming, which is its real subject: the sense of religious mission with its attendant violence, the consolidating force of the national press, the treasonous impulses of a ruling clique relying on the aid of European intervention, the proto-socialist colouring of the guerrilla opposition, and the misplaced and naïve solidarities of the fellow-traveller. Particularly, the attention Vargas Llosa gives to the political mythmaking of the 'word' – whether in the form of the prophetic utterances of the 'Counsellor' or the dispatches of the 'myopic journalist' (a central character of the novel) and those of Gall – is characteristic of the cosmopolitan writers of the Third World, who do not participate in the mythmaking but comment on it metafictionally. This feature is especially pronounced here since Vargas Llosa's source is da Cunha's legandary 'non-fictional' *Rebellion in the Backlands*.

If political mythmaking is the novel's unifying theme, it is also important for Vargas Llosa to show its attractions to all contestants. In the end, not even the thorough obliteration of Canudos, in which tens of thousands die horribly, can destroy the persistent self-delusion of the dispossessed. Asked by an army colonel what happened to the commune leader Abbot João, an old peasant woman gleefully says in the novel's closing lines, 'Archangels took him up to heaven . . . I saw them' (p. 568). Similarly, in one of the many conversations between Galileo Gall and the stoical landowner, the Baron Canabrava, the image-making of the other side is discussed:

> 'As is the case with many idealists, [General Moreira Cesar] is implacable when it comes to realizing his dreams. . . . Just think what's going to happen when that idealist has the monarchist, Anglophile insurgents of Canudos at his mercy', he said in a gloomy voice. . . . 'He knows that they're really neither one, but it's useful to the Jacobin cause if that's what they are, which amounts to the same thing. And why is he doing what he's doing? For the good of Brazil, naturally. And he believes with all his heart and soul that that's so.'[57]

It would be wrong, however, to think that Vargas Llosa was merely anatomising a general process – that his cosmopolitanism freed him from the same national obsession found in the writerly milieu he was implicitly critiquing. How can one miss his scornful caricature of liberation theology, for example, in the monstrous Christian 'base camp' that was Canudos? Or how can one fail to read in the confused proto-socialism of the 'Counsellor' a fundamentally reactionary cult of the personality? It is very unlikely that the, on some level admirable, fanatacism of the *jaguncos* with its horrible consequences was not inspired very directly by Vargas Llosa's own reading of Peru's Maoist rebels, *Sendero Luminoso* ('Shining Path'), the special occasion for his later novel *Historia de Mayta*, about a disillusioned Trotskyist. That particular kind of creative 'duplicity' has a good deal in common with Rushdie as well.

2
Anti-Colonial Liberalism

[T]he present is also history.

José Carlos Mariátegui[1]

[U]na cultura que no niegue el universo pero que sea capaz de poner en vigencia sus propias raíces, o sea, una cultura con dos rostros superpuestos, el universal y el nacional.

Tomás Borge Martínez[2]

World community and ghetto, cosmopolis and nation, global village and strategic hamlet – these are terms that seem increasingly to belong together. The pairings are bound by a dialectic found widely in the writing of decolonisation. For Fanon, 'it is at the heart of national consciousness that international consciousness lives and grows'; for Cabral, 'one of the aims of cultural resistance is the development of a *universal* culture aiming at integration in the contemporary world and its prospects for evolution'; for the popular Nicaraguan musician Francisco Seveño, 'to be "very Nicaraguan" is to be universal'. How does the writer account for both the many and the one – how capture a sense of the new unities while finding the allegiances on which identity thrives?

The question is a traditional one in discussions of cultural dependency, and revolves around the position of the 'cosmopolitan intellectual'. In *The Modern Culture of Latin America* (1967), for example, in a chapter entitled 'Cosmopolitan or Universal?', Jean Franco sketches out some of the features of that convention in Latin America.[3] Here cosmopolitanism represents an embrace of European artistic influences by writers who wish to mould the local culture in Europe's image. In this case, it is possible for even wildly dissimilar writers to represent that basic urge, and Franco finds examples in the insistently 'textual' work of Jorge Luis Borges as well as in the much more earthy,

32

humanist and outward-looking work of Pablo Neruda and Mario Benedetti.

Given what her book considers, that is a proper way of understanding the issue: it is a question of an artistic avant-garde, and cosmopolitanism is a matter of formal experimentation. The conflict of 'nation' and metropole is inevitably raised, but in this case the conflict takes place within the individual countries of Spanish America, or within the relative cultural homogeneity of Spanish America itself. But of interest in this chapter is the way that that conventional question has been altered by writers for whom cosmopolitanism has become an absolute value – who present their own 'Third-World' identities as a mark of distinction in a world supposedly exempt from national belonging. Today cosmopolitanism is propelled and defined by media and market, and involves not so much an élite *at home*, as it does spokespersons for a kind of permanent immigration.

Vargas Llosa and others like him play an important inter-mediary role in the reception of literature from the Third World. They hover between borders, the products of that peculiar 'weightlessness' that Salman Rushdie saw in his and others' 'migrant' consciousness. No writer more than Bharati Mukherjee signifies that partial transfer. Born in Calcutta, she later studied in Iowa, taught in Montreal and has now relocated permanently to New York. As such, she has begun to describe in her fiction and in high-profile articles for the *New York Times* the art of being 'in-between':

I have joined imaginative forces with an anonymous, driven, underclass of semi-assimilated Indians with sentimental attach-ments to a distant homeland but no real desire for permanent return. I see my 'immigrant' story replicated in a dozen American cities, and instead of seeing my Indianness as a fragile identity to be preserved against obliteration (or worse, a 'visible' disfigurement to be hidden), I see it now as a set of fluid identities to be celebrated. . . . Indianness is now a metaphor, a particular way of partially comprehending the world.[4]

Her situation (both personal and artistic) is as symptomatic as it is unrecognised. As she puts it, the community of American authors she has joined are for the most part still producing a

mannered and brittle 'minimalism' unaware of or indifferent to
the 'epic . . . washing up on its shores'. The characters who
people her fiction are those who fill America's cities: people
who have lived 'through centuries of history in a single lifetime
– village-born, colonised, traditionally raised, educated. What
they've assimilated in 30 years has taken the West 10 times that
number of years to create.'[5]

The issue here, then, is not only that familiar pattern of authors,
mostly middle class, who from the dominions travel to London,
Paris or New York as a rite of passage, 'civilising' themselves
before returning to high-level positions in the home intelligentsia.
That particular model is not specific enough to warrant a name;
it covers most of the Third-World authors who find their way on
to the Western bookshelf. What is at issue here is the intersection
of two kinds of 'cosmopolitan' – the new immigrant underclass
discovered eloquently in the writing of Mukherjee, and the kind
that, on another level, Mukherjee herself represents: that shifting,
'rootless' intellectual condemned by more embattled branches
of the anti-colonial struggle to a traitor's role. Seen against the
backdrop of 'Third-World' literary reception – that is, against the
backdrop of that literature's featured place in the major journals
and newspapers of Europe and North America – Mukherjee's
defiant challenge to traditional ways of conceiving the 'national'
deeply matters to a certain kind of anti-colonial tradition. We shall
try to sketch out some of the concerns of that tradition later in this
chapter.

At issue is not so much the accidents of place or privilege
but of political attitude – an attitude that translates into certain
shared aesthetic strategies that do not finally amount to a common
programme. In the epic narratives of Vargas Llosa, Isabel Allende,
Salman Rushdie, Carlos Fuentes and others – as in the fiction of
Mukherjee – allusion, metaphor, allegory and parable are all like
nationalism itself, 'janus-faced'. They are always a combination
of formal elements that are context-specific, and therefore resist-
ant to an imposed norm. But these writers nevertheless belong
together, quote one another and enter the public sphere as a
distinct community without a name. They do not yet have a name
because we are accustomed to grouping authors by language and
national origin, rather than by position or social function.

Although this book is about Salman Rushdie, it cannot explain
what he represents without explaining his own very different

sense of tradition. Despite attempts to make it so, his tradition, for example, is not (or at least not only) an Indian or a British one.[6] This attempt at grouping is not an attempt to fix Rushdie and the others into a spurious 'school' or common style, but to suggest a creative community, international in scope, that the publishing industries have actually unified in the minds of the Western public. Even politically, they certainly do not share the same positions on the contentious topics of socialism, NATO or the debt crisis. But for all their differences, they seem to share a harsh questioning of radical decolonisation theory; a dismissive or parodic attitude towards the project of national culture; a manipulation of imperial imagery and local legend as a means of politicising 'current events'; and a declaration of cultural 'hybridity' – a hybridity claimed to offer certain advantages in negotiating the collisions of language, race and art in a world of disparate peoples comprising a single, if not exactly unified, world.

Other writers could be added, but excluding them makes the tendencies more clear. In a way, the obvious model is V. S. Naipaul, whose writing – too much commented on to be of use here – also departs from theirs by largely abandoning any sympathy or acceptance of 'native' culture (Mukherjee's 'sentimental attachment to a distant homeland'). In his early fiction – *A House for Mr Biswas, The Mystic Masseur* – Naipaul created an ambivalent mockery of East Indian Trinidad that became a general inspiration. But the heavy weight he has since placed on the Western half of the cultural equation has cut him off from those who followed. Wilson Harris of Guyana and Wole Soyinka of Nigeria, for example, are not grouped here because, while their creative sensibilities are equally 'hybrid', they have not entered the international scene with the same pedagogical force. In spite of Soyinka's winning of the Nobel Prize and the relatively high level of critical interest in Harris's work, their books are simply too difficult for the parochial tastes of the Western public – too rooted in alien histories and mythological systems of their own making. They are not 'in-between' in the same way. On the other hand, Nadine Gordimer or John Coetzee of South Africa, along with others from the white Commonwealth countries, while clearly playing this mediating role, are probably better placed in some category of the European novel of Empire because of their compromised positions of segregated privilege within colonial settler states. They are too much like the fictional 'us' of the so-called mainstream, on the inside looking out. There are, of course, important differences of emphasis. For the Latin American authors mentioned here, the 'new' immigrations play nothing like the role they do for Mukherjee and Rushdie. The coming of the African slaves to the New World took place centuries ago, and Italians, English and Germans arrived along an entirely different axis of power. Immigration is a crucial theme, but more as a flowing out than a flowing in (as in the cinematic counterparts to this metropolitan interest in the Third World – the films *El Norte* and *Salvador*, for example). The Latin Americans' successful intervention into the metropolitan bookmarkets is, if anything, the model for the rest (and we shall see, for example, how important that model is for Rushdie), but their defiant worldliness takes a different form – a careful wavering between nostalgic nationalism and pan-Americanism, between satirisations of the juntas and parodies of the guerrillas, often presented in a voluptuous, experimental prose that has become expected in the wake of García Márquez. One thinks especially of Allende – brought up in Bolivia, Europe and the Middle East and, until lately, exiled in Venezuela – whose *The House of the Spirits* owes so much to the East German novelist, Christa Wolf, and whose lament for Chile loudly declares itself a political novel without really offering the oppositional politics it promises. Like Wolf's *The Quest for Christa T.*, it is primarily a study of the recovery of memory through writing. In a common gesture in this fiction, its 'typical' revolutionary, the character Miguel, refers to Salvador Allende's coming victory with characteristic stupidity: 'the election was a joke . . . whoever won, it would make no difference because you would just be changing the needle on the same old syringe, and . . . you cannot make a revolution at the ballot box but only with the people's blood'.[7]

Among other things, writers like Rushdie, Vargas Llosa and Allende show now unrepresentative much of the writing now being published from the Third World is. Their names are now more familiar than those of the radical Salvadoran poets, Claribel Allegría and Roque Dalton, or the Lebanese poet and novelist, Etel Adnan, not because they are necessarily 'better', but because they tell strange stories in familiar ways. Inevitably, the demands of Western tastes ensure selective criteria: the preference, first of all, for novels (an imported genre), which sell better than poetry, testimonials and plays even though these forms make up the majority of what is actually written in the Third World; the tendency to privilege writing in European languages, even though (in Asia and the Middle East particularly) there are developed, continuous and ancient literary traditions in such languages as Urdu, Bengali, Chinese and Arabic; the attraction to writing that thematises colonialism, but that does not do so from a strident point of view; and (in a way related to this last point) the attraction to writing that is aesthetically 'like us' – that displays the complexities and subtleties of all 'great art.'[8]

The aesthetic misunderstandings at work in this celebrity-making are, of course, also political ones. Just as in those revisionist theories of Marxism that see the Third World standing before the First as proletarian to bourgeois, there is a tendency to regard the work of even Oxford-educated colonials as a form of 'low' art. If that art happens to depict angrily and in some detail the mechanisms of oppression employed by imperialism, it usually ceases to be thought of as art at all, and is soon relegated to the 'black studies' or 'Marxism' sections of the local bookstores.

The writers mentioned above understand these guidelines fully and avoid a spurious labelling. But it is more than their artistic quality that allows them to do so. Even in the work of those who have not received the same acclaim, the aesthetic conflicts of reception cannot be seen, as they often are, in terms of the 'high' culture/'low' culture split so familiar in debates about the literary canon. Fredric Jameson's (in some ways) excellent essay on the 'national allegory' does this by arguing that the Third-World novel is for the most part 'socially realistic', that it is unable to 'offer the satisfactions of Proust or Joyce' with their 'rhythm of modernist innovation'. In fact, this statement is not true, even for those novels that are not 'modernist'. A different kind of innovation is at work – one that the contentious politics of decolonisation has obscured – and which has been called 'resistance literature' in the recent work of Barbara Harlow. One of the problems with Jameson's account is that it makes Third-World literature an important artefact or record, but an artefact without theoretical importance – obscuring its staggering abundance and diversity by making it a totality to be 'mapped' (a term that has its own unintentional ironies). To say that Third-World literature 'as a whole' is locked in the naïve aesthetics of European realism is to say that it can be described but not really engaged with, like an ethnographer studying human subjects in the proverbial rural village.[9] With the same assumptions, the metropolitan reader is surprised or delighted to find authors like Rushdie or Allende treating Third-World themes with 'sophistication', and that surprise has everything to do with their current popularity. But other equally 'sophisticated' novelists are not popular, and they are not because they are not 'cosmopolitan' in the specific sense outlined above.

This neglect in Western critical circles has nothing to do with the fact that the work of writers like Dalton and Adnan is 'political'. The prominence of politics in Third-World fiction – or rather, our own tendentious projection of politics on to a mythical 'Third-World' – is exactly what Western critics find attractive. It is a mark of novelty, shock value, contemporary relevance and the exotic, and more importantly, it makes a false distinction between 'their' literature and 'ours'. For example, on the issue of nationalism itself, Mary Layoun has correctly pointed out that 'in a perverse if nonetheless pleasing reversal, the most radical location or citation of the allegory of nationalism could perhaps not exclusively be situated in the Third-World novel at all but precisely in the universalizing postmodernist first-world text' – works like Thomas Pynchon's *Gravity's Rainbow*, E. L. Doctorow's *Ragtime*, Ralph Ellison's *Invisible Man* and many others.[10] The demand for Third-World themes in the literary marketplace as a result of the guerrilla victories, 'anti-terrorism' campaigns and oil embargoes that fill the headlines, has made it easier for many peripheral writers to find a hearing. But only within a field of reception already defined by metropolitan tastes and agendas.

In the interplay of class and race, metropolis and periphery, 'high' and 'low', and cosmopolitans have found a special home, because they are both capturing a new world reality that has a definite social basis in immigration and international communications, and are at the same time fulfilling the paradoxical expectations of a metropolitan public. They bridge the literary world's Manichean spaces, and do so by exhibiting a political-aesthetic that is itself double. On the one hand, they satisfy the unwritten guidelines of metropolitan taste by supplying the market demand for novelty, either as exotica, political exposé or simple *Schadenfreude*. But just as importantly they also deviate from these guidelines by being deliberately pedagogic; by historicising current events without processing them in the manner of the media, which (as Benjamin had noted) gives us information as if it were 'already read'.

They reinforce dominant tastes, but in a characteristically dual fashion – not in reluctant submission to values branded on to the skin of their cultures, but as participants in a new *world* literature, with apprenticelike devotion to a mind-boggling array of literary precursors from diverse regions and traditions. Thus, Vargas Llosa draws on Flaubert, Balzac and Da Cunha; Rushdie on Günter Grass, Italo Calvino and the storyteller of Baroda; Derek Walcott on Malraux, Yeats and the calypsonian Sparrow. But more importantly, they are writers for whom the national affiliations that had been previously 'given' as part of a common world view of the Third-World intellectual have lost their meaning.

By combining widely different traditions – previously ignorant of one another – and placing them within the same frame of reference, they inform First-World audiences about what they persist in refusing to see. Their embrace of the dominant literary creed exalting modernist 'complexity', 'subtlety', 'irony' and 'understatement' at the same time involves a vision of democracy, freedom, 'popularity', 'truth' – largely lost or devalued in the metropolis seen as an arena of disintegration and postmodern decentring. In this sense, one recalls how in Allende's *The House of the Spirits*, with all its narrative gamesmanship, the story subsides in its closing chapters into a deliberately prosaic, eye-witness account of the Pinochet coup. In that grim moment, the marvellous reality of the horse-dog Barrabas and the levitations of Clara return to the shadows letting the historical record find its rightful place.

For these writers, the cosmopolis is no longer just life in the capitals of Europe and North America, nor that place of refuge for the native intellectual seeking a break from the barbarousness of underdevelopment at home. It is rather (and simply) the *world* – polyglot and interracial. As Mukherjee writes in her story 'The Lady from Lucknow': 'I have lived a life perched on the edge of ripeness and decay. The traveller feels at home everywhere, because she is never at home anywhere.'

COSMOPOLITANISM AS THE ENEMY

To understand what Rushdie and others are responding to, one has to look at the arguments of decolonisation theory itself. To give a sense of the way that 'cosmopolitanism' as defined above violates an important Third-World rhetorical mode, one has to see how the concept has been formed historically. Paradoxically, the starting point for any study of cosmopolitanism and dependency – and indeed, one of the early elaborations of an aesthetic that might be called 'Third-World' – is the work of a European.[11] Antonio Gramsci, despite the close attention he has received in recent decades, has not usually been seen as a theorist of national culture in the dependency sense. There has, first of all, been a tendency to ignore the predominance of literary theory in Gramsci's work as a whole. Of the many studies written about him, most concentrate on the life and thought of an organiser and tactician: the activist of the Turin factory councils, the delegate to the first Congresses of the International and the political strategist of the Prison Notebooks.

Studies of his theories usually treat the familiar concepts of 'hegemony', 'organic intellectual' and 'war of position', while ignoring his interest in linguistics and popular culture as well as his specific references to European stereotypes about the Arab world, India and China. In fact, he left behind a body of work that exhaustively analysed the emergence of the 'cosmopolitan intellectual', which he saw as poised against the vital work of creating 'national culture'. What is more, Gramsci happens to display extraordinarily well that aspect in British society of national struggle *within* the European nation–state by its own embattled minorities. It is a discussion essential to understanding Britain's contradictory situation at present, a situation Rushdie has helped to clarify.

As we shall see, Rushdie captures this interdependence of nationality and class with a precision that owes something to his Indo-English background. For Europe, particularly in its major colonies, had left the traces of its exploration in a hierarchical structure of tongues, customs and complexions on modern 'national' soil. In Rushdie's India, the remnants of former imperial relationships are everywhere: in the Bombay servants with Portuguese names who worship a Jesus who is blue like Krishna; in English-speaking Saleem who 'translates' so that his many-tongued countrymen can understand one another on All India Radio; in the pornographic magazines of the Islamic ruling circles; in the massacre of the poorer rural 'blackies' of East Pakistan by their wealthier compatriots to the West.[12]

To see these relationships through literature is to limit one's audience since literature is bound by language. But broadening that audience is not simply a problem of translation. Rushdie, for example, would feel as many misgivings about portraying the lives of Pushtus and Kurds in Islamabad as in London, for his views veer from theirs at more than one angle. His 'Englishness' and 'Indianness' are fungible: not merely a distinction of language or habitation, but the aesthetic tracings of class – his 'bookishness' and 'intellectualism'. Once the imperial interchange is set in motion, fiction between nations illuminates fiction between nations-in-a-nation.

Few writers have been better situated to discuss these concerns than Gramsci, a writer whose influence on postwar British intellectuals (who more or less discovered him outside Italy) has been deep and general. As a European from the impoverished and segregated Southern regions of a divided Italy, Gramsci knew internal divisions first-hand. Like much of the Third World, Southern Italy bore the marks of illiteracy, peonage and the dominance of an industrialised North acting, domestically, like a foreign oppressor.[13] In a kind of low parody of the scientific racism that accompanied empire, the people of Milan and Turin actually considered Sardinians like Gramsci genetically inferior. And despite Italy's own involvements in colony-hunting in northern Africa during the 1920s and 1930s, the country itself had much in common with the British colony of India. As V. G. Kiernan pointed out: 'a great deal in Italy's social structure and the social psychology that goes with it, notably in the South, has its counterpart in India,'[14] In the words of Marx, in a passage Gramsci may well have known, the parallels were striking: 'Just as Italy has, from time to time, been compressed by the conqueror's sword into different national masses, so do we find Hindustan, when now under the pressure of the Mohammedan [sic], or the Mogul, or the Briton, dissolved into as many independent and conflicting States as it numbered towns, or even villages.'

These affinities suggest why many Third-World theorists have taken Gramsci as their own – particularly minority intellectuals within Britain and the United States (Cornel West and Stuart Hall, for example) and, as a body of work, above all Latin America, where the first attempt by a government in power to approach official cultural policy with a consciously Gramscian perspective can be seen in contemporary Nicaragua.[15] Well before they were published in English, the cultural writings of Gramsci found extensive representation in Gaspar Quintana's Cuban edition of 1973, although Gramsci's *Intellectuals and the Organisation of Culture* was already widely known from an Argentinian translation as early as 1960.[16] Thus, in Roberto Fernandez Retamar's seminal 'Caliban' essay of 1974, we find him reminding his audience that Gramsci's specific sense of the term 'intellectual' 'has already been used among us at the preparatory seminar of the Havana Cultural Congress, and . . . Fidel had returned to the theme in his speech at the First National Congress of Education and Culture'.[17] He is there also at the core of the cultural theories of communication and popular culture by the Chilean scholars, Armand Mattelart, Michele Mattelart and Ariel Dorfman.[18] Nor has he been used by those from the Latin American socialist countries alone. The Costa Rican writer José Luis Velázquez P.'s recent attack on the Nicaraguan revolution in *Sociedad civil y dictadura* (1986) models itself on Gramsci's theories of civil society.[19]

In general, the side of Gramsci's work most pertinent here concerns what he called 'national-popular' literature, a concept that has already received some attention. However, by not giving sufficient notice to the 'highly specific combination' of 'nation' and 'people' existing in Gramsci's Italy, most have missed the way it merges the ideas of class and *nationality* – a combination that is crucial for understanding the aura surrounding 'cosmopolitanism' as he meant it. As we shall see below, it is precisely this thrust that has given so much force to recent accounts of the contemporary arts communities of black Britain by Paul Gilroy, A. Sivanandan and others, and which helps explain the influence and importance of the writers outlined here.

Italy never achieved full political unification. Its inability to create a coherent national mythos was for Gramsci the result of its failure to develop a literature that could bridge Italy's diverse communities. For specific historical reasons, what had developed there was a professional *literati* that remained culturally segregated from what he called the 'popular national reality', a term that in the restricted field of literary production included folklore, *feuilletons* or serial literature, and the brand of 'propagandistic' fiction for mass audiences so widespread in Europe and North America that tended to use the pulp staples of crime plots, superman themes and entrepreneurial underdogs – forms that reinforced the existing structure of values while disempowering their readers with compensatory hopes, and furthering the misconception that the particular joys of such fiction were 'subliterary' and therefore below the dignity of serious study by the *literati*.

His emphases here are striking for several reasons. At a very early date he was already treating literature not as the 'spirit of the age' or some distilled high-literary 'tradition', but as a social institution with interventionary powers that underlined its role as a form of 'ideological conditioning' within what Perry Anderson calls the 'strategic nexus of civil society'. Similarly, he departed from most of the European critical tradition, including its Marxists, by generally ignoring *capolavorismo* – the exclusive study of 'quality' literature – and turning his interests instead towards literature as a contemporary and meaningful function of belief and persuasion. Inasmuch as he was interested in the much more common practice of literary 'appreciation', he politicised it in a prescriptive sense by pointing approvingly to individual authors who managed to combine the classics' verbal beauty and 'divine inebriation' with the ability to reach out and affect the 'uninitiated'.

For all the resonance these positions have for current conflicts of Third-World reception, his major contribution – and precisely that part of his work that is most consistently ignored – is his argument that the question of culture itself is nation-specific. In accounting for Italian cultural disunity, Gramsci assessed the unique character of Italian history from a philological point of view (he had earlier written a thesis on the history of the Italian language in 1918, and studied glottology at the University of Turin in 1911 and 1912). As we noted above, the discipline of philology accompanied the rise of modern nationalist rhetoric and contributed to it, providing the basis for our own contemporary practice of literary study, which has such a hard time bringing 'peripheral' literatures into its field of vision. From this perspective, Gramsci noted the following peculiarities in the Italian situation.

The underdevelopment – intellectually, literarily and economically – of early twentieth-century Italy could be traced to its origins in the Roman Empire itself. The problem, by

European standards, of Italy's late-becoming as a nation – inadequately realised by the collective struggles of the Risorgimento (1848–70) – obsessively occupied the Italian intellectual milieu of Gramsci's day and contributed to the rise of Mussolini and his pseudo-imperial ventures into Libya and Ethiopia. The stage had been set for this catastrophe by the distorted development of Italian intellectuals. When, in the nineteenth century, the project of nation-forming had remained incomplete, the cultural representation of the disenfranchised peasantry and impoverished city-dwellers in a total national *mythos* was the task of the day. And yet the essayists, columnists and professors already found the issue passé. The Italian intellectual's lifelessness and conservatism before the pressing question of the 'nation' could be pinpointed in the Roman imperial legacy:

> [It is] necessary to go back to the times of the Roman Empire when Italy, through the territory of Rome, became the melting pot of the cultured classes from throughout the Empire. Its ruling personnel became ever more imperial and ever less Latin: they became cosmopolitan.[20]

This historical uniqueness of Italy as hereditary descendant of the Roman Empire and, later, as Papal Seat, fundamentally disrupted the incipient national spirit enjoyed by the intellectual castes elsewhere in Europe after the Renaissance: 'From the 1500s on . . . Italian Catholicism was experienced as a surrogate for the spirit of nationalism and statehood, and not only that, but as a worldwide hegemonic function – that is, as an imperialistic spirit.'[21] Italy produced, therefore, what could be called 'imperial' intellectuals. On the one hand, they were entrenched within the ersatz universality of the Church, where they tended to fill the ranks of the reactionary Catholic hierarchy; on the other, they swarmed abroad to serve as technicians and specialists in other countries whose 'medieval cosmopolitanism [had] shed its skin'. They became, in effect, managers of the national classes in other parts of Europe.

It is no coincidence, actually, given this history, that the one European of his time to theoretically develop literary-political issues of such importance to decolonisation would have come from a land beset by imperial decline. The interdependency of the imperial encounter – an interdependency that helps explain

England's rich tradition of novels by Conrad, Forster, Rhys and others, which sensitively (if limitedly) depict the mutual deformations of world conquest – is here the occasion for an analysis that pierces the heart of European development, and from a specifically literary point of view. For Gramsci's philological approach, apart from stressing the literary character of nationalism's foundations, prodded him to see European history as a struggle among multiple language-based pockets of opposition to the imperial Church. It was precisely the rise of the vulgate tongues that finally dismantled the pernicious imperial unities of Rome and the Church, such that imperialism itself was seen as a *forced* or artificial unity of distinct and independent cultures.

What is essential to see here is the striking dialectic of his observations when considered together. The international situation, as he put it, had to be 'considered in its national aspect'. For not only were the nation's discontinuities of ethnicity and class analogous to the ethnic and linguistic rupture between states, but 'national' differences continued to exist *within* states, and provided excuses to many of the class disparities that persisted. 'Colonisation', then, for Gramsci was not only international but also domestic. In a presentiment of the more recent work of linguists like Voloshinov, 'language' included the new ways of thinking and new linguistic usage of emergent social groups generally, rather than those divisions now institutionalised in the university and suggested by his term 'the vulgate tongues'. Thus, in respect to the latter, he distinguished between the positive 'breaking away' represented by their first appearance, and the later attempt to force them into new unities by the 'elaboration of a "distinguished vulgate" [made possible by] a certain centralisation of intellectual groups, or to say it better, of professional literati' – an observation that, in this context, can be said to resonate suggestively with reference to the 'high' cultural norms by which certain works from abroad and not others are valorised, or by which writing in the world languages of Spanish and English, for example, are given preferential treatment.

Gramsci was not alone in his observations, as evidenced by the work of an exact contemporary from Peru, the journalist and activist José Carlos Mariátegui. Influenced by many of the same intellectual sources as Gramsci – particularly the nineteenth-century Italian critic, Francesco de Sanctis – Mariátegui exhibited a strikingly similar biographical profile. He

was sickly as a child, a cripple in later life, a theatre and art critic
in his youth, and a recognised founder of indigenous socialism
in the era of the Third International, with a critical methodology
that combined literary research and active commitment. Like
Gramsci, his attitude towards the attempt of the International
to form a uniform front of self-disciplining local parties set him
to analysing how national traditions might be reconciled with
'internationalism' – that is, how joint organisational work might
be reconciled with the unique problems posed by Peru's Andean
culture and large Quechua-speaking population. According to
Alberto Flores Galindo, 'Mariátegui ended up elaborating a specific method – Peruvian, Indoamerican, Andean – of thinking
about Marx. Predictably, it was precisely by being most Peruvian
that he became the most universal.'[22] On this basis, in a crucial
difference from Gramsci, he in fact opposed incorporation of the
Peruvian party in the Third International.

In this way representative of the centre/periphery conflicts
that characterise the cultural theories of decolonisation today,
he sought crucially to reapply in a dependency context many
of the concerns that had occupied Gramsci. In a much more
classic scenario than Gramsci's 'domestic colonialism', Peru
had endured generations of European economic pillage, most
recently in Britain's expropriation of Peru's rich sodium nitrate
and guano deposits in the mid-nineteenth century. The axis
of cultural valorisation and suppression and the role that the
indigenous intellectuals played in the process were therefore
fundamentally different – less a question of class, dialect and
ethnicity (although, as always, these were inevitably present
as justifications) than a conflict between states, Peru having
accomplished its formal independence almost a half-century
earlier. Remarkably, though, Mariátegui found himself facing the
same default of the intellectuals in creating a national culture.

There were, Mariátegui argued, three periods in a country's
literature: the colonial, the cosmopolitan and the national.[23]
The listing itself, in an ascendant scale of value, inverts the
Gramscian terminology in one sense, while preserving it in
another. 'Cosmopolitanism' was still an arrested, incomplete
middle stage, a negative quantity. But its deleterious effects
were the function in Peru's case (as in Latin America as a
whole) of unprocessed foreign importations of the cultural
values of an external oppressor – Europe – rather than the

legacy of rootlessness and managerial professionalism spawned by a position within the colonial relationship from the coloniser's side. Himself steeped in European literary history like his Peruvian contemporaries, Mariátegui could speak of the 'unity of European culture, maintained during the Middles Ages by Latin and by papal authority' and later 'shattered by the nationalist movement which individualised literature'.[24] And like Gramsci, he cheered on such shattering, and for the same reasons.

But given the vivid memory of invasion and dislocation, the stakes of challenging European imperial 'unity' in the Latin American context were much greater. The culmination of literary development in his emphasis was precisely the 'national' as declaration of otherness *vis-à-vis* the invader's culture – an emphasis that in the chauvinist atmosphere of Fascist Italy was not and could not have been Gramsci's. Not only the different colouring given the problem by the historically concrete issue of late colonial 'invasion' by the British, but the presence in Latin America of the Indian, and of the related complex of issues surrounding *mestizaje*, or the much earlier Europeanised but indigenous sector of *criollos*, combine to give the national problem for Mariátegui a different trajectory altogether, where the rapacious external factors of imperialism formed part of a 'felt' culture. The point here, however, is the fundamentally similar approach both arrived at in reference to literary cosmopolitanism. Thus, in dissecting the failings of the Peruvian intellectual, Mariátegui's complaints remarkably echo those of his Italian counterpart:

> In Peru, literature did not grow out of an indigenous tradition, history, and people. It was created by the importation of Spanish literature and sustained by imitation of that literature. . . . Peruvian writers never felt any ties with common people. Only the Inca empire and the colony were clearly defined, and the writers chose the colony.[25]

What is important to notice here in his comments – really a transposition of Gramsci's 'domestic colonialism' to a classical colonial framework – is the way that the language of class wears the garments of race and ethnicity, where each of those categories corresponds to a sub-population with its own histories and traditions possessing unequal potential in providing a basis for a not-yet-realised national culture. Mariátegui's focus is, therefore, the 'indigenous' as opposed to Gramsci's class-orientated 'national-popular' with its admiration for the universal appeal of such writers as Tolstoy, Shakespeare and the Greek tragedians. Similarly, the counterpart of the élitist *literati* is expressed by Mariátegui in terms of the race/class nexus embodied in the Latin American *criollo*, with paradoxical results. Denouncing the literary movement in Uruguay known as 'nativism', which reduced the Indian to a set of purely literary plots, themes and characters, Mariátegui argued that its exotic appetites were 'born of a cosmopolitan experience'. By contrast, he urged writers to immerse themselves in the indigenous spirit, and reorientate literature to reflect the traditions of those who made up four-fifths of Peru's population. Because of the narrowly mercenary, ill-defined philistinism of the 'native' white ruling class, this could only be done with the aid of (and the ultimate reaction against) Europeanisation:

> Our nativism, which is also necessary for revolution and emancipation, cannot be a simple *criolloism*. The Peruvian *criollo* has not yet liberated himself spiritually from Spain. His Europeanization, in reaction to which he must find his own personality, has been only partly completed. Once he is Europeanized, today's *criollo* will become aware of the drama of Peru, recognizing in himself a bastardized Spanish and in the Indian the cement of nationality. . . . Whereas the pure *criollo* generally conserves his colonial spirit, the Europeanized *criollo* of our times rebels against the spirit, even if only as protest against its limitations and archaism.[26]

It was Gramsci, however, rather than Mariátegui, who successfully translated these social observations into clear aesthetic preferences. National-popular literature exhibited, first of all, what he called a 'positive *contaminatio* of traditionally elevated art'. This familiar conflation of high and low art, however, with its resonances of class, did not exhaust the matter. Societies capable of producing national-popular writers for Gramsci (like ancient Greece and Renaissance England) typically experienced 'many and hybrid importations' from the cultures with which it came in contact. Such a literature had to manifest nationally the hybrid combinations of its locality brought about by such contact, and exhibit a vigorous 'spirit of combination' necessary for 'harmonizing the many contradictions of national life'.[27]

More specifically, and at the level of the art work itself, he distinguished between '*la lingua e i linguaggi*', the former referring to conventional linguistic usage and the latter to a personal alteration of that convention. His intention was to place limits on the arbitrariness and egotism of the individual artist's manipulation of language as in the European modernisms then in full swing. In the words of one Gramsci critic:

> If one arbitrarily distorts the *lingua*, he/she shows open disregard for the *lingua's* social and historical ('nazionale–popolare–culturale') defining ground, and that poet opts for an artistic 'monologue' over a cultural function contained in 'dialogue'.[28]

He consistently attacked under the rubric of 'byzantinism' that 'pathological manifestation of language (vocabulary)' of which all the 'artistic and literary schools and groups [are a] . . . cultural manifestation'.[29] These harsh attacks on the élitism of the *literati* were elaborated in a set of strict preferences that amounted almost to a political programme: the art of dialogue over that of monologue, the art of 'impassioned sarcasm' over that of 'irony', and the art of ingenuousness and spontaneity, which he associated with the 'sentiments and conceptions that the silent masses hold'.[30] Encapsulated in another of these couplings is a restatement, in aesthetic terms, of his earlier dichotomy between the cosmopolitan and activist intellectual. For irony, he argued, was the attitude of 'isolated intellectuals . . . indicat[ing] the distance of the artist from the mental content of his own creation . . . a distancing related to a more or less dilettantish scepticism belonging to dillusionment, weariness, and "*superominismo*" [supermanism]', whereas 'impassioned sarcasm' was the 'appropriate stylistic element for historical-political action'.[31]

To conclude, then, for Gramsci the 'cosmopolitan' – almost always negative in his usage – implied a superficial or 'picturesque' attachment to a cultural miscellany based on empire. A specific illustration could be found in his study of Esperanto, which he saw as the project of 'an intellectual élite seeking affinities with its own caste abroad'.[32] The aesthetic by-products of the attitude expressed themselves in 'egotistical inventiveness', 'bookishness', being devoid of 'impressions of collective life . . . the modes of thought, . . . the signs of the epoch . . . the changes that are occurring in customs, etc'.[33] We shall return to these points later by looking at the contradictory way in which they are expressed in the work of Rushdie himself.

THE AESTHETIC DIMENSION

We have looked at Gramsci and Mariátegui to give a sense of the stakes involved in the cosmopolitan challenge to national culture. While their arguments continue to enrich the debates that have been carried on in the postwar period (and we shall look at some of them below), they did not live long enough to witness the changes that have given cosmopolitanism a new character. Today it is based in part on real social changes, not merely predictable concessions to dominant culture by writers interested in carving out a career, or in escaping the suffocating atmosphere of a domestic culture which foreign travel has made seem 'backward'.[34] At the heart of those changes were the great postwar immigrations to the metropolitan centres. These immigrations – in the United States of Mukherjee and the Britain of Rushdie, for example – have in a sense muted the national question, not only because they have happened in the wake of (and partly as a result of) formal independence, but because they have been motivated by economic and cultural opportunity or flight from repression. In that way they deny the old pattern of need to create a national mythos in the country of origin. On the other hand, the immigrations have posed the national question more strongly than ever, although in a different light – namely, within the Western countries to which the new 'immigrants' now only half belong – countries which are being forced to account for the new composition of their collective make-up.

In this way, for example, Paul Gilroy discusses the expressive cultures of black Britain by showing 'that culture does not develop along ethnically absolute lines but in complex, dynamic patterns of *syncretism*'. The roving reggae 'sound systems' of urban black youth and the 'dub' poetry of West Indians living in London combine with the Notting Hill Carnival to create a cultural 'signature' that white Britain takes up as its own, and which re-emerges as new-wave hits on the popular song charts. At the same time, young West Indian and Asian playwrights find grudging acceptance of their own sought-after arrival in the mainstream by appointments at the Royal Court and National Theatres. Significantly, though, the appearance of a new British syncretism is balanced against another kind of reality – the sense of community that persists across the African and Asian diasporas. The two tendencies exist side by side:

> A new structure of cultural exchange has been built up across the imperial networks which once played host to the triangular trade of sugar, slaves and capital. . . . The cultural and political expressions of new world blacks have been transferred not just to Europe and Africa but between various parts of the new world itself.[35]

These global confrontations and blendings have produced new goals for art that both confound and enrich the older goal of finding the language appropriate to the place. *Race and Class* editor, A. Sivanandan, has outlined some of them. In a perfect example of the syncretism cited by Gilroy, he does this with the aid of quotations from T. S. Eliot:

> To 'positivise' his identity, the black man must go back and rediscover himself – in Africa and Asia – not in a frenetic search for lost roots, but in an attempt to discover living tradition and values. He must find, that is, a historical sense, 'which is a sense of the timeless as well as the temporal, and of the timeless and temporal together' and which 'involves a perception not only of the pastness of the past, but of its presence'. Some of that past he still carries within him, no matter that it has been mislaid in the Caribbean for over four centuries. It is the presence of that past, the living presence, that he now seeks to discover. And in discovering where he came from he realises more fully where he is at, and where, in fact, he is going to.[36]

The distinction here, however, is not merely between an older and more modern way of conceiving identity, but between positions within the fluid unities of post-colonial culture itself. For Rushdie and Mukherjee only peripherally belong to the world of Gilroy and Sivanandan, who are much more the offspring of Frantz Fanon, Amílcar Cabral and other embattled theorists of decolonisation. This is so in spite of the fact that Fanon and Cabral symbolise the classic nation-forming struggles that the quotations above importantly modify. But like those fighters for African independence, Gilroy and Sivanandan highlight the 'liberating rationality' of the black communities for whom it is impossible to 'act socially or cohesively without the structures provided by formal organizations'.[37] They privilege the vision of the oppressed, and argue that process lies in organising from below. Writers like Rushdie, Vargas Llosa, Mukherjee and Allende reject this view, although they are deeply aware of it. To a great extent their work is specifically addressed to it, and against it.

The cosmopolitan embrace – its articulation of a new world literature designed to capture the global juxtapositions that have begun to force their way even into private experience – involves instead a flattening of influences, which assemble themselves, as it were, on the same plane of value. By stressing the global nature of everyday life – not merely (as in Gilroy) at the locus of identity within the metropolis – they consciously allude to the centre/periphery conflicts raised by decolonisation, and modify them by enhancing the role of the 'West' as, alternately, foil and lure. And this is, after all, the real distinction between the new cosmopolitanism and what Barbara Harlow has called 'resistance literature', the literature of the independence movements: namely, the role of the West. It is not the older concept of influence alone that is at work – say, the attractions for Peruvian or Nigerian novelists of French symbolism, imagism, or *nouveau roman* – not in other words, the attractions of high capitalist, city culture as filtered through its art, but the image of the West as receptacle of 'democracy'.

The Uruguayan historian, Eduardo Galeano, has described how advantages in Western industrial technique became the lure for the managers of the domestic Third-World economy to 'imitate ape-like, the advances spread by the great corporations'.[38] The lure of 'technique' has been, not just metaphorically, at work in literary relations too: the priority given modernist 'innovation', 'invention' and 'discovery'. Some of the reasons for this artistic embrace of the West and of the rejection of the caustic mentality of 'resistance' so alive in the words of Sivanandan, for example, are spelled out in Derek Walcott's essay 'The Muse of History', and Walcott, although a poet rather than a novelist, belongs with the new cosmopolitans:

The common experience of the New World, even for its patrician writers whose veneration of the Old is read as the idolatry of the *mestizo*, is colonialism. They too are victims of tradition, but they remind us of our debt to the great dead, that those who break a tradition first hold it in awe. They perversely encourage disfavour, but because their sense of the past is of a timeless, yet habitable, moment, the New World owes them more than it does those who wrestle with that past, for their veneration subtilises an arrogance which is tougher than violent rejection. They know that by openly fighting tradition we perpetuate it, that revolutionary literature is a filial impulse, and that maturity is the assimilation of the features of every ancestor.[39]

That attitude could generally stand for the other cosmopolitan writers grouped here. It has a basis, however, in a more overt politics than is suggested by Walcott's distanced way of putting things. As Galeano points out, in the Latin-American context as elsewhere 'instead of the social class for which history clamored with small success, it was the government of the populist *caudillos* that embodied the nation and gave the masses political and economic access to the benefits of industrialization' – the Juan Peróns, Mohammad Mossadeghs, Gamal Abdel Nassers and Sékou Tourés. Cosmopolitan writing, especially where it overlaps with that related subgenre that Ahmad called 'the nationalism of mourning', tends to challenge the state itself, whose hostility to the arts is always easier to locate in neo-colonies like Zaire, Haiti or Brazil than in the West, precisely because they cannot argue as effectively in the world arena for their own good intentions.

The confusion between the skewed independence of the populist *caudillos* and the more obvious agents of the Third-World political nightmare (Pinochet, Namphy, Bokassa and so on) is very common here. The socialist alternatives of Cuba, Angola and Vietnam play virtually no role in this particular imaginative world, which enjoys the publicity and acclaim denied 'resistance literature', which, in turn, distinguishes among states precisely because its writers are contributing to the rise of a new state power. There is, then, an important difference between literature that demolishes the pretence of national sovereignty for the purpose of accusing those who have sold it out, and literature that questions whether independence itself is meaningful or desirable.[40] Cosmopolitanism blurs the two. It is a blurring based on a traditional (Western) framework of value in which artists and the state are seen to be incompatible. The apocalyptic finality with which Canudos, Macondo, Chile and India perish in the novels of Vargas Llosa, García Márquez, Allende and Rushdie ambiguously counters their passionate opposition to censorship and their struggle for human rights in the public forum. In the end, this ambiguity grows from a parodic or dismissive approach to decolonisation: as we see, for example, in the tyranny of ideal- istic guerrilla general, Colonel Aureliano Buendía in *One Hundred Years of Solitude*; in the portrayal of insurgency as opera buffa in the Juaja of Vargas Llosa's *Historia de Mayta* with its pathetic infighting among Trotskyists and Apristas; or in the mercenary cynicism of contras and Sandinistas in the Honduras of Mukherjee's story 'The Middleman'.

As suggested by Gilroy and Sivanandan above, attempts to deal with the human effects of decolonisation have produced their own aesthetic emphases, which are different from those of the cosmopolitan Third-World writers. It is, of course, not possible to discuss this vision 'as a whole' since it is not monolithic. But in general it focuses on a decisive valorisation of 'the people' and an insistence on 'national culture' – in the sense that culture itself is meaningless if not considered 'in its national aspect'. Two examples are suggestive. First, Amílcar Cabral, founder of the African Party for Independence – Union of the Peoples of Guine and Cape Verde (PAIGC), which came to power under his leadership in 1973 forming the state of modern Guinea-Bissau. It would be hard to find anyone with a more purely instrumental view of culture, or a more embattled consciousness than Cabral's. As a native Cape Verdean, he was among those twelve or so men who in the entire history of Guine had achieved a university degree.[41] Thoroughly assimilated into Portuguese culture, in fact, 'his attitude throughout his life', according to one biographer, 'shows that he never viewed the Portuguese as enemies'.[42]

And yet, despite this profile of relative privilege, his definition of culture and the role of the arts was dependent on what he called the 'people-class' – very much like Mariátegui's '*el indio*' and Gramsci's 'people-nation'. Under the conditions of Portuguese colonisation, the destiny of that shiftless, drifting, ill-defined sector, the intellectual, was clear. To be something

was to be fighting; decolonisation was an opportunity for intellectual self-realisation: 'it is the struggle in the underdeveloped
countries which endows the petite bourgeoise with a function'.[43]
In a celebrated formulation, Cabral argued that this middle sector
had to 'commit suicide as a class' by completely identifying itself
'with the deepest aspirations of the people to which it belongs'.
This is only Mariátegui's discussion of 'assimilation' raised to
the level of a pitched battle, for 'Europeanisation' as a contradictory literary influence becomes (although contradictory) no
longer literary. 'Culture' is a weapon of war. The foundations of
that belief derived from a central thesis: 'it is easier to dominate
a people whose culture is similar or analogous to that of the
conqueror'.[44] Thus, in 'National Liberation and Culture', Cabral
is a deeply pragmatic tactician who speaks of the value of culture
as a 'martial art':

> The ideal for foreign domination . . . lies in this alternative:
> either to eliminate practically all the population of the domin-
> ated country . . . or to succeed in imposing itself without
> damage to the culture of the dominated people, that is, to
> harmonize economic and political domination of these people
> with their cultural personality.

Culture became a vehicle for liberation only as that which
superseded 'culture'. For Cabral was deliberately numb to the
appeals of the aesthetic life, and Aimé Césaire's and Leopold
Senghor's universalising theory of 'Negritude' – apart from its
delocalised sloganeering for an external population to whom the
abstract notion of 'African cultural identity could actually mean
something – was to him an opportunistic dabbling in culture's
outward show. He remarked that it was no coincidence that these
theories developed among assimilated Africans in 'cultural cen-
ters outside Black Africa', and that 'this "return to the sources"
is not in itself an act of struggle against foreign domination and
does not necessarily mean a return to traditions.'[45] The 'return'
itself showed a zealous but also merely reactive response of an
alienated caste severed from those who did not need to 'return'
because they *were* the source.

Frantz Fanon too arrived at Gramsci's 'national aesthetics'
from another (and more severe) angle: as an active member of the
Algerian Provisional Government to Ghana in 1960, editor of the

newspaper of the *Front de Libération Nationale* and an FLN member from 1956 until his premature death.[46] Despite being steeped in the 'Negritude' sympathies of the journal *Présence africain* in his formative years, Fanon foreshadows Cabral in opposing the view that transformed culture into 'a cult or a religion . . . more and more cut off from the events of today'.[47] For him, however, the literary intellectuals took centre stage as the actors in a psychological drama of contesting national and imperial temptations. National culture is much more than a set of political goals; its presence is responsible for nothing less than the native's 'psycho-affective equilibrium'.

Thus, Fanon addresses those who wield pens but do not know who they are, those who condemn the 'exaggerated passion of the defenders of national culture' while hiding behind 'French, English, or German culture'; those intellectuals who would be a ' "race of angels" colorless, stateless, rootless . . . taking up a "universal standpoint" at the cost of psycho-affective injuries' (Fanon, *Wretched of the Earth*, p. 218). The meaning of his reference to the term 'universal' comes out in his scornful references to the 'European Cultural Society threatening to transform itself into a Universal Cultural Society'. It is, in other words, another look at Gramsci's 'imperial-universal'.

Fanon turned his attention to the characteristic attitudes of competing Third-World intelligentsias at various stages of their coming-to-self. In fact, Fanon had an explicit theory of stages: the stage of assimilation; the stage of remembering who one is; finally, what he called the 'fighting phase' in which one veers towards the 'people' – not exactly to lose oneself in them, but rather to learn how to move forward with them (*WE*, p. 222). He therefore diagnosed literature as the expression and formative component of colonial consciousness. Caught between folklore and the technical dazzle of the metropolis, the colonial artist in Fanon's thinking typically drifted into exoticism. Just as Mariátegui wrote of the purely literary 'nativism' of Uruguay, he knew that folkloristic motifs – even by writers proclaiming their desire for roots – had the potential for being only the reverse side of assimilationism, equally alienated, equally outside looking in. Writers often elevated ancient custom as the touchstone of authenticity, whereas, Fanon insisted, custom in this sense was actually the deterioration of culture, since it locked it up in a past sealed off from the vigorously altering effects of contemporary events. The task, on the contrary, was actually to assimilate downwards by locating the 'zone of occult instability where the people dwell'; nor was it an attempt to fetishise the supposedly fixed identity of a metaphysical 'people', but an attempt that recognised supple variations:

> A national culture is not a folklore nor an abstract populism discovering the people's 'true nature' . . . but the whole body of efforts by a people in the sphere of thought. (*WE*, p. 233)

The evolution of artistic form within this process was, however, uneven and corresponded to the colonial intellectual's level of development within the national struggle. They were concisely these: humour and allegory are elements of a borrowed aestheticism characteristic of an intermediary stage between assimilation and the 'fighting phase'. In the latter, a 'literature of combat' comes into its own in which the artist shifts from addressing the audience of the oppressor to addressing his own people. Here one uses oral tradition not as set pieces, but for bringing conflicts 'up to date':

> There is a tendency to modernize the kinds of struggle which the stories evoke, together with the names of heroes and types of weapons. . . . The formula 'this all happened long ago' is substituted for 'what we are going to speak of happened somewhere else, but it might well have happened here today and it might happen tomorrow'. (*WE*, p. 240)

The methods of historical and political allusion are in this stage prominent.

Fanon clearly had in mind here actual village storytellers rather than an urbane literary élite, although his focus is precisely how this 'progress of national consciousness among the people gives precision to the literary utterances of the native intellectual' (*WE*, p. 239). Thus, in tracing the impact on Algerian storytellers in 1952–3, he notes what in his schema is their highest attainment: 'comedy and farce disappear, or lose their attraction'; the drama of plot no longer centres on the 'troubled intellectual' and his 'tormented conscience'; 'formalism is abandoned in the craftsman's work'; the contemplative attitude is made 'unreal' and 'unacceptable' (*WE*, pp. 241–3).

Taken together with Gramsci's prescriptive aesthetics, these arguments are remarkable for the way they capture the hybridity of cosmopolitan writing at the level of political attitude – an attitude towards the 'people'. In its formal properties, not merely in its themes, that writing reflects the other and more familiar hybridity of being from many countries, of having conflicting racial and linguistic allegiances. For as we shall see later in the novels of Rushdie, these artistic features are brought into a new combination. Vigorously adopting Gramsci's 'positive *contaminatio* of traditionally elevated art', he nevertheless brings the language of the newspapers into the refined epic contours of the 'serious' bourgeois novel; capable of exhibiting 'impassioned sarcasm' with a vengeance, his ironies are also clearly a part of the 'isolated intellectual's' disillusionment and weariness; hardly leaving behind humour and allegory, his work is nothing if not an oral tale brought 'up to date'. It is, in fact, a 'literature of combat' in one sense, and one which even attempts to locate the people's 'zone of occult sensibility'. But it is not addressed to them.

3
The Art of Translation

*[There is a] rarity of good novels about the Far East,
which can only be written by people who are in some way
anomalous . . .*

George Orwell[1]

Many of the examples here have been drawn from Latin America
because the discussion of literary cosmopolitanism is so developed there. An important example is the recent work of Angel
Rama, whose term 'transculturation' (borrowed from the earlier
work of Fernando Ortiz in 1940) captures that special value in
writing that exhibits 'a simultaneous adherence to terms entirely
heterogeneous, or rather, a curiously satirical playfulness that
oscillates endlessly between the adoption of a European model
and the valorisation of national difference'.[2]

As argued above, the cosmopolitanism attacked in decolonisation theory is not all bad, even from the point of view of
the political stands staked out by those theories. As Jean
Franco points out, for example, the heterogeneity of race,
ethnicity and politics, which had always been the shameful
symbol of a muddled national identity (what Vargas Llosa
cultural 'fragmentation' and cultural 'poverty') later became
for him and other of the Latin American 'new novelists' of
the early 1960s a mark of cultural vitality. The literary intelligentsia was discovering in its very 'carnivalesque pluralism
the claim on metropolitan attention that had so long eluded
it'.[3]

Indeed, Rama notes how in the 1920s and 1930s, Alejo
Carpentier rediscovered the African rhythms of the Cuban
village by listening to the music of Stravinsky, and how Miguel
Asturias learned to marvel at the lyric imagination of Guatemala's
indigenous communities by studying surrealist techniques of
automatic writing.[4] Of course, to give a sense of the matter's full

scope, the surrealists and Stravinsky had earlier initiated themselves in the replenishing European cult of primitivism which had
come to them in the form of African music (filtered through North
American jazz) and African sculpture and design. In this sense,
Rama uses the term 'transculturation' as a more accurate way of
referring to 'acculturation', which had misleadingly suggested
(in the words of Ortiz) 'the loss or uprooting of the previous
culture'. In response, Rama insists that more attention be paid
to the criteria of selectivity and invention that actually exists in
all cases of 'cultural plasticity':

> If the community is lively, it will accomplish a selectivity,
> both of what exists within it, and what comes in from outside
> effecting invention in an 'ars combinatario' appropriate to the
> autonomy of its own cultural system.[5]

As far as it goes, the gloss is useful. But it does not really
account for the kind of cosmopolitanism in which the distinction
between inside and outside has been obliterated. In that sense, a
writer like Rushdie is like Carlos Fuentes, a 'Mexican' novelist
born in Panama, raised for the most part in the United States
and ambassadorially linked to France. It is not just immigration
that is at issue, since we are dealing with intellectuals for whom
'assimilation' is doubly impossible. Operating within a *world*
literature those traditional national boundaries are meaningless,
writers like Fuentes and Rushdie also possess 'calling-cards' in
the international book markets because of their authentic native
attachment to a specific Third-World locale. In that sense, as
Rushdie insists, he does not suffer from a feeling of 'rootlessness';
'the problem is that [he] comes from too many places . . . [suffers]
excess rather than absence'.

> If you are an extra-territorial writer you select a pedigree for
> yourself, a literary family . . . Swift, Conrad, Marx are as much
> our literary forebears as Tagore or Ram Mohan Roy. . . . [W]e
> are inescapably international writers at a time when the novel
> has never been a more international form . . . cross-pollenation
> is everywhere.[6]

It is not just an attempt to cover tracks when Fuentes,
for example, argues in his recent book of essays, *Myself with*

Others, that his very diversity allows him better to engage in dialogue, to embody that Bakhtinian *heteroglossia* valorised in recent North American criticism; or that, being from nowhere, he is also from everywhere in the sense described by Edward Said when he speaks of the exile's 'plurality of vision [which] gives rise to an awareness of simultaneous dimensions, an awareness that – to borrow a term from music – is *contrapuntal*'.[7]

The implicit question raised by the chapter above is whether this homelessness is only another version of Gramsci's 'imperial-universal', which might explain the eagerness of metropolitan critics to embrace the 'pluralism' of the cosmopolitan just when defensive nationalism is on the Third-World agenda. Or, on the contrary, whether it is in the spirit of Gramsci's 'national-popular', whose 'hybrid importations' make such a literature possible, as when Rushdie speaks of being equally from India, Pakistan and England: 'the frictions make sparks, and that's what writing is'.[8] At least in the case of Rushdie, one would have to say it is both. Almost certainly unaware of Rama's work, he echoes it, substituting for 'transculturation' the more authorial concept of 'translation', a key term throughout his work:

> I, too, am a translated man. I have been *borne across*. It is generally believed that something is always lost in translation; I cling to the notion – and use, in evidence, the success of Fitzgerald–Khayyam – that something can also be gained.[9]

'Translation' – a term provocatively borrowed from the realm of the purely literary – is a political programme. He does, however, refer at the level of language to specifically colonial politics in the sense that he familiarises alien histories and traditions while defamiliarising modernist form, and tries to do so without 'neutralizing their oppositional characters'.[10]

In this sense, the unusually close attention Rushdie has given the themes, styles and histories of Latin America are worth looking at, if only because the models of anti-colonial resistance displayed there are so unlike the familiar cycle of communalist violence, religious corruption and voiceless village life on the subcontinent. In fact, Rushdie spent the years of his apprenticeship during the rise of the Latin American 'new novel', whose influence and authority – particularly, of course, that of García Márquez – suggested what his more recent political memoir, *The Jaguar*

Smile: A Nicaraguan Journey finally proves: his search for reference points within Latin American decolonisation as provided by one dominant current-events issue of the 1980s – Nicaragua – and the ironies implicit in his personal yoking-together of the two Indies, East and West:

> I recognized a deeper affinity with that small country in a continent (Central America) upon which I had never set foot. I grew daily more interested in its affairs, because, after all, I was myself the child of a successful revolt against a great power, my consciousness the product of the triumph of the Indian revolution. It was perhaps also true that those of us who did not have our origins in the countries of the mighty West, or North, had something in common – not, certainly, anything as simplistic as a unified 'third world' outlook, but at least some knowledge of what weakness was like, some awareness of the view from underneath, and of how it felt to be there, on the bottom, looking up at the descending heel.[11]

Born in Bombay in 1947, the son of a Cambridge-educated merchant of Muslim background who was conversant in Persian, Arabic and Western literature, Rushdie (himself a Cambridge graduate) has lived in England since the age of fourteen. Recipient of the prestigious Booker McConnell Prize for *Midnight's Children* in 1981, Rushdie went on to become a topical journalist in prominent publications on both sides of the Atlantic on subjects ranging from George Orwell and British immigration policies to the recent wave of Raj revival films. *The Jaguar Smile* is an extension of this kind of journalism, which had already shown a strong interest in the example of Nicaragua, culminating in his membership in Britain's Nicaragua Solidarity Committee and his acceptance of an invitation in 1986 to attend the Seventh Anniversary celebrations of the Nicaraguan revolution in Esteli, which forms the basis of his reflections in the book.

If on the one hand this interest was perfectly natural given Rushdie's sense of authorial mission, since (in a familiar modern pose) he had argued in one essay that writers could not leave 'the business of making pictures of the world to politicians' seeing that it would be 'one of history's most abject abdication's', it was on the other, odd for him to see affiliations between India and Central America. This was so in spite of the fact that those links were in a sense already archetypal, having been set down graphically in Abbe Raynal's massive eighteenth-century study, *A Philosophical and Political History of the Settlements and Trade of the Europeans in the East and West Indies* – a book (as C. L. R. James notes in *The Black Jacobins*), that independence leader Toussaint L'Ouverture read for inspiration as a house slave on the eve of Haitian independence.[12]

Seeing these affiliations was odd because India had always been the consummate former colony, partly as a result of its present vastness and wealth, but also because of its central role in English imperial decline. If the Philippines was the first Asian nation to win independence, it did so with a restricted mandate under North American control, and left nothing so tactfully epic as the Indian liberation story whose components include the well-known Home Rule Leagues, Gandhi's *satyagraha* (non-cooperation) movement in the 1920s and 1930s, the Quit India movement of 1942 and the peaceful accession to power following the war.

India was not only within the Asian context, but within the popular memory (above all in the West) the great success story of political gradualism – of a kind of 'evolutionary' independence. The quite different stories of Indonesia, Malaya and Vietnam (which resemble the Central American struggles in this respect) are usually presented as stories of warfare, cruelty and mismanagement in which the particular agents of violence are less important than the repellent atmosphere of violence itself. And yet, for this reason, the Indian Emergency of 1975, the language riots in Bombay, the assault on the Golden Temple at Amritsar and similar happenings, have stood out disappointingly in popular accounts of India as a kind of backward sliding of the 'democratic' model, and these lapses have sometimes explicitly been compared to the policies of the Latin American military dictatorships. V. S. Naipaul, for example, wrote about the Indian Emergency: 'The overthrow of socialism, the beginning of the assault on the poor: Indian events given a South American interpretation'.[13]

The 'transculturation' of these legends of 'democracy' and 'totalitarianism' – located in some indeterminate space between the Indies of the East and West – involves a transculturation at another level: between the culture of 'news' and novel. At the same time that he absorbs the liberating clarity of the struggle

in the grotesquely underdeveloped and beleagured region of
Nicaragua, hoping to adopt its lessons for that part of India
which can be made to use them, he 'translates' current events
into the themes and images appropriate to an 'artist' – one whose
authority to write about Nicaragua for a Western public derives
from his being a writer of 'high' literary novels. In an earlier essay
on Orwell, he had argued that literature must be political 'because
what is being disputed is nothing less that *what is the case*' – a theme
he picks up again in the booklength memoir when he says that
the struggle within Nicaragua is a 'struggle between two kinds
of discourse, vying for supremacy'.[14] This allusion to the battle
of discourse is characteristic of Rushdie's fiction, which is fully
aware of the practical consequences of novels on state regimes.
But its Cabral-like edge, in which 'truth' and 'untruth' are the
projects and responsibilities of artists acting like directors of
culture, is muddled in his fictional treatment of Pakistan and
India, whose problematic politics – much more than Nicaragua's
embattled anti-imperialism – begs for the novel form as if to help
problematise them at an existential level.

In part, it is not simply that a political shift occurs in
the act of literary 'translation', but that India itself evokes a
distinct national essence: more than any other country on earth
it combines a technocratic, mass-information, computer society
with an ancient, traditional and oral one – the two distant ends
of the historical spectrum frozen together. For India is a land
of over 700 million people in which over half are permanently
impoverished, in which three out of four are illiterate. It is a
'nation' the size of Western Europe with as many states as Europe
has countries, and with over sixteen major languages; and yet it is
also the land with the largest middle class in the world, possessor
of microchip factories, a country with more scientists than any
but the United States and the Soviet Union, a land in which 70
per cent of the population is in range of television, and in which
over 25 000 television sets can be found in its rural villages.[15]

The point is that Nicaragua, by virtue of what it represents
politically, could not for a writer like Rushdie be the subject of a
novel. Instead, it is the site of another balancing-act altogether –
between another kind of 'truth' and 'untruth'. It was a place, as he
puts it, where one could acquire 'the ability to distinguish between
the PLO and the IRA' – between a legitimate liberation force and
an army maddened by injury into a policy of vengeance.[16] His

frankly partisan support of the government there leaves no doubt about the camp in which Nicaragua should be placed. There are admiring portraits of every Sandinist leader except the Minister of Culture, Ernesto Cardenal, whom he finds to be too uncritical of Cuba and who directs an office (that for Rushdie, at least) is appropriately nicknamed 'Minicult'.

It is no accident that cultural policy specifically would be singled out for attack. Within the predominantly Western aesthetic that Rushdie occupies (and from which, at the mid-way point, he bridges the two Indies), culture always provides the occasion for a passion play on freedom and democracy. In this case, it allows Rushdie to retain a dignified balance appropriate to the 'serious novelist' according to the social codes accepted among his sceptical English and North American audiences. Inevitably, and by a sleight-of-hand, 'untruth' in a more unthreatening literary sense gradually comes to the fore: namely, 'Latin America as the home of anti-realism', a feature it is supposed to share with India (according to one of the book's anecdotes) through the agency of Rabindranath Tagore. In this way, we find Rushdie writing that in the city of Matagalpa, García Márquez's 'Macondo did not seem very far away'. And thus, he opens the book with a quote from the travels of Columbus saying 'instead of [the lands of the Great Khan] another, also rich, beautiful and plenty of fantasy, was discovered: America'. The influence of García Márquez on Rushdie in a sense passed through Nicaragua. The Anglicisation of 'magical realism', and the saleable 'Third-Worldism' it represents, required the adoption of a specific attitude towards the colonial legacy.

Part of that attitude had to do with the invocation of 'fantasy' itself, which has a different sense here than in those theories that discuss it as a mode of literature involving the explosion of desire (Rosemary Jackson), a hesitation between the natural and the supernatural (Tzvetan Todorov) or a complement to mimesis (Kathryn Hume).[17] In this case it is a genre that serves an ideological role as a genre: namely, as the imaginative expression of 'freedom' in the way, for example, that 'popular culture' in certain *New York Times* feature articles about teenagers in Warsaw and Moscow is nothing more than a signifier for what socialist countries cannot freely enjoy (discos, blue jeans, *Interview* magazine and so on). This is not to suggest that Rushdie uses this Cold War coding to attack Nicaragua, but only that the popular features of Latin American 'unrealism' in literature are overlayed on to his political observations in order to legitimise them.

Many of the similarities between Rushdie's *Shame* (1984), for example, and *One Hundred Years of Solitude* are, in fact, casual. When Third-World writers set out to describe the transformation of traditional societies, they tend to have, as both novels do, saga structures, a reliance on the unifying presence in the narrative of a matriarch who spans the generations (Ursula, Bariamma), and scenes suggesting the matriarchal origins of the oral tale. But the combination of elements in common suggests a much more direct influence. Both display a calculated and disorderly leaping to the future and past; both demonstrate the corruptibility of popular generals (Aureliano, Raza); the mimicry of Holy Writ; the cranky stubbornness of a father who pursues his ideals (José Arcadio, Mahmoud); a girl whose marriage is continually put off (Amaranta, Arjumand); an idiot child (Rebecca, Sufiya); a foreigner who is jilted in love (Pietro Crespi, Eduardo); scenes before an execution in a condemned man's cell (General Moncada, Iskander); the use of nicknames for beauties who have an appetite for jilting their suitors (Remedios the Beauty, the Virgin Iron-pants); illusory suicides of prominent political leaders who are supposedly shot through the chest (Aureliano, Iskander); scenes in which the protagonists are haunted by men they unjustly killed (José Arcadio, Raza); a crusty, ageless mystical counsellor who returns after death (Melquíades, Maulana); and (finally) the overall stylistic veneer of humorous fantasy and matter-of-fact violence.

Midnight's Children had also borrowed from *One Hundred Years of Solitude*: the miraculous happenings of the magicians' ghetto where ventriloquists 'could make stones tell jokes and contortionists . . . could swallow their own legs' (p. 237); like Macondo's gypsies, there was among the Midnight's Children a 'sharp-tongued girl whose words already had the power of inflicting physical wounds'. But there it is not primarily García Márquez but Günter Grass who gives Rushdie, in *The Tin Drum*, a model in the figure of a physically deformed and morally reprehensible hero with magical powers.[18] What Rushdie borrows from García Márquez is nevertheless unique in one respect: he theorises his own use of fantasy, and does so by referring to colonialism.[19]

García Márquez himself had made an issue of influence by habitually citing the Italian explorer Antonio Pigafetta, whose

Voyage to the New World inspires all of his work. Pigafetta 'wrote on his passing through our Southern America, a strictly factual account that nonetheless seems like a work of fantasy'.[20] The comment is an ambiguous one since it wavers between pride in the inspiration provided by 'our' America and scepticism about the accuracy and the intentions of Pigafetta (for example, is 'a strictly factual account' Garcia Marquez's judgement or, as is likely, Pigafetta's dubious claim?).[21] Apparently these features are not limited only to the explorer Pigafetta. The same balance of satire and sincerity is found in García Márquez's comments on another fantastical explorer:

> Daily life in Latin America shows us that reality is full of extraordinary things. In this respect, I usually mention the North American explorer F. W. de Graff, who at the close of the last century made an incredible voyage through the Amazonian world in which, among other things, he saw a stream of boiling water and a place where the mere sound of human voice provoked torrential downpours.[22]

García Márquez had spoken of Pigafetta to a European audience in his Nobel acceptance speech, with an admiration that was at the same time sincere and backhanded. The conventional problematics of 'truth' and 'fiction' are here expressed in an imperial context by a Third-World author whose acknowledged debt to his former masters is a lesson in how to lie appealingly. His fiction is their 'news'. And by implication – if the irony is taken far enough – his novels have a greater claim to truth than their non-fiction, for their fantasies are the result of the strangeness of a world to which they are alien, while his reports to the metropolis are authoritative because native. It is thus that he ironically converts ill-will (in the form of his own implicit reprimands, and presumably in that of Pigafetta's and de Graff's ulterior motives) into a complaint, without relinquishing his subdued references to the probable causes of the explorers' fantasies: namely, that they invented wonders in order to justify the expense of their ventures or to sell books upon their return; or that they intended to make future conquest appealing by the allure of their extravagant imagery.

While these complaints linger in his ironies, García Márquez defuses them by suggesting that the explorers in one sense had no choice but to rely on fantasy. 'We have had to ask very little of the imagination as our greatest problem has been the inadequacy of a convention or a means by which to render our lives believable.'[23] The 'unbridled reality' of the colonial world cannot simply be reported; it has to be 'translated' or 'borne across' – and bearing-across is also, literally, 'metaphor'.

As he attributes his choice of form to the inheritance of European colonisation, García Márquez wilfully inverts the common neo-colonial dilemma of having to write in the language of the former colonisers. For it is not a question of a language involuntarily accepted but of an entire artistic outlook voluntarily assumed. The logic behind this new emphasis is plain. It places responsibility for the present on the only ones today capable of mastering the situation, instead of reliving the sins of the past. By proclaiming that his discourse derives from imperialism's early myth-makers, he envisions an influence so deep that it infuses all thought. But at the same time, the influence is *their own* possession, and therefore capable of being transformed for constructive purposes. The power of the former rulers is in fact diminished, for the conqueror himself has apparently been conquered by a reality which he is powerless to describe in any way other than the language of fantasy.

Among the accounts of former explorers, it is significant that García Márquez did not mention Bartolomé de las Casas, whose *Destruction of the Indians* recorded the cruelties of the *conquistadores* toward the indigenous peoples of the New World. It is a rare example of a work that overcame the apparent free interchange between truth and fiction in the conflict of alien peoples on either side of the colonial nexus. De las Casas's outrage – his ability to conceive of the Indians as sentient, moral beings – challenged the notion that the illusion of realism in the explorers' accounts was a result of their ability to describe violence impassively, neutrally and as a simple matter of fact. It was especially to avoid the righteous indignation of De Las Casas that García Márquez borrowed just these features of imperialist style (which Rushdie picks up again in *Midnight's Children* when he refers to the aesthetic legacy of the boorish military man Shiva). With wonderful irony, he explains how they had been passed down to him through his grandmother:

> My grandmother . . . used to tell me the most terrifying things without showing any signs of emotion, as if they were things

that she had just seen. I discovered that that imperturbable manner and that wealth of imagery was what contributed most to the verisimilitude of her stories. Using the same method as my grandmother, I wrote *One Hundred Years of Solitude*.[24]

Rushdie and García Márquez may describe these methods as being more *real* because of the way in which the news media desensitise our response to catastrophes, making them seem almost normal. And it is this kind of criticism that both authors relate to the 'postmodern' experience of dominant metropolitan cultures which can no longer portray the battles of nation-forming in the language of heroism. Their shockingly inappropriate juxtaposition of humorous matter-of-factness and appallingly accurate violence, both ironically alludes to the blasé reporting of contemporary news and the preventable horrors of current events. Fantasy is thus never merely an embellishment and, in García Márquez at least, there lingers a confidence in a reality which fantasy can allow us to rediscover:

I believe that the imagination is nothing more than an instrument for elaborating reality. And fantasy, or invention pure and simple – like in Walt Disney, without the barest contact with reality – is the most detestable thing possible.[25]

If in *Midnight's Children* Rushdie is more careful than García Márquez to show the political and juridical legacy of colonialism (that is, if there is more 'real history'), he borrows, in *Shame*, García Márquez's concern with colonialism's legacy to the imagination. Thus it is, for example, that the hero's discovery of home has already been filtered through the accounts of strangers reporting on observations made in a foreign land: 'In what books the young fellow immersed himself . . . the Burton translation of the Alf laylah wa laylah, and the Travels of Ibn Battuta, and the Qissa or tales of the legendary adventurer Hatim Tai . . . ' (*Shame*, p. 28).

Both García Márquez and Rushdie in this way temper and subvert the routine appeals by writers of anti-colonial commitment to 'native' discourse by showing not only the inevitability but the benefits of what has been left behind. Their discourse, instead of telling a story reviling Europeans for their dishonourable past, stylistically alludes to that past and appropriates it for their own use. The background to this 'appropriation of the appropriators' is already evident in Rushdie's first novel, *Grimus*.

GRIMUS – HOME AS EVERYWHERE

It is an early failed novel like *Grimus* that shows most clearly what Rushdie is up to in the later work. With the exception of G. V. Desani's autobiographical confessions at the beginning of *All about H. Hatterr* (published in England in 1948), few novels could have codified so well the feeling of being 'neither here nor there'. Published in 1975, *Grimus* is a prefiguring – a volatile playground of Western and Eastern literary sources that mix together uneasily in a sustained and uninterpretable allegory.

But *Grimus* at first gives no indication of Rushdie's future interests. The tone is speculative and intellectual; the style coldly clever and obviously, although obscurely, allusive. Historical references are rare and oblique. The hermaphroditic hero, Flapping Eagle, is an American Indian on a quest for his lost sister, who he eventually finds on a Mediterranean island under the control of Grimus, an expatriate European magician whose power emanates from a miraculous stone rose. The very placing of the quest within the Mediterranean suggests the symbolic topography of the novel – a midway point between Orient and Occident. In the opening pages we find Virgil Jones, a pedantic Englishman, and his lapsed Catholic mate, Dolores O'Toole, reading in rocking chairs on a beach and philosophising at length 'about the parade of history', as the body (still living) of Flapping Eagle washes to the shore at their feet.

It would be hard to find a novel that demonstrated better the truth of Fanon's claim that a culture that is not national is meaningless. For if novels do not necessarily have to be set in one location, or be resistantly pure to foreign importations, they must be anchored in a coherent 'structure of feeling', which only actual communities can create. Even the idiosyncratic pastiche of, say, a novel by Thomas Pynchon can be apportioned space on the known territories of a given culture map. *Grimus* fails even though it is carried off with professional brilliance simply because it lacks a *habitus*. The expectations created by the American South-west setting of the opening, for example, are violated by the wilful migration to a fantastic Middle East. It doesn't know where it is and 'tries on' cultures like used clothing.

Here we have a composite picture of many national traditions without the forcible enclosures of the conqueror – or rather, the conqueror is played ineffectually by the tentative narrator. As one writer has put it, 'the text is characterised by its very heterogeneity, its refusal to adhere to any *one* particular semiotic code, any *one* narratological scheme'.[26] Nevertheless, although they are camouflaged, Rushdie's cultural origins in the Orient are given a certain priority by the fact that the book's central myth is taken from the *Shahnameh* ('Book of the Kings'), a tenth-century ethical history of Persia, whose semi-legendary characters, for example, include the 'Simurg' – 'a huge bird who has seen the destruction of the world three times and has all the knowledge of the ages'.[27] The metaphysical questioning does not itself separate it from his later novels – only its one-sidedness. There is no relief. If the conflict between Third-World peoples and European colonisers is evident here, it is carried out in terms so metaphorical as to be unrecognisable.

At the same time eclectic and tongue-in-check, the novel from the start takes on the aura of a kind of cryptic handbook – a series of codes that outline intellectual positions rather than pursue a narrative goal. With an opening allusion to the mythical Simurg, the hero is named Flapping Eagle, an 'Axona' Indian, who with his sister Bird-dog, had been shunned by his community for violating its laws forbidding contact with the outside world: 'The god Axona had only two laws: he liked the Axona to chant to him as often as possible, and he instructed the Axona to be a race apart and have no doings with the wicked world.'

Passages like these fill the novel, and establish its mood of uneasiness and disproportion. If Flapping Eagle's heroism comes precisely from seeking the 'outside world', there is little room here for heroes, and he finally flees home not out of principle but because he is forced to. For he is the victim of every proverbial village prejudice, an outcast from birth. His mother, for example, dies bearing him so that he is considered the offspring of bad magic and (like the Phoenix) is given the name 'Born-from-Dead'; his unwarriorlike sensitivity (in that social code, his 'womanliness') marks him with the hermaphroditic alias 'Joe-Sue'; and he is (as, in fact, Rushdie elsewhere describes himself) inexplicably 'fair-skinned'.

His sister leaves Axona after drinking an elixir of eternal life given to her by a shady pedlar with the sibilant, serpent name of 'Sispy'. After several years of hesitation, Flapping Eagle follows her in his happy Fall, leaving the garden of antiquarian codes and religious bigotry. After a series of adventures, he is washed up on the shore of Calf Island, where he is revived by Virgil and Dolores, who, with British assurance, inform him that the island is peopled exclusively by immortals who can no longer bear living – a discovery that a starstruck young emigrant from India, coming to the English metropolis, would naturally make once seeing its decay first-hand. That Flapping Eagle's journey is just that kind of allegory is borne out by the image of ascent that occupies the rest of the book, as though scaling Calf Mountain in search of Grimus was a physical rendering of the act of climbing the ranks of British opportunity. The novel's portrayal of Flapping Eagle's coming-to-self takes place alongside his gradual apprenticeship within the European guild, progressing at each new level of the mountain's many ledges. Thus, the body of the book describes his meetings with the immortals, who represent an extremely diverse group of Russians, Irish, French, English, Abyssinians and others with middle names like Quasimodo and Napoleon – who engage with him in long philosophical discussions about language, myth, order and the identity of Grimus, the European 'magician'.

Given this parable of crude acculturation, he binds together the European hodgepodge with an Eastern religious myth in order to preserve himself. If the Simurg myth is everywhere present in the book's repeated themes of apocalypse, it is the omniscience of the individual entrepreneurial 'creator' that Rushdie brings to the surface with intentional unfaithfulness and an already Westernised will to interpret the 'word' for his own uses:

> There is a Sufi poem in which thirty birds set out to find the Simurg on the mountain where he lives. When they reach the peak, they find that they themselves are, or rather have become, the Simurg. The name, you see, means Thirty Birds. Si, thirty, Murg, birds . . . the myth of the Mountain of Kaf.[28]

Sufism is Islamic mysticism. Not a sect as such, or an official branch of Islam, it nevertheless exists throughout the Islamic world in brotherhoods, whose existence is often denied by the official guardians of the Faith (in Saudi Arabia, for example).

Much of what goes on in Rushdie's allusions to Islamic tradition — not only here in *Grimus* but throughout his writing, especially in *The Satanic Verses* – is unintelligible without an understanding of Sufism. Rushdie has claimed, in fact, that the Islam practised in India differs from that of the Arab world by its wide acceptance of Sufi traditions. Originally Sufis were ascetics: those who lived in voluntary poverty, reproaching those who relied too heavily on the Law and the Word and relying instead on a form of intellectual transcendence. Not at all a secular movement, Sufis nevertheless tended in practice to undermine Islamic Law by their conviction that faith was a personal responsibility and that its personal expression was necessary for the social welfare. The truth was more important than the rules set up to approach it. Naturally, they despised the formalism and intellectual dogmatism of the Islamic clergy, who despised them in turn.

Its invocation here in a Persian poem recalls perhaps the legendary origins of Sufism in the work of the early Persian convert, Salman Al-Farisi, as well as the fact that, being the area through which the Aryan invasion of India occurred, Persia (which plays a similar role in *The Satanic Verses*) was historically the stepping stone to Europe and the legendary proof of a common heritage. In this way the international cast of the island-mountain of Calf complements this particular choice of literary source-material in a Persian narrative poem.

The meaning of Sufism within the Islamic tradition suggests, however, even deeper correspondences. Although devoutly orthodox in its call for every Muslim to attain a profoundly meditative attachment to Quranic teaching, it exalted the 'inner tribunal' rather than the public one as defined by the clerisy. The charge of heterodoxy naturally dogged it from its inception and tended to attract to it over time 'foreign decorative elements' which caused some scholars to search (incorrectly) for a non-Islamic origin. The preferred mode for expressing their highly individualised visions of God was a verse form that departed from the rigid rules of Arabic prosody, and was 'intended to provoke among listeners a psychic excitement by aesthetic means so as to realise a sort of artificial ecstasy'.[29] As Tarif Khalidi points out, 'by re-enacting within themselves the Prophetic experience, they often spoke like prophets, and for this reason were to earn the suspicion or hostility of their fellow Muslims'.[30] Much more than being limited, as Rushdie implies, to the Simurg poem, the imagery exploited by *Grimus* partakes fully in a developed tradition of Sufi verse that repeatedly re-enacts a journey to God (as in Muhammad's journey to heaven) seen as 'ascent' or 'flight'. Khalidi explains that 'like a bird flying higher and higher in great spiral patterns, Sufi awareness may be called a centripetal force, each state drawing the Sufi closer and closer to the center . . . [becoming one with the] Ocean of God, a loss of individuality in the identification with wholeness'.[31]

But the novel's all-encompassing intentions would not be possible if it were not also based on the literature of the West. The hero, whose age has been arrested at precisely thirty-four years, three months and four days (half way through life's journey), scales Calf Island (really a mountain jutting up from the sea) with the help of a guide named 'Virgil' Jones. Rushdie recalls, that is, his own English muse. The host of discounted immortals who tell Flapping Eagle their stories along the way are a prelude to the decisive moment before Grimus, when Flapping Eagle beholds Grimus's magical stone rose. If the *Purgatorio* and the *Paradiso* supply this imagery, the *Inferno* is invoked by a foreign counterpart through an allusion to the mountain of 'Calf' – spelled in its Quranic form 'Qaf', the title of a chapter in the *Quran* that looks forward to the final Day of Judgement when God shall ask Hell, ' "Are you full?" And Hell will answer: "Are there any more?" '. The word 'qaf' is also the name of the letter 'q', and therefore the prototype of *Shame*'s 'town of Q', or modern Quetta in Pakistan in which the unwelcome alternatives to this escape to the West are explored more fully.

Grimus deliberately mixes contemporary authors, historical personages and legendary beings in a kind of international compendium of myth. Side-by-side are references to Kafka's Joseph K., Sinbad's Roc, the Old Man of the Sea, the Ancient Mariner, Odysseus, the Phoenix, Chanakya (an ancient court philosopher), Jonah, Oedipus and Jocasta, Napoleon, Chekhov and the Valkyrie. The plot outline is taken from Dante, but the mood and situations of the novel's core are based closely on Kafka's *The Castle*. And the final effect of the book is a bringing-together of Eliot's sublime pessimism in *Four Quartets* (which he quotes in an epigraph, and through which he filters Dante) and the stance of complacent philosophical scepticism associated with one of the few well-known Persian poems in English, *The Rubaiyat* (which he quotes from as well).

This display of international influences, only partially and secondarily rooted in the East, is at the same time a mapping out of allegiances and an attempt to decide what fictional forms his ethnic and racial alienation in England might take:

> He was Chameleon, changeling, all things to all men and nothing to any man ... [He saw] a man rehearsing voices on a cliff top: high whining voices, low gravelly voices, subtle insinuating voices .... He asked the man what he was doing. The man called back – and each word was the word of a different being: I am looking for a suitable voice to speak in. (*Grimus*, p. 36)

Although in retrospect passages like this clearly describe the experience of a young Indian author among the English, the context of *Grimus* makes them highly abstract. Because of the many layers of mediation, Rushdie is able to record his feelings of exile with a directness that his later, more explicitly political books would make appear too crude:

> Stripped of his past, forsaking the language of his ancestors for the languages of the archipelagoes of the world, forsaking the ways of his ancestors for those of the places he drifted to, forsaking any hope of ideals in the face of the changing and contradictory ideals he encountered, he lived, doing what he was given to do, thinking what he was instructed to think, being what it was most desirable to be. (p. 36)

At this point, he finds no advantages in being a composite man. Incorporating influences is simply a matter of fictional experimentation.

The journey to Qaf's summit is a mental one: 'Analysts of the mythical mountain of Qaf have called it a model for the structure and workings of the human mind' (p. 292). His analogue for Dante's concentric circles or fosses has been a series of inner and outer 'dimensions':

> It was the nearest they would get to escape, and also the most dangerous of the Inner Dimensions. They stood at the very fringes of Flapping Eagle's awareness, close to the point

at which his senses merged with the void. This was unmade
ground, the raw materials of the mind. (p. 101)

The paradoxical inversion of these solipsistic wanderings, this
'burrowing away, away from the world, into books and philos-
ophies and mythologies, until these became his realities' (p.
307), is the chance, on another level (again, thinking only as a writer
of fiction), to create a world – an opportunity he describes as
a 'minor branch' of 'the Divine Game' called Conceptualism:
'I think, therefore it is' (p. 79). The consequence of Rushdie's
exile, the bridge he forms between isolated Axonas and deserted
Qaf's, his ability to reintroduce foreign myths out of context and
substitute parts of them with their alien others – all of this gives
him an advantage as an author: the kind of status he increasingly
associates with the political misleaders of Indian and Pakistani
(not to say, British) politics. It is, however, not understood that
way here. Thus the powers conferred by the stone rose at the
point Flapping Eagle reaches his goal, allows him to 'enter into,
and become, a thousand thousand other people, live an infinity
of lives, and acquire the wisdom and power to shape [his] own'
(p. 316).

   Until this point, the multicultural experience of exile (like
immortality) conferred advantages only at the expense of his
own identity. Here he sows the seeds of the moral relativity of
his later historical fiction by referring to his own actual features:
'His face was such, his skin was such, that in many places he
could pass for a local. . . . For a tyrant, he slew rebels; in a free
state, he denounced tyranny' (p. 36). That interesting crossover
between 'race' and political outlook, in a typically jarring and
extraneous aside, begins to inch towards satire: 'He lived the same
physiological day over and over again'. Atypically, he continues
by giving the jest a local reference: 'His body: an empire on which
there was no sun to set' (p. 37).

   Instead of exemplifying what Rushdie later discarded, *Grimus*
prefigures with unusual clarity Rushdie's major interests. Even
in the area that seems most different, he provides evidence of
his eventual practice: namely, an underlying attachment to
Indian culture and the multiple overlapping of various national
myths. For example, Calf Mountain (Persian, Quranic, Dantean)
is described in passing at one point as being 'rather like a giant
lingam weltering in the *yoni* that is the Sea' (p. 66). The *lingam*

and *yoni* are respectively phallus and vulva, the customary inconography of the Hindu god Shiva. Rushdie's allusion to this iconography is appropriate at this point given Flapping Eagle's hermaphroditic past and the sterility of the immortals on Calf. Rushdie invokes Shiva (who in addition to being a fertility god is also proverbially a 'Destroyer') once again when he explains Flapping Eagle's name: 'The Eagle has an interesting significance in Amerindian mythology. Am I not right in saying that it is the symbol of the Destroyer?'[32] Thus, either the Indian expatriate fertilises the barren cultural landscape of England or threatens to destroy its former supremacy.

But Rushdie could not have expressed his art of mythical transposition better than to have made his exiled hero an American 'Indian' – a people bound to the Indians of the East by the geographical ignorance of their European colonisers. In *Grimus*, the political content of this reference is submerged in a way it would not be in his later fiction. Born in the environs of 'Phoenix', Flapping Eagle instead represents a reincarnation of the nonconformist in an intolerant land. The Amerindians and the Indians are bound together in Rushdie's mind negatively: the religion of Axona mirrors the strict rituals and hypocrisy of Islam, Judaism, Christianity and Hinduism: women are chattel; those open to foreign influences are repudiated by a community of bigots.

The heart of this quest is a transcendent vision of heterogeneity – heterogeneity made beautiful, as it were, in the being of Grimus. But as in the later works, here Rushdie associates an inverted or jumbled order with divine or supreme creative powers, which are not demonstrated narratively but only talked about. The degree to which Rushdie is able to conceive of this crystallised 'otherness' only in terms of fictional craft and intertextual plan is shown by the physical imaging of this otherness in a language game. His examples are the palindrome and the anagram – the most important of which is 'Grimus' itself, the anagrammatic embodiment of 'Simurg':

The Divine Game of Order. The Game extends far beyond mere letter-puzzling; the vast mental powers of the Gorfs [large god-like 'frogs'] make it possible for them anagrammatically to alter their very environment and indeed their own physical make-up. (p. 77)

Nor is Rushdie insensitive to the nationalist themes he will later work through in detail. Nowhere in his essays or interviews is the content, say, of *Midnight's Children* so directly described as in *Grimus*, published in 1975, the year he begins writing his novel of India:

> I became engrossed in the notion of race memory; the sediment of highly-concentrated knowledge that passes down the ages, constantly being added to and subtracted from. . . . I have achieved the ultimate harmony: the combination of the most profound thoughts of the race, tested by time, and the cadences that give those thoughts coherence and, even more important, popularity. I am taking the intellect back to the people. (p. 160)

Burying it in an allusion to Odysseus, Rushdie recognises that these literary expressions of a 'race' or 'people' lead only in one direction: 'To be in K [on Kaf] was to return to a consciousness of history, of good times, even of nationhood. . . . It made a big difference to the home-seeking man' (p. 162).

But where is home? His next novels were to examine the possibilities more sensuously and fully than here.

4

The National Longing for Form

What new criteria will black literature bring into play at a time when polarization of cultures thrives through instant news, instant camera and instant technology? This is why I think that fiction needs to assert its peculiar scale . . .

Wilson Harris[1]

I myself believe that the history of Ganesh is, in a way, the history of our times.

V. S. Naipaul[2]

Until the appearance of *Midnight's Children* in 1980, India's literary agents in the West were, for the most part, obscure intellectual tourists or Indian academics writing in the yellowed volumes of Delhi publishing houses. Srinivasa Iyengar has noted, for example, that at the very moment that Commonwealth fiction was finally getting attention, Indo-English literature – despite its comparative quality and volume – had no following comparable to that of Africa and the Caribbean. In the United States and in Britain, the social conflicts making news in those regions were enough to make their literatures a going issue, whereas India and the Raj (much less the Independence struggle itself) were already an old story.

The problems of Western reception, however, go beyond this apparent anachronism. For the Indo-English masterpieces have been trying to overcome larger cultural barriers than those of other post-colonial novels. Flourishing in a highly developed literary tradition of several millennia, working off of a set of standard invocations and stories from a voluminous array of epics and holy books, the novels can require an extraordinary immersion in literary and historical background: Vedic, Puranic and epic traditions with their centuries-long Sanskrit commentary; the civilisations of

Mohenjo-Daro, the Aryans, the empires of the Mauryans, Mughals and British; an uncanny mixture of village television programmes, nationwide Hindi cinema-viewings and oral storytelling; and, on top of this, the grafting on to this intellectual legacy of the British canon itself. Added to this is the paradox that the Indian novel (unlike others in the British colonies) flourished first not in English but in Bengali and Hindi.

Occupying the British mind before the sharp clashes of the decolonisation struggles in the 1950s and 1960s, the Indo-English novel became known in the West before the image of anti-colonial 'struggle' became a selling point in Western critical circles. Thus, some of the most prominent Indo-English novelists, already with secure reputations before 1947, were noticeably indifferent to the kind of anti-colonial preoccupations of, say, Chinua Achebe in Nigeria, or Vic Reid in Jamaica, whose work followed the rhythms of the decolonisation process itself. Mulk Raj Anand, for example, active on the socialist Left in the 1930s and a contributor under George Orwell to the BBC foreign service, emerged with the early novels *Untouchable* and *Coolie* – a part of the rich Indian tradition of fictional reform that in many ways was more far-reaching than novels about the national movement; R. K. Narayan, despite his *Waiting for the Mahatma* about the impact of Gandhi on a southern village, spent his time chronicling the human comedy of Malgudi, a fictional microcosm of his own Hindu 'pan-India'; and Raja Rao, who emigrated to France rather than England precisely to avoid the suffocating colonial question inevitably raised there, shifted between the Proustian reminiscences of a Brahmin abroad in his *The Serpent and the Rope* and a chapbook of small-town Hindu social customs during the Gandhi days in *Kanthapura*.

The success of *Midnight's Children*, particularly in the English-speaking West, has to be appreciated with these obstacles in mind. It was not just the victory of the latest (modern) example of the Indo-English novel, but a quite deliberate presentation of the whole tradition to a naïve reading public. As such, the book's acclaim in India has a lot to do with its putting the Indo-English imagination on the map. The frequently ecstatic reviews of *Midnight's Children* all get their energy from this fact. But what has always been overlooked is that the book is at the same time a critique of that tradition, as well as a meticulous catalogue of the doubtful literary devices of Third-World novelists themselves, seen as collaborators in the doubtful politics of the independence

process. In this sense, Rushdie consummates the ironic propo-
sition of the British-based Indian novelist, G. V. Desani (his most
obvious precursor): 'Mimic me Truth successfully (that's to say,
lie to me and achieve belief) and I'd credit you with Art, Skill,
Imagination and intimate intelligence of truth.'³

One obvious reason for *Midnight's Children*'s successful intervention in the Western literary scene was its familiarity to readers
of other well-known satirists of nationalism and dependency
mentioned above (all of whom Rushdie has either reviewed or pub-
licly recognised). Rudolph Bader, for example, has shown how
closely *Midnight's Children* mirrors Grass's techniques in *The Tin
Drum*: the structuring of historical memory through photos and
newspaper clippings, the wilful exoticism of dwarfs, magicians,
gypsies and cripples; the mixing of 'fairytale style . . . court evidence, school essay, public speech and other variations of the
narrative mode' until the effect is one of 'simultaneity of past,
present and future'.⁴

But the subtlety of Rushdie's critique of the imperial relationship
is usually lost in this source-hunting. For the duality of the colonial
'in-betweener' is found at the structural level too, as we saw in
the discussion of García Márquez. The formal aspects of Grass's
vigorous postmodernity becomes in Rushdie's hands simply
another version of the oral storyteller's spiralling digressions and
intentional nonlinearity, as suggested by Rushdie's reference in
one place to the Indian storyteller of Baroda:

> [W]hen he was telling his stories, the number of people who
> gathered to hear him was 600 000. Baroda has a population of
> 400 000. That's to say the number of people who arrived was
> 50 per cent greater than the population of the town that he
> was performing in. And this sea of people sat in a field for a
> weekend and listened to this man tell stories. If ever there was
> a way of making a novelist feel humble, that was it.⁵

The novel is deliberately designed to evoke both simultaneously.

It is the story of Saleem Sinai, born with 1001 other Indian
children in the hour of midnight, 15 August 1947 – the moment
India is formally granted independence from England. By virtue
of his propitious birth, each of the children possesses a distinct
magical power, whose force is greater the closer the child's
birth occurs to the stroke of twelve. The most powerful among

them turn out to be Saleem and his rival, Shiva – the latter with bulbous knees that give him the power of war, the former with an over-large nose that gives him the power of 'seeing into the hearts and minds of men'.

India's new national leaders acclaim the Children's arrival, and identify them with an auspicious national destiny. Nehru personally writes to the infant Saleem to say: 'You are the newest bearer of that ancient face of India which is also eternally young. We shall be watching over your life with the closest attention; it will be, in a sense, the mirror of our own' (*MC*, p. 143) – a comment closely borne out by the novel's events in which the personal travails of Saleem and his family metaphorically correspond to key events in India's postwar history.

We find in *Midnight's Children* an ironic awareness on Rushdie's part of the same English 'Novel of Empire' that he is trying to overcome. He jestingly opens the novel with a character he names 'Dr Aziz', in reference to the Aziz of E. M. Forster's *A Passage to India*. Similarly, by virtue of Saleem's telepathic powers, all the magical Children of Midnight are assembled together in a 'Midnight's Children's Conference' (MCC), whose members never actually meet but who communicate with one another through Saleem's mental transmissions – a kind of All-India Congress: a bitter allusion to the passage in Paul Scott's *The Jewel in the Crown* in which the Anglicised Indian, Hari Kumar (Harry Coomer) is said to belong to the 'Mayapore Indian Club. The Mayapore Chatterjee Club. The MCC. The Other Club. The wrong one' – in other words, not the famous British refuge of colonial privilege, the Marylebone Cricket Club.[6] Rushdie even mimics Scott's method of introducing the novel's defining themes in a painting's iconography. In Scott's case, a painting is discussed (alluded to in the novel's title) in which a native prince bequeaths to Queen Victoria a bejewelled crown. In *Midnight's Children* this becomes a painting of the young Sir Walter Raleigh sitting at the feet of 'an old, gnarled net-mending sailor . . . whose right arm, fully extended, stretched out towards a watery horizon' (p. 142). This invitation to conquer foreign lands mortifies Saleem when he recalls later how his parents, inspired by the painting, dressed him up to look like 'an English milord', and how his *ayah* would rock him to sleep singing confidently: 'Anything you want to be, you can be.'

The novel, however, is much more than a sardonic reflection

of these 'orientalist' precursors, and exists on a different order
of reality. It is distinctive, for example, in the way that it systematically sets out in discursive fashion all the key historical
roadmarkers of the Indian postwar period, inserting them into the
narrative like newspaper reports or like textbook lessons in modern
Indian history: the massacre at Jallianwallah Bagh in Amritsar in
1919: the Partition of 1947; Nehru's First Five-Year Plan in 1956;
Ayub Khan's coup in Pakistan in 1958; the India-China war of
1962; the India-Pakistan War of 1965; the creation of Bangladesh
in 1971; and the Indian 'Emergency' of 1975, when Indira Gandhi,
convicted by the Allahabad High Court of election malpractices,
suspends all civil rights and gaols her opponents.

Although *Midnight's Children*, unlike his next novel, *Shame*,
presents itself as a written form, and its narrator Saleem assumes
the role of a modern Valmiki (the author of the *Ramayana*), Raja
Rao has made the point that the digressional obsession of the
Indian imagination – the deliberate timelessness of its historical
reportage – is as much a quality of Indian literature as Indian oral
tale: 'The *Mahabharata* has 214 778 verses and the *Ramayana* 45 000.
The *Puranas* are endless and innumerable. We have neither punc-
tuation nor the treacherous "ats" and "ons" to bother us – we
tell one interminable tale.'[7]

The sober playfulness with the notion of a co-present modernity
and antiquity repeats itself in a still larger contradiction: that at the
same moment Rushdie insists on these native allegiances, he seeks
to cancel forever the heroic terms of the Indo-English historical
novels. The idea is not that the entire Indo-English tradition is only
a prelude to its culmination in Rushdie, but that Rushdie playfully
alludes to earlier moments of Indo-English fiction as though he
were its culmination. It is part of his joke. If, for example, the
post-independence novel of India turned to problems of individual
self-realisation, Rushdie cleverly made his hero's self-realisation
depend on the whole history of India: the teleology of the one
and the many fused at the point of independence. If the Indian
historical novel used the raw material of the ancient epics,
Rushdie thematised that very impulse to use mythology and
the Indian novel could therefore read itself. If the Indo-English
novel was born in the national movement and dedicated itself to
drawing its heroic contours; and if the Indo-English novel was at
times a massive and formless genre in its effort to tell all, Rushdie
pushed these elements one step further by refusing to stop his

story at its apparent culmination (the moment of independence), and by applying all the rhetoric of the political heroic age to the unheroic bungling of modern India itself.

If it is just as easy to ignore Grass and find a source for *Midnight's Children* in K. Nagarajan's *The Chronicles of Kedaram*, for example, with its self-conscious and confidential narrator, or Manohar Malgonkar's *A Bend in the Ganges*, which has been called 'not so much a . . . historical drama as an erratic national calendar', it is equally incomplete. By far the most significant historical jump in *Midnight's Children*'s time-frame is not so much temporal as thematic. No one has seemed to notice that the very staple of a major branch of Indo-English historical fiction, Gandhi's National Movement, is impertinently excised from the narrative outright, which rushes from Amritsar in 1919 to Agra in 1942 without so much as a passing comment! Thus, the story of Indian nationalism is erased from the book that documents its sad outcome, and the most dramatic illustration of Rushdie's argument is an absence.

What is new and what is old in Rushdie's rendering of the Indian tradition is therefore easy to misunderstand. The sophisticated exile commenting on Indian culture from a European country is certainly not new: we find it already in the characters Savithri and Ramaswami in Rao's *The Serpent and the Rope*. Presenting 'an intricate design of myths, allegories, fantastic and supernatural episodes [and] extravagant situations of comedy' against a modern historical background is not new either, for it can be found in the novels of Sudhin Ghose, among others.[8] But it would be hard to find other contemporary novelists who display Rushdie's taste for theoretical commentary on the, in some ways, indistinguishable features of Western and Eastern, 'developed' and 'developing', literary style. Style is, of course, also social attitude, and for Rushdie the attitudes have not been formed in isolation (as if to emphasise that incommensurability of foreign cultures found in Forster, for example) but as complementary poles in an imperial relationship.

Critics tend to talk about the ingeniousness of the Rushdie style or the cleverness with which he burlesques history, but not the obvious fact that his writing is less *in* the novels than *about* them. Characterisation in any conventional sense barely exists – only a collection of brilliantly sketched cartoons woven together by an intellectual argument. Narrative never follows the emotional logic of the characters' lives, but the brittle, externally determined contours of 'current events'. Rushdie deliberately prevents his readers from being caught up in a story with its own 'organic' life, that progresses uninterrupted, and that creates a completely imagined world. We are instead always being shown 'the hands holding the strings' (*MC*, p. 72), are having the metaphors cut short by an on-the-spot explanation, are being directed to the future or the past, the beginning or end of the book, instead of being ushered on to 'what-happened-next'.

What we have, in other words, is an extreme case of that de-aestheticising of literature that Bakhtin found typical of the novel form, it being (like other genres) a 'zone of valorised perception', but one responsible for the process in which the social function of literature is called into question and made an object of artistic treatment. Given Rushdie's interests, that 'social function' derives from the intermediary role played by the Third-World cosmopolitan author. Detaching himself from his own characters the better to study them, Rushdie is best seen as a critic for whom 'fiction' in the monumental sense of high modernism is no longer preferable: as in the polemical sense in which Brecht called himself not *Dichter* but *Stuckschreiber*. His novels, in short, are metafictions, and their range of interest neo-colonial. That is, they are novels about Third-World novels. The discussion of *Midnight's Children* should then begin with a look at one of its principle interventions, which is an attempt to explain in the Indian context a problem found nearly everywhere in the Third World, and widely described in its fiction – namely, the rise of the domestic collaborators, the corrupt neo-colonial élite. Of course, much more than represent this élite (as, for example, in Chinua Achebe's *Man of the People*, or in Earl Lovelace's *The Wine of Astonishment*), Rushdie links it to the production of Third-World fiction itself.

CHAMCHAS AND OTHER SELLOUTS

As a critic not only of India, Pakistan and England but of the 'fictions' of national discourse, Rushdie has been aware of the privileges separating Third-World authors from the realities they describe. So, he wonders, with what native authority can the colonial exile speak? Rushdie has been obsessed by this dubious position, which he expresses in the experiences of his many Westernised characters – for example, Aadam Aziz in *Midnight's Children*, who had been 'branded as an alien' for studying medicine in Germany, and was 'therefore a person not completely to be trusted' by the village poor. In the more recent novel, *Shame*, the sense of being foreign is even stronger, and its rebukes are directed for the first time against the author personally, who imagines the Pakistani commoners saying: ' "Outsider! Trespasser! You have no right to this subject. We know you, with your foreign language wrapped around you like a flag: speaking about us in your forked tongue, what can you tell but lies?" '[9]

So, it is with a sense of self-reproach that Rushdie declares himself an enemy of the *'chamcha's'* in a *Times* article of 1983. Literally 'spoons', the *chamchas* are for Rushdie those collaborators under independence who have propped up the post-colonial status quo; even after the departure of the Raj, Rushdie observes, the Empire continues to grow fat by being 'spoon-fed'.[10]

In a novel like *Shame*, dependent on the mode of fantasy, there was the danger, especially among Western audiences, of simply continuing the warped vision of the European explorer by viewing the land as a spectacle, a fund of imagery. Although he writes about his native land, he carefully abstracts its features and makes them exotic, as if to reflect the uncomfortable similarities between himself and an adventurer stationed in London selling Oriental wares to a public whose tastes he knows from several decades of travel.

This tentative, but explicit, comparison between the early reconnaisance work of imperialism's first scouts and Rushdie's own novels of information, reveals his awareness of the contradictory sides of his impact in Britain. Not only is he potentially an 'impostor' to his Pakistani readers, but a potential traitor as well. Translating the coercive acts of European conquerors into the forms of his writing did not necessarily mean correcting them. García Márquez's playful recognition of an imperial legacy in style becomes in Rushdie an identification of motive as well: 'I too, like all migrants, am a fantasist. I build imaginary countries and try to impose them on the ones that exist.'[11]

There is no necessary connection between the cosmopolitan author and the post-colonial élite, yet on an imaginative level, Rushdie repeatedly associates the two – for example, in *Shame*'s Omar Khayyam Shakil. As his name implies, Omar is a character only articulated *through* the English, just as the *Rubaiyat* is known to us only through the free revisions of the Victorian poet, Edward Fitzgerald. We see the pattern of Omar's significance to the novel before we see his precise role. Tainted by the English in name, Omar comes from a family whose entire heritage has English blemishes. An illegitimate child with three mothers, he has a father who is most likely 'an Angrez sahib'. Omar's grandfather has a reputation for learning that is based on a library secretly purchased from an English colonel.

Omar's stylish clothes, his cigars, his European education are obvious marks of his foreign identity, but they are not the decisive ones in his pervasive English makeup. The Shakil household betrays a history of collaboration, in which many of the English imperial habits are symbolised. His family's livelihood depends on pawning furniture that had been acquired by their 'rapaciously acquisitive forebears'. Like an imperious Westerner empowered by technology, Omar looks down on the town of Q from an upper floor of his ancestral home ('Nishapur') using a telescope through which he sees 'the world . . . as a bright disc, a moon for his delight' (*Shame*, p. 30).

The ability of the colonial power structure to impose its forms *in absentia* is reflected in a cultural system designed to enforce consent. Thus, Omar learns to manipulate his friends with the techniques learned from a European do-it-yourself hypnosis manual. And, more like the English than in any other way, Omar knows no shame – there is no counterpart in English, says Rushdie, for the word *'sharam'* (shame). For this reason, Omar, like the English, cannot comprehend certain 'dialects of emotion' like 'embarrassment, discomfiture, decency, modesty, shyness, the sense of having an ordained place in the world'. He belongs to that stratum of colonial society that has to be trained to lack a conscience, to deflect the uneasiness resulting from questions of his disgraceful origins, his tarnished birthright. But, in spite of these alliances, he is not the social equal of the Angrez sahibs. The only access that he and the other residents of 'Nishapur' have to the outside world is a dumbwaiter, a mark of their subservience.

Omar's erudition, his privileges, his cultural proximity to the English are all prefigured in Rushdie's earlier fictional counterpart, Saleem Sinai. However, *Midnight's Children* being a more explicitly historical work than *Shame*, Rushdie adds a theory of collaboration to the portrait of the Anglicised native – one that is central to his understanding of the failure of nationalism in India and Pakistan. At the heart of the theory is the *'chamcha'*, first raised in the portrait of Saleem's uncle Mustapha Aziz, whose wife,

> the half-Irani would-be socialite Sonia . . . had been driven certifiably insane by a life in which she had been required to begin 'being a chamcha' (literally a spoon, but idiomatically a flatterer) to forty-seven separate and successive wives of number-ones whom she had previously alienated by her manner of colossal condescension when they had been wives of number-threes. (*MC*, p. 467)

In *Midnight's Children*, we find the image of the *chamcha* in those 'leaders whose fortunes [were] built originally on the miseries of fleeing Hindu families', the same group described by Rushdie's contemporary, Tariq Ali, as the Punjabi bureaucrats and Muslim aristocrats who declared the viability of Pakistan with little other motive than to enrich themselves, speaking Urdu and writing in Persian to a peasantry that spoke Bengali, Punjabi, Sindhi and Pushtu, all the time claiming that they constituted a community. In *Midnight's Children*, Saleem's English parentage and his membership in the Aziz household (obviously patterned on Rushdie's own) slowly merges with the actions of the landholders, religious charlatans and military henchmen who control the state. Estrangement becomes collaboration.

The *chamcha* does not merely utilise the appeal to the nation but epitomises the appeal's oppressive legacy. Fashioned as a weapon against occupation, it merely completes the occupation by recasting the Empire in native form. Thus, in one scene from *Midnight's Children*, the war over the Rann of Kutch, highlighted by desperate communiqués summoning popular support against efforts 'to subvert the state' (p. 404), is shown to be a cynical swindle. The real motives behind the war 'didn't get into the papers: the pressures of internal political troubles in Pakistan – Ayub's government was tottering, and a war works wonders at such times' (p. 404).

The logic of Rushdie's harsh self-treatment is at first hard to grasp. Personal privileges do not after all amount to *betrayal*. But his affiliations with the vilest of *chamchas* makes some sense when one considers his and their roles in communicative fictions. In the conflicting official radio accounts of the war, 'Nothing was real;

nothing certain' (p. 406). Sincere, patriotic sacrifice is forged in 'the fantasies of our rulers' (p. 405).

If the *chamcha* continues the logic of imperial domination, he does so using indigenous forms: the Christian civilising mission becomes 'Jehad . . . Holy War . . . the mujahid philosophy of Syed Ahmad Barilwi', who invites the Pakistani troops marching into Kashmir 'to make sacrifices "as never before" ' promising that, if they are martyred, they will be 'bound for the perfumed garden! Where the men would be given four beauteous houris, untouched by man or djinn; and the women, four equally virile males!' (p. 405-6). And the culminating wars – the war for Bangladesh and the Indian 'Emergency' – were wars *within* the nation. Far from being exempt from cruelty, these homemade wars show the 'patriots' to be more furious than their predecessors. Rushdie reserves the most shocking descriptions and the bitterest emotions for his treatment of the fraternal conflicts:

> Bloodhounds track the fleeing enemies of national unity. . . .
> And newspaper offices, burning with the dirty yellowblack
> smoke of cheap gutter newsprint, and the offices of trade
> unions, smashed to the ground, the roadside ditches filling
> up with people who were not merely asleep – bare chests
> were seen, and the hollow pimples of bullet-holes . . . [O]ur
> boys, our soldiers-for-Allah, our worth-ten-babus jawans held
> Pakistan together by turning flame-throwers machine-guns
> hand-grenades on the city slums. (*MC*, p. 426)

In exploring his own culpability for the events of the novel, Saleem determines responsibility not only by his acquiescence ('nor was I to blame for Sino-Indian border skirmishes in the Aksai Chin region of Ladakh . . . [but] I did nothing to alleviate it'), or by his sharing of the desires and human failings of the more visible culprits, but specifically as a writer – a creator of communicative fictions. Guilt is centred in, and emanates from, the writer himself, extending to all his creations. This conforms to the book's central trope in which Saleem contains India's multitudes within him (p. 457). Authorial ambiguity translates into bi-polar morality in which every group has a good and a bad expression.

In a celebrated passage of the novel, Saleem's parents, fleeing the horrors of Partition, move to Bombay where they buy an estate from the Englishman, William Methwold, a descendant of an East Indian Company officer who in 1633 (when their Portuguese rivals still had a foothold in India) had had a vision of 'a British Bombay . . . defending India's West against all comers'. Methwold stipulates that Ahmed and Amina may have the house cheaply but must leave everything just as it is – furniture, dishes, paintings . . . everthing – in the same way that, under similar conditions, Lord Mountbatten signs over the British claim to India.

The genealogy of guilt thus begins with Empire, which like the natives, is split into two parties: benevolent 'civilisers' like the Englishman, Methwold (with their pinkish skin, bibulous habits, mercenary intentions and carefully parted toupés) and cold-hearted keepers-of-order like the infamous perpetrator of the Jallianwallah Bagh massacre, General Dyer (with their waxed moustaches, ingenuous pronouncements of white supremacy and willingness to kill for the sake of propriety).[12] In their wake come the Westernised and nativist Indians, neither of whom represent a wholly positive or negative political force.

As a follower of European humanism and Western democracy, the hero of the book's opening chapters, Aadam Aziz, represents in one sense genuine progress, a break from small-town prejudice and oppressive social practices, having studied medicine in Heidelberg and having been unable to retain his Muslim faith upon returning to India; he frees his wife from the chadoor and struggles to limit the influence of religious sectarianism.[13] On the other hand, his European idealism – repeated in the novel in other guises, especially by Aadam's college friend the German anarchist Oskar Lubin and his rival in love, Quasim the Red – fuels what Rushdie calls the 'disease of optimism', religious fanaticism's reverse image and the complement to nationalism in its Eastern form. His natural contestants – religious believers like the Muslim fanatic Syed Barilwi and Saleem's Christian *ayah* Mary Pereira – display their own kind of idealism, which despite its notorious results, possesses native roots the élite Western ideas do not yet have in India.

Rushdie's fictional counterparts in both *Shame* and *Midnight's Children* belong to the first group, although he depends (as we shall see) on the second. In one of the novel's more pointed jokes, Saleem's 'mother', Amina Sinai (daughter of Aadam Aziz), aims for and wins a *Times of India* contest offering an award to those mothers who give birth at the exact moment of Indian independence.

She, however, shares the prize with a neighbour named Vanita, wife of a poor accordian-player named Wee Willie Winkie. As it turns out, the child is not really Willie's but Methwold's, who Vanita has been seeing on the sly. To complicate things still further, a hospital midwife, tormented by her unrequited love for the Christian rebel, Joe D'Costa, *switches the babies* of Amina and Vanita, imagining this irreverence will somehow please him. Vanita's child (really Amina's) is named 'Shiva'; Amina's child (really Vanita's) is named 'Saleem'. Thus, having presented himself as the offspring of Aadam Aziz and Ahmed Sinai, Saleem is really the true son of an Englishman.

As an illegitimate, half-English pretender, Saleem lives with the Aziz family on the Methwold estate in Bombay, composed of 'three-story homes of gods standing on a two-story Olympus, a stunted Kailash!' (*MC*, p. 108). Here lives India's élite, Muslim, Parsee and Hindu:

> These were the people amongst whom I spent my childhood: Mr Homi Catrack, film magnate and racehorse-owner . . . also old man Ibrahim Ibrahim with his goatee and sisal, his sons Ismail and Ishaq, and Ismail's tiny flustry hapless wife Nussie. . . . On the ground floor lived the Dubashes, he a physicist who would become a leading light at the Trombay nuclear research base, . . . And, finally, on the top floor, were Commander Sabarmati and Lila – Sebarmati who was one of the highest flyers in the Navy, and his wife with her expensive tastes. . . . . Selected by William Methwold, these people who would form the centre of my world moved in the Estate and tolerated the curious whims of the Englishman – because the price, after all, was right. (*MC*, p. 112)

Rushdie's diagnosis of Indian nationalism requires a fluid and comprehensive meaning of the *chamcha*. In the Methwold community, as elsewhere in the book, religious mission, national myth and secular demagogy flow into one another in the process of establishing a stable state, and we are reminded again of Benedict Anderson's point about the affinity of modern nationalism with 'religious imaginings'. Thus, Mrs Dubash turns out to be a 'cipher beneath whose blankness a true religious fanaticism lay concealed', and Saleem himself is given the last name 'Sinai', denoting (as he says) his status as 'a prophet in the wilderness' ('like Maslama, like ibn Sinan! No matter how I try, the desert is my lot'– p. 471).

It is consistently difficult to tell in Rushdie's parodies where complicity begins and ends. As he mocks the deadly and apparently eternal religious allegiances of the East ('Saleem' a typically Arabic name denoting a gentleman, good-hearted and generous; 'Sinai', a name suggesting the Mosaic Covenant) he chooses to draw our attention to his name's significance precisely in a passage where he presents himself to his uncle Mustapha Aziz (who, in the classic scenario of the *chamcha*, prospers as a result of the Indo-Pakistan War) to explain 'with proper solemnity and humble but resolute gestures – my historic mission to rescue the nation from her fate' (p. 471). The messianic pose is quickly punctured by Mustapha who assures him that all is safely in the hands of President Indira, the 'reformer', to which Saleem responds violently, repudiating Mustapha and his own *chamcha* past: 'O vile unhelpfulness of lickspittle uncles! O fettering of ambitions by second-best toadying relatives!' (p. 471).

But here, once again, we see Rushdie beginning to undercut any positive associations he manages to build up. For earlier he had expounded on the name 'Sinai', relating it to the historical figure Ibn Sina, a tenth-century Arabic philosopher and Sufi adept, famous in mediaeval medicine; and then to Moses 'of commandments and golden calves'. In Saleem's words, Ibn Sina, although a doctor and logician, was known legendarily as a 'master magician', and Moses as the prophet who never quite arrived in the Promised Land. In other words, the secular and historical status of the doctor Ibn Sina is jostled together with the religious image of the prophet, as though repeating the qualities of the Midnight's Children themselves – possessors of supernatural powers that owe their force to the declaration of Indian independence. No faction has a monopoly on approved means and creeds, and all share the attributes of their others.

To take the point through still another metamorphosis, Rushdie then has Saleem flee to the 'Magicians' Ghetto' in his continued efforts to 'rescue the nation from her fate'. These 'magicians' we learned from Amina's affair with Qasim (alias Nadir Khan) are actually activists in the Indian Communist Party who organise tirelessly and ineffectually against Indira's rule, only to be outlawed and forced underground a few years later. It has only been moments since this reference to the adherents of 'the disease of

optimism', in its most secular and idealistic form, followed a
reference to Saleem's true spiritual predecessors:

> At the time of the prophet Muhammad, other prophets also
> preached: Maslama of the tribe of Banu Hanifa . . . and Hanzala
> ibn Safwan; and Khalid ibn Sinan was sent to the tribe of Abs; for
> a time, he was followed, but then he was lost. (*MC*, p. 365)

Like these now-forgotten rivals of the Prophet, Muhammad –
who, despite their pretensions, put no stamp on history and
moved no mountains – Saleem is destined for the desert. A cross
between the secular philosopher Ibn Sina and the failed prophet
Ibn Sinan, 'Sinai' finally means simply 'barrenness, infertility, dust;
the name of the end', and so prepares us for the castration of the
Midnight's Children during the Emergency, Saleem's future as
'bits of voiceless dust', and the apocalypse of history with which
the novel closes.

The religious connotations of 'Sinai' had re-established from
above what an early phase in Saleem's life had established from
below. Before Saleem had confronted uncle Mustapha, he had
recently been saved by Parvati, another prominent Child of
Midnight, a benevolent witch from the 'Magicians' Ghetto', who
found him in a military procession in a half-witted trance, still
suffering from amnesia. It was in this state that his sister – an
infamous sycophant of the Pakistani military, who becomes their
Mata Hari and takes the name 'Jamila Singer' – had conscripted
him into the Pakistani army to be used (because of his olfactory
powers) as a human bloodhound, tracking down Bengali, 'enemies
of the nation'. His true membership in Pakistan (literally, the land
of the 'ritually pure') required that he be 'purified'. But this 'purifi-
cation' expressed itself only as Saleem's temporary idiocy induced
by a blow to the head in the bombing of Pakistan by India.

In Rushdie's syncretic jumble, Saleem's temporary idiocy
and his compliant membership in the military is compared
grandiosely to the state of being 'unable to bear the suffering
of the world . . . capable of not-living-in-the-world as well as
living in it' like the one who 'sat enlightened under a tree
at Gaya . . . [and] taught others to abstract themselves from
worldly sorrows and achieve inner peace' (p. 418). The depths of
degraded material ambition evidenced by the land-grabbing war,
and Saleem's pathetic role in it as cannon fodder, are somehow

recast in the stereotypical imagery of sublime Eastern religion, and a religion ludicrously inappropriate to Muslim Pakistan. Saleem – who is physically described as being fat and partially bald at this point – becomes, in short, the Buddha:

> I (or he) accepted the fate which was my repayment for love, and sat uncomplaining under a chinar tree; that, emptied of history, the buddha learned the arts of submission, and did only what was required of him. To sum up: I became a citizen of Pakistan. (*MC*, p. 419)

Complicity from below is acquiescence; complicity from above is the foisting on others of a private vision. Parvati, we recall, who saves Saleem from this condition of unquestioning acceptance, is the only Midnight's Child of humble origins born in the new Delhi Magicians' Ghetto – home of the reds. Here he is taught resistance, but also learns that 'no resistance is of any use against the cracks' (p. 473) – the fissures within the Indian state that physically repeat themselves in Saleem's own skin. That is, despite the welcome absence of religious and regionalist bigotry in this secular, enlightened socialist community, sectarian battles abound:

> Fire-eaters and sword-swallowers applauded the guerrilla tactics of the Naxalite movement; while mesmerists and walkers-on-hot-coals espoused Namboodiripad's manifesto (neither Muscovite nor Pekinese) and deplored the Naxalites' violence. There were Trotskyist tendencies amongst card-sharpers, and even a Communism-through-the-ballot-box movement amongst the moderate members of the ventriloquist section. (p. 476)

Rushdie finally conceives of the ghetto and the rest of India as representing respectively two warring 'religions' – 'Communism' and 'Businessism' – that are at once irreconcilable and complementary (p. 474): 'A renegade Businessist, I began zealously to turn red and then redder, as surely and completely as my father had once turned white, so that now my mission of saving-the-country could be seen in a new light' (p. 474).

The extremity of Rushdie's rejection of this involvement in 'nationalism' *qua* sectarianism in all its variety, arises clearly in the example of his neighbour Mrs Dubash, who transforms her son Cyrus into 'India's richest guru . . . Cyrus-the-great', alias Lord Khusro. If the most notorious *chamchas* of *Midnight's Children* are the Muslim rich who inhabit the Methwold estate, and if the Muslim League has already been singled out for its ugly part in fomenting nationalist hysteria, Rushdie makes sure here to provide a ruthless parody of religious charlatanism in its Parsee form with some Hindu borrowings:

> Know, o unbleivers, that in the dark Midnights of CELESTIAL SPACE in a time before Time lay the sphere of Blessed KHUSROVAND!!! Even MODERN SCIENTISTS now affirm that for *generations* they have LIED to conceal from the People whose *right it is to know* of the Unquestionabel TRUE existence of this HOLY HOME OF TRUTH!!! Leading intellectuals the World Over, also in America, speak of the ANTI-RELIGIOUS CONSPIRACY or reds, JEWS, etc., to hide these VITAL NEWS! The Veil lifts now. Blessed LORD KHUSRO comes with Irrefutable Proofs. Read and Believe! . . . send Donations to PO Box 555, Head Post Office, Bombay – 1.
> BLESSINGS!   BEAUTY!!   TRUTH!!
> Om Hare Khusro Hare Khusrovand OM. (*MC*, pp. 322-3)

The outrageous insincerity of this leaflet-cum-commercial is deepened by an illiterate, and quite sober, meanness. Khusro's pitch seems able both to provoke laughter and fear, as it mixes together 'scientific' justifications with crude misspellings, combines anti-Enlightenment harangues with pragmatic persuasions, clutches at the sublime while evoking the degraded here-and-now. In another stab at Eastern religious obfuscation, Little Cyrus the guru sham becomes an avatar of Cyrus the great, founder of the Persian empire, the birthplace of Zoroastrianism, the Parsee's faith. His conjuration of 'Bottomless deeps of Celestial Space-Eternity' is given a contemporary and local edge with a description of how 'American guitarists came to sit at his feet', not failing to bring 'their cheque-books along' (p. 323).

The combination of phony populism and religious mission in the service of a swindle mirrors that found in an earlier scene featuring the 'Ravana gang', which had posed as 'a fanatical anti-Muslim movement' during the Partition riots for the purpose of running a protection racket among the Punjabi shopkeepers: 'behind this façade of racial hatred, the Ravana gang was a brilliantly-conceived commercial enterprise' (p. 80).[14] So Rushdie elaborates in these microcosms the forces at work in the larger historical actors behind independence and partition – the Jinnahs (Muslim), Desais (Hindu), Boses (secular) and others, of all and any creed and shade of skin. The nation is a commercial enterprise.

Khusro's accretious motives, prettified by his supposed devotion, exemplify in miniature the nation's use of sacred origins to achieve its real goal: a viable domestic market. Even to this extent, Rushdie had internalised the sociological bases for his satire as if glossing Eric Hobsbawm or illustrating Hans Kohn. One value of Rushdie's fictional treatment of this more or less standard irony about greed and sacred right is his specific identification of the deceptive means of the modern state. Greed is not greed in general but a component in the drive of a recognisable underdeveloped country (which is named) to consolidate its power. The commercialisation of religion is portrayed not as a sign of our irreligious age, but as an age-old, well-honed tool in public-opinion management. Similarly, as Tariq Ali has pointed out, *Midnight's Children* is 'a portrayal not simply of wicked individuals, but of the collective frenzy of a desperately frightened ruling class', an aspect in which it is 'unique in Indo-English literature'.[15]

Behind his caustic parody of selfish civic liars is a theory about the intricate inner workings of an international political system. It is this system which Rushdie is always dismissing but which he is always conveying to the reader in great detail. It is a feature that distinguishes Rushdie from other post-colonial novelists in English, but it is not the only one. For Rushdie extends his critique to the point where 'communications' as a feature of contemporary political control comes to embrace fiction itself, including his own. In this sense, Khusro's commercial success is shown to be dependent on his access to the *media*: 'I saw the hoardings trumpeting the coming of Lord Khusro Khusrovand Bhagwan' (p. 324).

We are being prepared, in other words, for *Shame*'s revelation later when Saleem laments that 'telecommunications . . . were my undoing' (p. 354), recalling that Saleem before his drainage operated as a walking 'All India Radio' transmitting and receiving messages among the Midnight's Children. The association of a 'bad' mass media with the person of Saleem is borne out of his reactions to Khusro himself when he recalls how in childhood he had egged Khusro on to his first guru enterprises, and had even supplied him with his first copies of *Superman* comics – the model for his later religious profession. He softens the crudeness of Khusro's venality, by comparing his broadcasts to his own: 'set beside Cyrus's India, my own version seems almost mundane' (p. 323). Both equally, although in different ways, believed themselves to be saviours of the nation.

So the motifs of communication and the *chamcha* come together. Saleem's complicity with the media, and the importance of its forms to the national message of the novel, are brought out clearly when Saleem compares his writerly practices to the techniques of a Bombay talkie, filled with heavy-handed fictional devices ('a calendar ruffled by a breeze, its pages flying off in rapid succession to denote the passing of the years' – p. 414), and cheap illusionist entertainment. The significance of film as a pervasive form of mass persuasion – the earmark especially of Rushdie's native Bombay – is discussed thematically in the novel in the form of references to the screenplays of Saleem's uncle Hanif, whose documentary realism fails miserably with the sensation-hungry public (and in *Shame*'s tale of the equally ill-fated Mahmoud, owner of the 'Empire Talkies' theatre in Dehli, bombed by sectarian extremists for failing to take sides).[16] But in the passage where Saleem imagines the images on a movie screen seen from only a few inches away, film represents the form whose illusions become less coherent the closer they are scrutinised. Like the newspaper clippings – another mass media form out of which Saleem 'rearranges history' in his communication with Captain Sabarmati – the heroic images of the screen are composed of confusing fragments whose abstract arrangement is obvious when seen up close.

Rushdie's implicit reflection on the responsibility of the media's various 'broadcasters' in the postwar era (including, like himself, the authors of mass-circulation novels) is a reflection on the specific type of nation he is analysing. The nexus of fiction and nationalism in this period occurs within the borders of the nation–state – that is, in the apparatuses of ideological control: 'Divorce between news and reality: newspapers quoted foreign economists – PAKISTAN A MODEL FOR EMERGING NATIONS – while peasants (unreported) cursed the so-called "green revolution" ' (p. 399).

Thus for Rushdie the topic of the nation is inevitably the

topic of the *state*, its flesh and blood rulers and their impact
on their subjects. The disease of nationalism is thus not an
impassive judgement or a simple assessment of one of many
possible historical strategies, but is for Rushdie a question above
all of human rights – of torture, military campaigns, smashed
printing presses and phony referenda. He concentrates on the
imaginative and communicative forms at the state's disposal, in
order to create a scepticism necessary for guarding against the
mendacities, not only of governmental communiqués, but of his
own fiction.

'Telecommunications' are Saleem's undoing, then, both as
victim and as author. Far from exempting his own writing from
the mind control needed to impose one's own view on the world,
he treats his novel as if it were a paradigm of the state lie. On the
logic that Saleem contains all within him, and that the particular
'national longing for form' of India is expressed as 'the urge to
encapsulate the whole of reality', such that (in a glancing look
backward to the solipsism of *Grimus*) no crime committed within
the pages of *Midnight's Children* is committed without Saleem's
complicity:

> Because the feeling had come upon me that I was somehow
> creating a world; that the thoughts I jumped inside were *mine*,
> that the bodies I occupied acted at my command; that, as
> current affairs, arts, sports, the whole rich variety of a first-
> class radio station poured into me, I was somehow *making them
> happen* . . . which is to say, I had entered into the illusion of the
> artist, and thought of the multitudinous realities of the land as
> the raw unshaped material of my gift. (*MC*, p. 207)

It is significant that the 'illusion' of responsibility here is one
of power rather than one of guilt. In other words, just as he
is not innocent, neither is he the only guilty one: 'why should
I assume that I alone have had the powers of secret knowledge?'
(p. 351).

Thus, the key moments of Indian history occurred because
Saleem was their agent: 'the war [for the Rann of Kutch] happened because I dreamed Kashmir into the fantasies of our rulers'
(p. 404). Again, Saleem is a culprit not because he fails to resist,
or because he conspires for personal gain, but rather because he
proliferates *metaphor* and masters illusion ('dreams'). In the coup

of Ayub Khan, for example, Saleem helps plot troop movements by shuffling pepperpots around a banquet table in a demonstration for Ayub's generals. 'What began, active-metaphorically, with pepperpots, ended then; not only did I overthrow a government – I also consigned a president to exile' (p. 349). Similarly, in the secession of Bangladesh, 'I remained responsible through the workings of the metaphorical modes of connection, for the belligerent events of 1971' (p. 420).

Nevertheless, these sweeping claims to be the imaginative source of history, eventually lead to a repudiation of the individual as a moral being. In their reflections on the aesthetic features of insurgent nation-forming, Fanon and Gramsci (in different ways) had both commented on the subtle shifts in political attitude that occurred in the transformation of popular artistic expression into 'high' literature. The disparity between Rushdie's journalism and his fiction rests in the moulding of his politics to the demands of form. Thus, in *Midnight's Children* Rushdie's interpretation of human rights has pushed him to gauge history's importance by its effect on the 'personality': 'I am coming to the conclusion that privacy, the small individual lives of men, are preferable to this inflated macrocosmic activity' (p. 518). If 'psychology' and 'myth' are the modes in which literature escapes real history, Rushdie's historical novel surprisingly depends on them.

Just as Brahma dreams the universe, so Rushdie generates Indian history within the universe of the novel, and each person becomes the receptacle of the 'sum total of everything . . . everyone everything whose being-in-the-world affected was affected by mine' (p. 457). From this Chinese-box vision of a myriad of 'I's, each one of which contains multitudes, it is a small step – given the depressing history he lays out – to locate India's failures (or any other nation's) within the individual.

His first step in this direction occurs well within the bounds of *Midnight's Children*'s trope of Saleem the universal man, and has no further significance: 'Religion was the glue of Pakistan, holding the halves together; just as consciousness, the awareness of oneself as a homogeneous entity in time, . . . is the glue of personality, holding together our then and our now' (p. 420). However, Rushdie eventually reduces this to a more extreme and apparently unjustified position: namely, 'what you were is forever who you are', and 'each of us . . . [gets] the leaders we deserve' (p. 440, 518). These views weaken his critique of national folly by implying that folly is endemic – that it is 'human'. Torture, censorship and repression must be ingrained, as we see when we learn that Mary Periera's ditty was a deception (at least as Saleem concludes): 'Anything you want to be, you kin be' (p. 457). From 'can' to 'kin', heredity means changelessness.

MIDNIGHT'S CHILDREN AS POSTMODERN EPIC

Rushdie's analysis of the *chamcha*, although played out in Indian dress, belongs, as we said, to that larger tradition of the 'nationalism of mourning' found virtually everywhere in Third-World fiction. Indeed, it would be hard to find examples of contemporary Third-World novels that did not make some reference to it.[17] And yet, cosmopolitan balance, generated from a basic insecurity about national identity, demands that any critical mimicry of national fiction entail as well a 'going to the people' – or in Rushdie's case, rather an account of what this fictional gesture involves. In this sense, Rushdie dutifully casts the only unquestionably 'native' and authentic national spokespersons in lower-class dress.

In *Midnight's Children*, the portrayal of class tensions between *chamcha* and 'people' begins with the verbal battles that take place between the voluble and filthy boatman Tai Bibi and the foreign-educated Aadam Aziz; it continues in the conflicts between the poor accordian-player Wee Willie Winkie and the Methwold household, and is consummated in the life–and–death struggle between the changelings, Saleem and Shiva, over the birthright of India itself. As Rushdie's counterpart, Saleem narrates the story from the painful and inaccurate distance of privilege; he therefore requires assistance from a plebeian commentator to temper his erudition and, as he puts it, his 'purity of accent' (*MC*, p. 254) or so the cliché of national fiction goes. In *Midnight's Children* the role of plebeian commentator is performed by Saleem's servant and mistress, Padma, who is not part of the story proper but occupies selected 'asides' in which she participates with Saleem in composing the novel we are reading.[18] Her relationship is not with Saleem the character, but with Saleem the narrator and author looking back on the events of his younger self, the mirror of Indian history.

Here the book's narrative problems are both discussed and enacted. Padma's marriage designs on Saleem, for example, suggest the union of populist sentiment and local élitism necessary for any complete national rendering. Saleem's temporary bout with fever and his subsequent delirium are made to stand for the author's visionary style. In this supra-narrative role, Padma also literally intervenes in the composition of the book Saleem is writing, by presenting in her comments an alternative, popular aesthetics.[19] Padma is not only a passive receptor, or a disembodied voice of the national conscience, but a literary *critic*, whose authority rests on her being a member of the lower classes. Significantly, her advice is hardly ever followed, but it ostensibly tempers the shameful cosmopolitanism that would make the writing inauthentic. Her presence is Rushdie's playful acknowledgement of a tradition of national literature which his peripheral status allows him to criticise even as he participates in it.

Midnight's Children therefore elides an older view of the nation with a contemporary and neo-colonial one, in which national *mythos* merges with a humanist critique of the *polis*. The familiar 'nativist' rhetoric of much Third-World fiction is therefore both appropriated and parodied. Although much of *Midnight's Children* unfolds within a modern and political mode, repeatedly recalling the sectarian violence of contemporary Indian political life and the class tensions against which any national unity is artificially constructed, it is nevertheless designed to suggest the living presence of India's mythical past, not as 'vital tradition' but as false consciousness. It is neither a documentary portrayal of postwar Indian politics, nor a representative of the more common approach to myth in the Indian novel described by Robin Lewis: 'to redefine Hinduism and infuse it with new meaning, so that India's past, its myths and its history, could provide an element of continuity in the search for a national identity'.[20]

For all its patches of straight history, meticulously accompanied by direct allusions to practical politics in the storyline, *Midnight's Children* filters day-to-day controversy through the medium of Indian mythology, thereby reversing the direction of most Indian nationalist fiction, which relies on a history with an appropriately solemn attachment to folklore.[21] If all the key figures of the novel have dual roles – one in the here-and-now, one in the ridiculously charged world of folklore – they are fighting not only over current

policy but over fictional style itself, which is hopelessly impli-
cated in directing and limiting the political terrain on which the
battle is taking place.

The pivotal act of the story (the baby-swapping of the two
central characters, Saleem and Shiva) announces Rushdie's
uncertain, contradictory acceptance of the *chamcha* role, for
it allows him to emphasise at will the lower- and upper-class
backgrounds which are both a part of his heritage. But it also
exemplifies what is striking in Rushdie's contribution to postwar
national fiction – a critique of *today's* political demagogy by
pointing to the explicitly mythological costumes and folkloric
rhetoric of the national leaders. The narrative commentary of the
Padma subplot intentionally splinters the narrative and keeps it
at a distance, 'under study'.

The contest between Saleem and Shiva is further portrayed as
a debate between parties in a parliament chamber. It takes place
in the arena of Midnight's Children's Conference, a microcosm
of the Indian government, where Saleem (the 'little rich boy')
argues against the 'endless duality of masses and classes' while
the working-class Shiva insists that 'there is only money-and-
poverty . . . have-and-lack' (pp. 306–7), an understandable view
for one who has been robbed of his place in the family of a
well-to-do Muslim businessman. These contemporary political
antagonisms are continued later when Saleem's 'son', the hope
of the next generation, proves to be the offspring of Parvati the
slumgirl and Shiva the beggar. If *Midnight's Children* attacks the
political mythmaking of Indian national politics, it does so using
Indian myth.

As an avatar of Hinduism's greatest deity, the character Shiva
automatically suggests the presence of traditional mythology. His
fight with Saleem is not only poor against rich, village wisdom
against cosmopolitan snobbery, but East against West. 'Shiva'
bears the mark of Hinduism; 'Sinai' (Saleem's last name) the
mark of the Judeo-Christian covenant. But Shiva, the fearful
image of *ressentiment*, also possesses the sexual (creative) potency
that Saleem lacks, thereby linking national progeny with the lower
classes as an elemental, autochthonous force. While Saleem's dispute with Shiva takes the form of an argument between humani-
tarian liberalism and blind sectarian revenge, their differences
exist on a much more elemental level: 'I disliked the roughness
of his tongue, the crudity of his ideas' (p. 271). Their dispute

involves class, not as profession or place in production, but as cultural vision and as national style. It is in this sense of literary nationalism that Padma's narrative lessons have to be seen.

Rushdie first of all goes out of his way to establish Padma's plebeian credentials, which he lays on with exaggerated thickness. ' "Padma" means lotus, and in the traditional Indian conscious- ness, the lotus symbolises one who was born in slime and mud but is able to reach out to the higher things of life. In other words, the name is suggestive of the ability to capture the essence of both worlds, the sordid and the beautiful.'[22] She 'stirs a bubbling vat all day for a living', calls Saleem 'city boy', is illiterate and has a name common among 'village folk' that means 'The One who Possesses Dung' (p. 22). Saleem's occasional revulsion for Padma's bodily smells and habits carries to the cultural and personal level the same class tensions found between Saleem and Shiva. In tacit reference to the well-schooled appreciation of 'culture' in many Third-World writers, Rushdie expresses well the ambivalence with which lower-class forms are usually absorbed. Because of Padma's crudeness, her relationship with Saleem is often strained. A mistress, but also a servant; a counsellor, but also a harpy, she seems both to revolt and impress him. Described distastefully as 'thick of waist, somewhat hairy of forearm' and as 'definitely a bitch-in-the-manger' (p. 21), Saleem later suggests an intimacy that is unfulfilled: 'I must go to bed. Padma is waiting; and I need a little warmth' (p. 36). We know at this point, however, that Saleem is impotent. He relies on her, but cannot make love to her; their relationship is symbiotic, but at cross purposes:

> How I admire the leg-muscles of my solicitous Padma! There she squats, a few feet from my table, her sari hitched up in fisherwoman-fashion . . . my admiration extends also to her arms, which could wrestle mine down in a trice, and from which, when they enfold me nightly in futile embraces, there is no escape. Past our crisis now, we exist in perfect harmony: I recount, she is recounted to; she ministers, and I accept her ministrations with grace. (*MC*, pp. 324–5)

The sexual tension Rushdie creates by describing Padma's legs is blunted and distorted by his focus (partly fearful) of their strength. What seems like sexual attraction is really a cold respect. 'Perfect harmony' exists only as a lull between crises, in a relationship of mixed loathing and submission. Padma's 'ministrations' are also her aesthetic interference; her 'solicitations' are both petitions and harangues.

The writer's appeal to plebeian virtue is always a sublimation of poverty, an elevation of raw material. While it is necessary to allow the plebeians to speak, it is only to have them call the bluff of the artist–voyeur. In *Midnight's Children*, the implicit dishonesty of the claim to cultural unity is therefore revealed precisely in these gestures to the 'people's' immemorial national essence. For Saleem rejects Padma's aesthetic counsels. They condition, but do not dictate the form of his writing. He feels the duty, and even at times the desire, to seek out her advice, but not the inclination to follow.

Padma's plebeian strengths of storytelling are repeated in the story proper by several characters: Mary Pereira, Saleem's Christian ayah, whose gift for preserving memories he compares to Padma's making of chutney (p. 252), and above all, by the boatman Tai, whose chatter, says Saleem, 'was fantastic, grandiloquent and ceaseless' (p. 9), whose age no one could remember, whose verbiage was endless and his talk 'magical', and who was illiterate ('Literature crumbled beneath the rage of his sweeping hand' – p. 11). Tai is a drunk who refuses to wash, whose bodily smells offend his passengers, who only has two teeth (both made of gold), and who 'set history in motion' by providing Aadam Aziz with a prophecy counselling him to follow his nose. A labourer whose profession is to carry the wealthy across the river in his *shikara*, Tai's store of memory keeps the entire community aware of its past. At the same time – and it becomes important in Rushdie's discussion of Western democracy – he is associated with small-town ignorance and reaction: 'Tai-for-changelessness opposed to Aadam-for-progress' (p. 124). Thus Padma represents aesthetically not only 'earthiness of spirit' (p. 177) but 'ignorance and superstition'; her 'down-to-earthery' predictably and depressingly jumbles together with its opposite: a 'contradictory love of the fabulous', inevitable in that, like all true 'folk', she is the heart and soul of the nation's original sense of self as described in the primal literature of mythology, the true national novelist's only reliable source material. She is the 'Lotus calyx, which grew out of Vishnu's navel, and from which Brahma himself was born' (p. 233).

As presented in the novel, then, Padma's plebeian aesthetics

are not surprising, although they are paradoxical: a naïve sense
of realism (she wants to know simply 'was it true?'; confronted
metaphorically by a talking photo, she asks 'How can a picture
talk?'), a scorn for Saleem's pretentious speech and his 'abstract
ruminations', an uncritical acceptance of the 'reality' of Saleem's
characters. But Saleem's condescension is not valorised, and we
are not supposed to reject her crudeness merely on the grounds
of our own sophistication. The uniqueness of Rushdie's allegory
of narrative composition is that here Padma's lower-class impulses
in art merely symbolise the fatal immaturity of her class in the
struggle for a meaningful democracy on a legitimately 'Indian'
terrain. When Padma gives Saleem's characters an exaggerated
importance, it is because she resents any breaking of the narrative
spell:[23]

> I must interrupt myself. I wasn't going to today because Padma
> has started getting irritated whenever my narration becomes
> self-conscious, whenever, like an incompetent puppeteer, I
> reveal the hands holding the strings. (*MC*, p. 72)

She advocates instead 'the world of linear narrative, the universe
of what-happened next' (p. 38), but it is not the kind of advice
that can solve the problem of excessive fiction. On the contrary,
being an illiterate, she is simply 'jealous of written words', because
Saleem dedicates more time to writing than to her, and she is
unable to resuscitate his 'other pencil' (p. 141).

While it is true that Padma is Saleem's typical audience,
bringing to the surface the reader's thoughts and questions,
his 'necessary ear' (p. 177); and while it is true that she is his
principal critic (p. 30) – she is, aesthetically speaking, much
more important as an image of the Indian masses' gullibility
– a translation of her readerly naïvete into social terms. It is
with misgivings that Saleem refers to her unquestioning faith in
his narrative: 'I vouchsafe daily glimpses of myself – while she,
my squatting glimpser, is captivated, helpless as a monogoose
frozen into immobility by the swaying, blinkless eyes of a hooded
snake' (p. 142). Her gullibility ('folkloric simplicity') is part of the
fictional status quo she represents, and is responsible for her failure to challenge the demagogy of India's national leaders. Thus,
even though Saleem points to the errors of memory that mar his
work, the plot inconsistencies, the unreliability of his facts, he can

still be assured that Padma and the people will believe him. His
writing becomes a process of imposing his vision on others, and
he is able to conclude cynically: '[i]n all literature, what actually
happened is less important than what the author can manage to
persuade his audience to believe' (p. 325).

According to the book's major trope, Saleem contains within
himself '630 million particles of oblivious dust' (p. 37), one for
each soul of the Indian masses, whose terrible force threatens
to destroy him in the act of his enormous empathy. As a
consequence, in the logic of the narrative he must record his
tale before he explodes (which, in the final pages he does), and
before his tale is in this way lost to the world. From Padma, the
domestic servant and unsatisfied lover, Saleem learns the techniques of pickling, displayed throughout the tale by her boiling
pots of chutney, always within smelling reach of Saleem's writing
desk. As he records Indian history for posterity, each new chapter
corresponds to one of the twenty-six pickle jars he methodically
adds to the shelf beside his desk. *Midnight's Children* is therefore
what Rushdie calls a 'chutnification of history'.

Keeper of the casaundy jars above Saleem's writing table,
Padma is naturally a preserver of traditions. But she is not,
surprisingly, a symbol of memory, which is a *historical* quality
directly at odds with the repetitive logic of folklore. Rushdie
makes this distinction at one point when Saleem counterposes
his own 'wild god of memory' to Padma's 'lotus goddess of the
present' (p. 177). At another point, she dismisses the past as so
much 'funny talk' (p. 531), and so apparently speaks for India,
characterised in another place as a 'nation of forgetters'. To the
popular mind, a story is what one lives through; to Saleem, it is
what one tries to learn from.

If Padma's value is her contact with the people, she also
represents precisely what is wrong with postwar India. We get a
clue of this in her reaction to Saleem's historical account of the
catastrophic India–Pakistan war of 1965. There Padma sheds tears
for the deaths of the major characters (Naseem, Zafar, Amina)
but seems oblivious to the historical lessons. She instead reduces
them to a cliché: 'O, mister, this war . . . kills the best and leaves
the rest!' (p. 413). Elsewhere, Rushdie calls this inappropriate
bathos 'Bombay-talkie-melodramatic' (p. 523) – the mind-dulling
insipidness of the popular mind at odds with history and addicted
to the equally insipid Bombay film. Folklore's incessant repetitions

mould history itself into a fixed pattern in which there is no escape from injustice and deception because the ones being deceived are unprepared or unwilling to change.

A good example, and one that exemplifies Rushdie's encyclopaedic style, occurs in the description of the love affair between Lila Hindustan and Homi Catrack, which he compares to those of several legendary lovers: 'Once upon a time there were Radha and Krishna, and Rama and Sita, and Laila and Majnu . . . ' (p 311). Yet even here he emphasises the inescapable pattern of behaviour already codified in ancient myth and continued willy-nilly in the civilised, still-unfolding present: 'The world is full of love stories, and all lovers are in a sense the avatars of their predecessors'. This intellectualised observation on the ways of history complements the similar, although unschooled, observation by superstitious village folk of the continued reality of myth in everyday national life: 'According to Mary, the country was in the grip of a sort of supernatural invasion . . . an old Sikh woman woke up in her hut and saw the old-time war of the Kurus and Pandavas happening right outside! It was in the papers and all . . . she pointed to the place where she saw the chariots of Arjun and Karna . . . rakshasas have been seen many-headed like Ravana' (p. 293).

The contradiction between *chamcha* and people is not resolved except in the sense of a convergence, in which each seems to assume the other's poorest qualities. In one sense, Padma and Saleem can both be thought to advocate, alternately, 'old time fabulism' and writing in a 'plain unveiled fashion' (p. 328). To show this convergence more clearly, Rushdie has cosmopolitanism come full circle in the fate of the Midnight's Children Conference (MCC), whose members (the hope of the new nation, many of them from humble backgrounds, after decades of political debate and organising) degenerate into the 'Midnight-Confidential Club'. If Padma represents linear narrative and the universe of 'what-happened-next', she does so because she is arrested in a world of immediate sensation, without interest in history or 'criticism' in the broad sense. But this is just what the Midnight-Confidential Club – the degenerate form of the fledgling Parliament of India – comes to represent: 'Here you are in a world without faces or names; here people have no memories, families or past; here is for *now*' (p. 541).

In Padma's narrative counsels, Rushdie pretends that *Midnight's*

Children inconclusively divides itself between popular-ethnic history and 'scientific' accounts by erudite humanists like Saleem, since neither is preferable in terms of relating 'what-actually-happened'. The anoymous popular masses are plain and sensible, but also sentimental. If they have the numbers to alter history's flow (and Saleem is eager to point out that Padma 'may be capable of altering the ending of my story by the phenomenal force of her will' – p. 530), they lack the sceptical intelligence to do so. On the other hand, the isolated individual author is capable of 'making history' in other and equally ironic senses – by distorting the facts and rhetorically forcing others to believe him, or by fictionally reshaping events as though the events themselves were being reshaped. If he suggests that he himself *is* India, by containing its variety and by purveying the illusion of causing its events to happen, then he resembles no one so much as Indira Gandhi following her suspension of civil rights in 1975: '[W]as my life-long belief in the equation between the state and myself transmuted in "The Madam's" mind, into that in-those-days-famous phrase: *India is Indira and Indira is India*?' (p. 501).

The alternate compliance and antagonism between Padma and Saleem (often symbolically represented by their inability to consummate sexual union) reflects the ambivalent relationship of literature and folklore, seen as upper and lower classes, or as Eastern and Western influences. The 'national longing for form' is not merely a longing for nationhood but a parody on the level of imaginative form, of ridiculously disparate *social* elements yoked together unsuccessfully.[24] *Midnight's Children* repeats that failed collaboration, composed in the process of our reading.

What, however, saves the novel from merely repeating the past is its own self-criticism. Rushdie alludes to folklore in such a way that we are made to see not an idealisation of primordial, native virtue – a characteristic of the 'folk' in the literature of early European nationalism – but a sensuous individual member of the contemporary Indian working class, with all its post-nineteenth-century political connotations. The fact that she represents the conservative fixity of tradition, arresting the story, making it tame and predictable, suggests the political failures of the Third-World socialism prevalent in modern decolonisation struggles. Conceived as always at the level of verbal conflict, the lower classes are deceived, the upper classes deceive, in their respective places within a literary hierarchy. History is 'altered' by rhetorical devices – either after-the-fact revision (the rewriting of history) or persuasion of those who can in fact change it. We have so far been examining Rushdie's theoretical discussion of national 'myth' in *Midnight's Children*'s narrative asides. We shall now consider 'national form' in Rushdie's comic perversion of classical Hindu mythology.

ELEPHANTIASIS OF STYLE

Midnight's Children's use of classical Indian myth relies above all on a single episode – the union of Parvati and Shiva, and the subsequent bearing of their elephant-headed child Ganesh. Other figures in the Hindu pantheon – Brahma (p. 253), Vishnu, Arjuna, Bhima (p. 239) and others – are usually mentioned only in passing, although Saleem's rivalry with Shiva in the MCC seems to mirror the rivalry of the gods Brahma and Shiva in one Hindu creation myth.[25] It is this relatively small cast of mythical characters, at any rate, that carries the weight. It is perhaps important to point out in this context that the novel has been read by its Indian audience as being a book unmistakably written by an author with a Muslim upbringing, conveying 'the sensibility of Islamic alienation from the rest of India'.[26] Rushdie, however, is hardly Islamic in any hard sense, although he has certain emotional attachments to Sufism as *Grimus* and *Shame* both show. That reading of his work nevertheless reminds us that his intended audience is a Western one, where the full range of his satire's targets (and he leaves no one out) can be appreciated naïvely, without sectarianism, but also without the fear of loss.

As the fruit of the union of Parvati and Hinduism's 'great god' Shiva, Ganesh is perhaps the most central of all – a god of good fortune and a sign of fecundity in a novel full of impotence and illegitimacy. His influence envelops the entire novel, from the opening pages where Aadam Aziz is said to have a nose 'comparable only to the trunk of the elephant-headed Ganesh' (p. 8) to the concluding chapter (two generations and 500 pages later) where Saleem's 'son' Aadam Sinai is described as 'the true son of Shiva-and-Parvati . . . [the] elephant-headed Ganesh' (p. 500). Earlier, other elephantic features had given the most important

Midnight's Children their special powers: Saleem's telepathy and insight derived from his large nose; Shiva's talent for war, from his bulbous knees. Spanning in this way all the generations of *Midnight's Children* – a novel that expresses national destiny in the form of family lineages – Ganesh is central partly as a symbol of the continuity of the generations. For it is only Aadam Sinai who carries the lineage of the Midnight's Children into the second generation. He is the only second-generation baby of Indian independence, since all the surviving Midnight's Children – now of parenting age – had been sterilised during the Indian 'Emergency'.

By offsetting this general lack of procreation, Aadam displays the propitious side of Ganesh, his proverbial ability to overcome difficulties. Traditionally, Ganesh is 'the typical embodiment of success in life and its accompaniments of good living, prosperity and peace'.[27] But in this very reference to procreation and good-tidings, Rushdie alerts us to another version of the Ganesh myth. According to this version, when Parvati attempts to seduce Shiva he refuses to engender a son because he wishes to divorce himself from the chain of rebirth. In this sense, Ganesh becomes acceptable to him only because he is not truly a child but a monster; not a son but some unnatural mixture. Ganesh is therefore at once a promise for the future and an end of the line, and Rushdie is implying that both qualities potentially apply to the first and last generations of *Midnight's Children* – to 'Aadam' Aziz, the patriarch (after Forster) of the Westernised Indian, and to 'Aadam' Sinai, the only offspring of the first generation of independence . . . the beginning of the end.

Like Ganesh, Shiva plays a dual role. However, his contradictions are even more elaborate. On the one hand, a 'Lord of Beasts', on the other, a Lord of the Hunt, he is 'at once the planter of seed, who gives life, and the destroyer, whose wrathful power can strip the skin from a tiger with the flick of his smallest finger'.[28] Although a symbol of masculine sexual potency, he is closely associated with female power, and he contains simultaneously within him the qualities of *tapas* (asceticism) and *kama* (sexual desire).[29] His place in a novel riven by castration and impotency is plain; most of his permutations concern sexuality. In effect, Shiva 'unites within himself the dangerous and the beneficent aspects of the fertility process'.

Rushdie's use of the Shiva myth is much more fully realised

than that of Ganesh, if only because Shiva is a character within
the novel. For the most part, Rushdie's Shiva varies only slightly
from myth and recites the more common epithets. For example,
Rushdie tells us about Shiva's 'gifts of war': '[Shiva is] the god of
destruction, who is also most potent of deities; Shiva, greatest of
dancers; who rides on a bull; whom no force can resist' (p. 264).
But in the novel, Shiva is also portrayed as a lower-class bully,
whose ideas are crude, his tongue rough, his intentions criminal;
a thug, in fact, who participates in election fraud, relies on 'ter-
rifying, nonchalant violence' (p. 262), and conceives of the MCC
as a 'gang' that he must control. He is socially Saleem's opposite:
a working-class tough, born of wealthy parents, Saleem being the
'rich kid' born of beggars. When late in the book, Shiva becomes a
famous major and socialite at the very moment Saleem is stuffing
envelopes in the tawdry meeting halls of the Magicians' Ghetto, it
becomes clear that the significance of their relationships depends
on the interchangeability of their roles. Their world-views clash as
they vie for control over the MCC in a conflict of complementary
opposites.

While other plebeian figures in *Midnight's Children* had been
too susceptible to national fiction (Padma, with her gullibility;
Mary, with her belief in mythical visitations during moments of
national strife), Shiva is completely immune to the 'high principles' pronounced by the nation's apologists. He is not therefore
a corrective to plebeian credulity, however, since his cynical lack
of principles (although it keeps him from being a dupe) simply
mirrors that of the nation's misleaders, who are only less frank
than he in stating their intentions. While Saleem is inspired by
the Prime Minister's letter to the Midnight's Children, Shiva calls
it 'crazy stuff' (p. 264). Saleem recounts the magical properties of
the nation's first children, while Shiva sees them all only as 'freak
kids'. Saleem insists that despite his and Shiva's superior powers,
the MCC must remain a loose federation of equals, whereas Shiva
demands an oligarchy: 'Everybody does what I say or I squeeze
the shit outa them with my knees.' While Saleem struggles to
discover the purpose of their group, Shiva denies the world has
purpose:

> For what reason you're rich and I'm poor? Where's the reason
> in starving man? God knows how many millions of damn fools
> living in this country, man, and you think there's a purpose!

Man, I'll tell you – you got to get what you can, do what you
can with it, and then you got to die. That's reason rich boy.
(*MC*, p. 264)

This two-dimensional ruffian nevertheless represents well the
complexities of his prototype in Hindu myth – a destroyer and
a propagator, a stud who reviles the begetting of children. Thus,
as a returning war hero ('Major Shiva'), he is portrayed as a tall
mustachioed ladies' man and a 'cuckolder of the rich' who
'strew[s] bastards across the map of India' (pp. 487–8), but also
as one who goes into a rage when hearing his exploits have led to
a pregnancy. Enormously fertile, he also makes possible the mass
sterilisation of the Midnight's Children when he turns informer
and betrays them to the authorities. The contradictions of Ganesh
and Shiva are suggested also in the rivalry of Saleem and Shiva,
who together represent the essential polarities in the conflicting
forces of the nation. Socially, as we saw, the conflict is between
what Rushdie called 'masses and classes'. But politically – and
the MCC is primarily a political body – their rivalry represents
a conflict between belligerence and diplomacy, election fraud
and democracy, thuggery and persuasion, material interest and
'humanism', treason and loyalty.

Thus, according to Rushdie, to understand this rivalry is to
'gain an understanding of the age in which you live' (p. 515),
because it represents, in other words, a social truth as invariable
as the lessons of myth. It is essential to Rushdie's point that neither
Saleem nor Shiva, despite their differences, be associated permanently with one or the other side of the dichotomies just listed.
Saleem, for example, insists that *he* is a traitor too – that he too
eliminated opponents when it was suitable (for example, when
his actions lead to the killing of the characters Jimmy Kapadia
and Homi Catrack).

The point, then, is that Rushdie's use of classical Indian myth
goes so far as to replicate while modernising the Hindu concept
of the world as a series of irresolvable dualities. To the degree that
any modernising of legend involves irony, Rushdie's is no exception. But by portraying the contemporary world as a place where
mythical patterns still fit, despite animated talk of the 'future', he
embraces the core of Hindu myth more sincerely than his earlier
dismissal of Padma had implied. The use of Hindu mythology –
despite Rushdie's rejection of its superstitious aspects and the

supposed *sacredness* of national traditions – is in this way both sardonic and sincere. It captures what Hindu scholar Wendy O'Flaherty calls the essence of Hindu myth, which 'treats correlative opposites as well as correlative identities as essential relationships', such that myths are always stories 'told and retold in an eternal search for the impossible solution'.[30]

Rushdie's embrace of these essential mythical dualities is best seen in the rivalry of Saleem and Shiva, which recalls the legendary rivalry between Shiva and Brahma. Saleem, that is, stands for Brahma, the god who created the universe when Shiva, who had been assigned the task, went into a thousand-year abstinence. According to this myth, Shiva returns to destroy the world with fire, angered by Brahma's pre-emptive creation. When he is finally appeased, he breaks off his *linga* (that is, castrates himself) and plants it.[31] The myth is important to *Midnight's Children* not only because it imagines fertility to be a counterpart of castration, but because it suggests the aesthetic competition between Rushdie's sources. It imagines the competition between Shiva and Saleem to be one between 'the two valid forms of creation'.[32] Brahma, as we know, is the god who *dreams* the world. Shiva, we learn, is the god who allows it to exist by declining to use his immeasurable power for destroying it.

As author, Saleem, like Brahma, imagines the whole of Indian history and contains it within him. His 'impotency' reflects his inability to change historical events except in so far as he convinces others to believe the doctored versions of his tales. Because Shiva and Brahma are 'correlative opposites', and because 'the two gods participate in aspects of each other so deeply that they exchange roles almost at random', Saleem/Brahma displays the largely negative or inverted capacity of Shiva for generation: that is, his impotency (lack of practical political power) directly strengthens his fertility *as a writer*.[33] For his part, Shiva, member of the angry masses, has the power to change events but uses it in ways that will not produce meaningful change. Like his namesake, he represents 'supra-ethical and supra-personal dynamic evolution', a poor foundation for a rational, democratic politics.[34]

The implications for Rushdie's view on authorical creation are here as important as the political lessons. Like folklore (as we saw), classical Indian myth suggests to Rushdie the forms of appropriate national style. It is within and through the characterisations of these primary mythical figures that Rushdie suggests the literary forms the national novel might take, and in so doing he alludes to what he earlier called India's 'national longing for form' (p. 359). Parvati, Shiva and Ganesh each represent distinct aspects of the national style found in *Midnight's Children*. Parvati-the-witch is presented to us as a resident of the 'ghetto of magicians' and 'the conjurers slum' filled with 'fakirs, prestidigitators and illusionists'. Aesthetically, her powers of 'conjuration and sorcery' are the powers of making appear real what is not: 'the art which required no artifice' (p. 239). Although an aspect of all style, illusion appears through *Midnight's Children* in specifically Indian forms, beginning with the popular linking of magic and Eastern mysticism (Lord Khusro, Ramram Seth) and India's national medium of illusion – the Bombay cinema. The consequences of faking reality are dealt with thoroughly in the case of Saleem's Uncle Hanif, the film-maker who persists in writing screenplays about the detailed inner workings of a pickle-factory while the public desires melodrama. His ultra-realistic, completely uncompromising documentaries are a failure with the public, but he is none the less quite clear on the problems of faking reality. Although the naïve dilemma of 'fakery' is a truism in fiction, in Rushdie it is something more – a plague upon political discourse, and so, in Rushdie's case (who combines the two), a double-bind.

Shiva, on the other hand, provides Saleem with the skills of a sensationalist reporter. But as with Parvati, there is no simple relationship with reality:

> Matter of fact descriptions of the outré and bizarre, and their reverse, namely heightened, stylized versions of the everyday – these techniques, which are also attitudes of mind, I have lifted – or perhaps absorbed – from . . . Shiva-of-the-knees. (*MC*, p. 261)

Here, apart from representing in almost the very same words, the aesthetic of García Márquez as bestowed to him by his grandmother, is represented the other problem facing the historical novelist – not distorting, but aestheticising reality, allowing it to be consumed *as if* it were fiction through a screen of desensitising verbal invention. It is especially a problem, Rushdie implies, in India, where the population is so great and various that it is easier to grasp it as a panorama than as a collection of individual lives:

> [The technique's] effect was to create a picture of the world of startling uniformity, in which one could mention casually, in passing as it were, the dreadful murders of prostitutes . . . while lingering passionately on the intricate details of a particular hand of cards. (p. 261)

The dangers of distorting, on the one hand, and aestheticising, on the other, lead Saleem to create various counter-techniques that go even further than his general narrative self-consciousness in cautioning against a single authoritative version of history. Of course, the subplot of Saleem and Padma (as we saw) was one of these techniques: the creation of a detailed active world whose events (sometimes allegorically, sometimes discursively) cast doubt on the reliability of the story and systematically analyse the elements making it up. Some of the reflections on narrative truth in these passages provide the strongest warnings against friendly fictions (the kind of fictions likely in the camaraderie of a new nation freed from 'foreign' influence), and sometimes go so far as to equate Saleem's activities as a form of communication – in the sense that in the novel he is portrayed as being both the author and, by force of his telepathic powers, the 'switchboard' of the MCC, a one-man 'All India Radio' – with totalitarian rule. For example, in one such passage he portrays himself as a kind of unwitting Big Brother when he explains how his mental transmissions had the power of entering minds at will:[35]

> I went to some pains to alleviate the shock of my entry. In all cases, my standard first transmission was an image of my face, smiling in what I trusted was a soothing, friendly, confident and leader-like fashion, and of a hand stretched out in friendship. (p. 262)

For Rushdie, writers enter our minds this way. When literature provides essential information; when it knits together entire polities; when it is capable of contributing to the 'disease of optimism' – then the 'lie of fiction' (normally a truism in literary criticism) acquires a more dangerous character.

And this is why Saleem rejects linear narrative, both as Padma's 'what-happened-next' and his own orderly historical chronology of events. The basis for his rejection is found in the aesthetic influence of Ganesh, as the offspring of both Parvati and Shiva, and as Saleem's figurative 'son', who represents the culmination of all national technique. For Ganesh is the medium through which the entire story is filtered, because he is (in addition to his other attributes) traditionally depicted as a scribe to whom Vyasa is dictating the *Mahabharata*, an office Rushdie explicitly associates with Padma, the midwife of *Midnight's Children*. For example, when Padma temporarily abandons Saleem, he alludes to another variant of the myth when he complains: '[h]ow to dispense with Padma? . . . When Valmiki, the author of the Ramayana, dictated his masterpiece to elephant-headed Ganesh, did the god walk out on him halfway?' (p 177). And, at another point, Padma attempts to cure Saleem's impotence with the virility herb *feronia elephantum*, and suggests after an illness that Saleem take a vacation for a day at 'Elephanta' (p. 252).[36]

But it is in another capacity than as a medium that Ganesh provides the culmination of national style, whose common element (Rushdie continually points out) is the 'Indian disease, this urge to encapsulate the whole of reality' (p. 84). There are several embodiments of this urge in the course of the novel: Lifafa Das, the peepshow man, who cries out as he walks the streets of Delhi displaying his vast collection of picture postcards: 'See the whole world, come see everything!' (p. 83); or the painter friend of Nadir Khan 'whose paintings had grown larger and larger as he tried to get the whole of life into his art' (p. 50); or the spittoon of Rani of Cooch Naheen, in which mix the juices, without prejudice, of all religions, castes and classes; and, consummately, Saleem's twenty-six pickle jars.[37] The style is from Ganesh, Rushdie implies, simply because it represents *Midnight's Children*'s and India's *elephantiasis* of style – a feature of Saleem too, of course, who admits earlier to being 'a swallower of lives' and in which 'consumed multitudes are jostling and shoving' (p. 4).

It is from his perspective of containing the whole world that Rushdie develops his attack on linearity. He first of all does this simply by pointing to the discontinuities of a story built out of 'scraps of memory', aromas, 'wind-blown newspapers', 'shreds', and 'fragments' (pp. 509–10), a process allegorised in the novel in the story of Aadam Aziz's courtship of the landowner's daughter, Naseem who, feigning sickness, has Aadam (a doctor) inspect her through a white sheet in which a hole has been cut, one part at a time; or (more literally) in Saleem's secret message to Commander Sabarmati, which is made up of random syllables clipped from newspaper headlines.

But more than this, he deliberately breaks continuity by interrupting the narrative with patches of straight history. If he calls these interludes 'Public Announcements' it is with a sense both of their real informational content and their inevitable overlapping with the reporting of 'current events' in the media. And because throughout the novel he has associated the media with illusion (Bombay cinema) and thought-control ('All India Radio'), he is not only protecting us from narrative tyranny by breaking the narrative spell, but is also refusing to privilege the very information that breaks it. Discontinuity is not only formal but sequential. Because Saleem contains all within him, it is possible for ends to precede beginnings, for the novel's time line to be embodied within him. This is the sense of the so-called 'coming attractions' – another device for interrupting linear narrative.

This formal assault on orderly fictions provides the only way out of the Saleem–Shiva duality. It is precisely their rivalry that produces a third element – Ganesh, whose style amounts to the chaotic 'sum total of everything' – an appropriate paradigm for India's national form, not simply because of India's mammoth diversity, but because all-inclusiveness finally undermines the idea of national distinctions themselves, which are orderly and bordered. 'Everything' means not just India. If neither Saleem nor Padma create 'true' national images, it is because the truth of postwar nationalism is international.

5
The Artist as Demagogue

A nation isn't a sudden creation, it's a slow ripening, year after year, ring after ring. Ha, that's a good one! Sow the seeds of civilization, he says. Yes, unfortunately, it grows slowly.

Christophe, in Aimé Césaire's *Le Roi Christophe*

I'm a British subject, not proud of it, and I carry the burden of shame.

UB40

The differences between *Midnight's Children* and *Shame* are based on a continuity and a contradiction: namely, that in *Midnight's Children* the masses speak in a written form through an epic scribe, the prototype of Valmiki; whereas in *Shame* it is the Pakistani élite who speak in an oral form through a matriarchal storyteller. The popular and the literary are intentionally crossed.

In *Midnight's Children*, Rushdie perfected the use of orality as a mode of modern writing to allegorise the complementary mimicry of East and West. It was a writerly *tour de force* because he was able to recreate an entire history of cultural conflict on the plane of style, which he simultaneously reinforced by a very discursive narrative commentary. As we began to see in the allegories of structure in *Midnight's Children* – for example, the fusing together of cinematic slogans ('Coming Attractions') with the spiralling digressions of the rural bard – the traditional and the avant-garde, realism and postmodernism were being forced together.

The movement from one novel to the other was also, however, an act of desperation. Rushdie had said that *Shame*'s first draft was 'very very depressing, unbelievably morbid', and that he later reworked it 'in the language of comedy'.[1] In fact, his sensitivity

118

to the abominable conditions of Pakistan led to a proliferation of irony that turned any potentially positive political value into a future catastrophe. As if in response to the unacceptability of Pakistan's dim political prospects, the historical 'two-sidedness' or ambivalence of *Midnight's Children* resurfaced in *Shame* as historical pun. Its comic tyrants were so bitterly drawn that they induced only horror, and the comic relief Rushdie promised came primarily in the form of hopeless mockery on the verbal level, a willy-nilly distancing in a 'postmodern' mood of automatic, and humourless, parody.

The two novels at first seem different in national subject alone – the former neatly embracing the territories once known as British India, and the latter, India's post-Partition rival, Pakistan. In this way, Rushdie seems to be devoting each novel (as a clearly bordered work of art) to a single national creation, departing in this way from the early cosmopolitan syncretism of his first novel *Grimus*, and looking forward to the as yet unanalysed component in his tripartite identity – the England of *The Satanic Verses*.[2] Thus, in those places where *Midnight's Children* deals with Pakistan, it does so only in the context of the subcontinent as a whole. By contrast, *Shame* covers a central episode in Pakistan's internal life, which it portrays as a family squabble between Iskander Harappa (Zulfikar Ali Bhutto) and his successor and executioner Raza Hyder (Zia ul-Haq). History in *Shame* is a history filtered through the ambitious self-images of its protagonists – the history they in effect 'try on' to inflate their importance. Our relationship to history is therefore more mediated and more purely instrumental. For Saleem Sinai (although he doubts his own motives) tries to incorporate multitudes, while Bhutto, Zia and others only reduce real events to their size. As though fearing reprisals, *Shame* does not present history openly but hides it in allusive references to the past which are buried in casual placenames and family titles and ironic reincarnations of figures from legend.

Iskander Harappa, for example, whose estate in the Punjab is referred to as 'Mohenjo', recalls the ancient Indus Valley Civilization ('Harappan'), situated in the area of central Pakistan. Its most important archaeological site at Mohenjo-Daro is thereby a subtle reference to Bhutto's reign of terror, since it recalls Mohenjo-Daro's other name – the 'mound of the dead' and the site is located just outside Larkana, the Bhutto family home.[3] Similarly, 'Iskander' is a variant of 'Alexander', the famous

Macedonian conqueror who invaded the part of India that is
now Pakistan in 326 BC, and who gives his name to the chapter
in *Shame* dealing with Bhutto's rise: 'Alexander the Great'. Because
the chapter sets out to puncture the inflated image of Bhutto as a
democratic reformer, Rushdie also uses the name 'Iskander' to tie
Bhutto to the real-life ex-major-general Iskander Mirza, a 'shrewd
reactionary timeserver' of the Punjabi bureaucracy, alluded to in
Midnight's Children as 'Brigadier Iskander', one of the commanders
in the fraticidal war against East Pakistan.[4]

A similar operation is at work in the name of Raza Hyder, the
counterpart of Pakistan's other great postwar ruler, Zia ul-Haq,
Bhutto's *'semblable et son frère'*, according to Rushdie in a later
essay.[5] 'Raza', an alternate form of 'raja', of course suggest the
'Raj' – the British governmental authority that ruled India from
1858 to 1947. The quintessential *chamcha*, Raza continues the
Empire's practice of evoking the profoundest spiritual principles
of religion and tradition to justify a strategy of tyranny and theft.
More importantly to the Pakistanis themselves, despite his nationalist declarations, he represents no improvement over his British
predecessors. Combining 'anti-imperialist' talk and freebooting
ways, he recalls the legendary hero Hyder Ali, the infamous
ruler of Mysore, a scoundrel and freebooter from the South.

Iskander's crony, Omar Khayyam Shakil obviously recreates
the famous mediaeval Persian poet, astrologer and mathematician
Omar Khayyam, who was also by legend (like his counterpart in
Shame) a doctor. As shown by the corruption of his texts, the
doubts about his being an author at all, the incomparable number
of translations of his work and the tendency of *Rubaiyat* collections
to include the poems of other Persian poets, he is not for Rushdie
an individual poet but a figurehead for Orientalist poetry in the
West, and is indeed one of the few well-known Eastern poets in the
West. Judging from the *Rubaiyat's* reception, he is in that sense a
composite image of Eastern sensuality, the original Epicurean. The
joke, of course, is that *Shame's* Omar acquires his Epicurean habits
in Europe, and unlike the uncouth 'richkid' of *Shame* who writes
nothing, the historical Omar was withdrawn, concise, respectful,
tactful, having written an essay on obligation in which he used
his philosophical knowledge to serve social aims, counselling to
'avoid animal passions', and arguing for 'Justice and Order . . . in
society by means of hope of reward and for punishment in the
next world'.[6]

The name 'Sufiya' Zinobia comes, of course, from the Muslim mystics, the 'Sufis'. It is appropriate for her, not only because the Sufis have usually been forced by persecution to live a semi-clandestine existence, but because their central tenet is that 'love rather than fear [should be] the determinant of man's relation-ship with God'.[7] As her blushing registers the shamefulness of her father's tyrannical rule, love seems an appropriate emotional label for her, until this too degenerates into the blind savagery of her arbitrary beheadings, and the sect of love becomes just another version of Zia's demagogic order carried out under an Islamic pose.

These perversions of Indian and Muslim legend are a way of suggesting the characters' own pretensions. They are not reserved only for the victors (the generals and landholders); they belong to the smaller parts too. In other words, Rushdie does not reflexively channel his ironies into a critique of the regime alone; the disease of power he isolates here infects the whole society. For example, Omar's brother Babar, the Baluchi rebel, is a pathetic version of the Mughal Emperor Babur ('the Great'). Pinkie Aurangzeb, Iskander's mistress and member of the Karachi *demi-monde*, takes her name from the last great Mughal monarch and a fanatical anti-sensualist. And Omar is based not only on Omar Khayyam but on Muhammad Iqbal, the leader of the Muslim League, the Punjab's great poet-philosopher, and the 'imaginative founder of Pakistan'.[8] Like Omar, Iqbal's sense of destiny changed after a trip to Europe. But, unlike Omar, he did not return with crates of cigars and pornographic magazines. Disgusted with European decadence, he turned devoutly to Islam and was central in for-mulating the intellectual basis for an independent Pakistan.[9] In short, everyone is precisely the opposite of what they seem, and the morbidity of the first draft lingers in this 'comic' version of epic as *opera buffa*.

If *Midnight's Children* was a novel whose key historical events involved huge and nebulous collectivities – Gujaratis, Kashmiris, Dravidians, Sikhs and Bombay Christians with Portuguese names, in *Shame* those events are seen strictly in the higher echelons. Their differences have as much to do with the direction from which they analyse political power as with the fact that they focus on different 'nations'. What Rushdie called in *Midnight's Children* the 'national longing for form' would therefore account for the two books' formal dissimilarities, which Rushdie indicates by consigning to each country a kind of 'shadow' genre that itself becomes thematic. They are India's and Pakistan's spiritual characteristics translated into literary slogans in the spirit of *Midnight's Children*'s unhappy Uncle Hanif, the documentary film-maker, who sadly observed that India's natural form was the 'melodrama', because melodrama is everything essential to the Bombay cinema, with its Bombay-talkie truisms, naïve sectoral passions, uncritical beliefs and obvious villains. Pakistan's authoritarian generals, on the other hand, with their swagger sticks and military regalia, are called forth best by the 'comic epic'.[10] Somewhat later, in the course of Rushdie's ever fertile imagination, these shadow genres take on other incarnations: for India, 'historical novel'; for Pakistan, 'modern fairy tale'.

Here history is not only briefer and more picturesque than in the earlier novel, but composed of different events. Apart from vague allusions to the war in Afghanistan and the Iranian revolution, the focus is local, courtly and familial. While touching on the suppression of the Baluchi rebel movement in the Western provinces, for the most part the novel centres on the rise of Bhutto, his execution in 1979 and the succession of (the recently deceased) Zia ul-Haq, covering a much shorter and more contemporary period (from 1947 to the present), and concerned less with the problems posed by independence from England – the political and juridical similarities that make the new nation a parody of imperial rule – than in responding to one form of the Islamic revival. Rushdie has pointed out elsewhere that Pakistan is distinct from the well-publicised Iranian case precisely in the absence of a genuine mass movement (which he argues India had) – an absence the literary form attempts to project metaphorically.

The departures from the narrative strategies of *Midnight's Children* are worth looking at in some detail since they exemplify the fictional coding that Rushdie employs in his analysis of the varieties of neo-colonial failure. Most striking, for example, is the fact that the many subplots of *Midnight's Children* give way in *Shame* to a composite narrative built from a series of juxtaposed, and basically self-contained, parables: the parable of Omar Khayyam's birth at Nishapur; of Omar's rebellious younger brother Babar, the Baluchi rebel; of the unlucky Partition-era movie house owner, Mahmoud the Woman; of the sacredly vengeful Sufiya Zinobia, assassin of the turkeys. Similarly, All-India Saleem – the universal poetic consciousness – gives way in *Shame* to a train of discrete individual points of view with equal narrative weight. It is a book with more than five 'heroes', all equally 'in it for themselves'. The critique of an entire population's collective memories, moulded into yet another government-of-the-few mouthing populist slogans, becomes the critique of a still-unfolding history which its participants cannot fully formulate, despite its archaic and mediaeval moralities and social practices. *Shame*'s lessons are provisional, immediate and emotional rather than part of a great design – more like prayers, notes or meditations than the encyclopaedia of *Midnight's Children*; and they are brought to the surface in an undigested state, communicated experientially through the medium of style.

In the discussion of García Máquez and the 'fantasy' of European exploration, Rushdie understood the writer's imaginative link with imperialism to be ongoing and not merely inherited as a form of writing. But when considering Pakistan, where national cohesion more than normally depends on a military and juridical enforcement of community, rather than an (albeit deluded) communal sharing of felt 'nationality', he saw the state depend on more and more imaginary claims. Pakistan is, even theoretically, untenable – or, as Benedict Anderson had put it, 'insufficiently imagined'. By contrast:

> [India] was a fiction invented by the British in 1947. Even the British had never ruled over more than 60 per cent of India. But it was a dream that everyone agreed to dream. And now I think there actually is a country called India.[11]

Shame is simply meaner, seedier, a bad joke. Earlier, invoking the proverbial myth-life of India with its pundits, fakirs and mahatmas had allowed Rushdie to exploit the satirical capital found in the overactive imaginations of its 'naïve' villagers. Here, the problem is not idealising the past but simply 'rewriting history' – not myth as 'false consciousness' but myth as the government lie one knows to be a lie but cannot contradict for fear of reprisal.

What remains in the latter novel is Rushdie's goal to steer between the *mohajirs* (immigrants) and the 'natives'. He maps out a narrow middle road 'between the Cantonment and the old town', as it were, avoiding, on the one hand, the illusory comforts of ineffectual sloganeering (like that of the Left sectarian card-sharps in the 'Magicians' Ghetto) and, on the other, more 'rewritten history', another layer to what he calls Pakistan's historical 'palimpsest'. And here again he portrays his own novels as a kind of colonisation, imposing themselves on reality in the form of a desire for conquest. For the Utopian vengeance of the novel's ending – the retributive death of Raza/Zia – is a merely fictional resolution of political problems Rushdie believes to be unresolvable. Literature is always Utopian, which is the central problem since, as he says in *Midnight's Children*, optimism is a 'disease'.

SHAME'S HOLY BOOK

If nationalism, as Benedict Anderson had argued, is an ideology that reinterprets religious modes of thought and amounts to a 'secular transformation of fatality into continuity, contingency into meaning', Rushdie drove the idea to its limits by making Pakistan the apotheosis of nationalism.[12] He transforms this 'modern fairy tale' into its religious variant – the modern 'Holy Book', not to reproduce the tired 'book-Book' imagery of modernism, with its authorial prophecies and its deification of style, but as an historical reference to the uses of a specific Holy Book – the *Quran*. Of course, Pakistan's claim to nationhood is based on its religious differences with India. Thus, the similarities between nationalism and the religious impulse achieve exaggerated proportions in the religious nation – nationalism's purest form.[13]

In many superficial ways, *Shame* parodies the style of sacred texts in general. It is riddled with portentous capitalisations ('Rim of Things'), elliptical utterances and absurdly elaborate number symbolism.[14] Omar's three mothers with their 'trio of manservants' lived in a town which witnessed a triple murder, and encountered Raza's three grandmothers who had three brothers. The story is about three families (Shakil, Hyder, Harappa), three countries (England, India, Pakistan), three religions (Islam, Zoroastrianism, Hinduism) and three capitals (Quetta, Karachi, Islamabad). The familiar significance of the number 'three' in religious and folkloric texts is not the point; rather, it is the monstrous exaggeration with which it is carried out – another signal that the genre is the message.

The details of style sometimes suggest the *Quran* specifically. For example, the novel's run-on-words ('wentwithoutsaying', 'whichwhichwhich', 'nothing-that-you-will-be-unwilling-to-do') probably mimic the practice of Arabic calligraphers, who often connected adjacent letters when copying the Arabic in order to create a pleasing visual effect from the continuously patterned line. Similarly, *Shame*'s genealogical trees, inscribed for the reader's benefit immediately after the title page, are like the 'groves of genealogy' that Raza's faithful wife Bilquis finds 'inscribed in the back of the holy book' (*Shame*, p. 77), a passage that intentionally confuses the common practice of writing one's own family lineage in the inside cover of the household Holy Book, with the genealogies of the sacred text itself, as if to show the disingenuousness of the religious pose and the authoritarian logic of theocracy.[15]

Since the patriarchs of the clans described in *Shame* (Harappa, Hyder) are the chief historical villains of recent Pakistani history, and since the *Quran* is the text that gives Pakistan its authority as a nation, Rushdie launches his assault on the politics of the Pakistani state from a novel whose formal features have been borrowed from that same *Quran*, in its being both a Holy Book and a specific product of Islam. Thus, again, the authoritarianism of the literary spokesperson merges with that of the simple tyrant.

In interviews, Rushdie has insisted that the narrative asides of *Shame* are unlike the 'Public Announcements' of *Midnight's Children*, which provided contemporary factual intrusions into the always deceptive narrative. Instead, the asides are the would-be transcriptions of an oral tale. No one, Rushdie says, would find the author's anecdotal breaks in the narrative unusual if they were hearing the story recited. What seems like a calculated literary device, he claims, is only the written simulation of the very common practice among storytellers to interrupt themselves.[16] But of course, it is also (and he does not mention this) the calculated device of one wanting to mirror the 'recital', which is what *Quran* literally means.

Since a gesture towards orality always suggests national authenticity, Rushdie is implicity claiming to have revealed that feature of Islam which not only distinguishes its sacred text from those of other religions, but makes it especially appropriate for Pakistan – namely, its authoritarianism. This is, naturally, not just the secular view of a Muslim-born Indian intellectual, but one who matured in England – who embraces the European Enlightenment openly (as in *Shame*'s invocation of 'liberty, equality and fraternity' and its not altogether ironic comparison of Zia ul-Haq to Robespierre), who feels refreshed by images of Western popular culture (he mentions Batman, Superman and Randolph Scott westerns), and who weaves into the fabric of *Shame* that most Western of political challenges, feminism, in the persons of *Shame*'s only rebels: 'the Virgin Ironpants', who rejects a marriage proposal on the grounds that 'this woman's body . . . brings a person nothing but babies, pinches and shame', and Iskander's wife Rani Humayun, who patiently embroiders the history of her husband's crimes in elaborate visual images in a series of eighteen shawls. There are also the victims, Pinkie Arangzeb, a mistress grown old before her time, and Naveed 'Good News' Hyder, who eventually hangs herself because she is perpetually made pregnant by her husband.

None of this is to suggest that there is not something offensive about the way Rushdie often depicts women, beginning with the images of Padma as *Bharat Mata* and continuing more clearly in the strangely demeaning characterisations of *The Satanic Verses*. The point is only that in *Shame* women are the key to his political analysis in a number of interrelated ways, for the very reason that, as Thomas Lippman points out, 'there is probably no issue that has more unfavorably influenced the Western world's image of Islam or more preoccupied lawmakers in Moslem countries than the status of women'.[17] It is an analysis that consequently declares itself feminist in the text of the novel itself:

> Repression is a seamless garment; a society which is authoritarian in its social and sexual codes, which crushes its women beneath the intolerable burdens of honour and propriety, breeds repressions of other kinds as well. . . . Contrariwise: dictators are always – or at least in public, on other people's behalf – puritanical. (*Shame*, p. 189)

Rushdie's consistent, playful association of Islam with authoritarianism operates in the conviction of writing for an audience that will eagerly accept this kind of joke.[18]

According to those preconceptions, played artfully by Rushdie, the *Quran* is, unlike the Bible, a divine work revealed in its entirety to only one man (Muhammad), who himself assumed 'the position

of a theocratic ruler' using the text 'for making public his com-
mands'.[19] It is not that the text is less 'popular', for it is widely
known that the Prophet's revelations were revered by the people
and preserved with scrupulous care. It is only that the direction
in which authority flows is top to bottom (that is, just the opposite
of folklore). For the purity of the written text of the *Quran* was
historically ensured by destroying variant copies when they first
began to appear in the early process of transcription. Far from
being associated with the private, authorial consciousness, this
frightening 'fixity' of the written word in *Shame* becomes the mark
of communal, oral and religious works like the *Quran* which have
never been subject to revision.

Recalling the eternal image of the *Quran* as 'transcribed speech',
Rushdie further parodies his Quranic borrowings by assembling
his story from newspaper clippings and anecdotes, reversing the
condition of sacred textual permanence and relying instead on
'current events', which are immediately set to paper, quickly consumed and thrown away. Rushdie had developed this method of
tension between Western and Eastern genres already in *Midnight's
Children*, where Saleem describes how 'wind blown newspapers
visited my shack to inform me. . . . There were other pieces of
information; and from these, I must build reality' (*MC*, p. 509).
We see the same technique in *Shame*, where Rushdie describes
how he created the character Sufiya Zinobia. In an interview
conducted shortly before the novel's publication, he refers to his
sources as two young Pakistani women about whom he read in
the London newspapers – the one killed by her devout father for
dating an English boy; the other pummelled in the Underground
by white hoodlums. He combines these two cases and gives the
fictional result the cross-cultural name 'Anna Muhammad', from
which – although English in origin – we get the idiot daughter and
avenger of Pakistan's strongest general.[20]

Moreover, the invocation of Sufism implicit in Sufiya's name
once again suggests the close attachments Rushdie feels for that
particular brand of Muslim heterodoxy. It was the practice of the
Sufis to appeal directly to the masses and to reject the dogmatism
of the clerical scholars (the *'ulama'*). Not only were they upstarts
against the social and religious institutions of Islam, but because
they believed in a more personal and individualistic relationship
of the devout believer to Allah, they developed verse forms that
intentionally mimicked the utterances of the Holy Book. In the

words of Tarif Khalidi, it was 'as if these fragments of verse were, consciously or otherwise, an emulation of Koranic revelation'.[21]

These and other examples of his practice are provocations, an overturning of the Islamic concept of ⁿidjaz, 'which describes the uniqueness of the Koran . . . which is inimitable'.[22] Nevertheless, if a Quranic parody is going to be effective satire, it must display what Islamic orthodoxy denies. In the words of Edward Said: 'the desire to create an alternative world, to modify or augment the real world through the act of writing . . . is inimical to the Islamic worldview'.[23] *Shame* inverts this particular Islamic tradition by making its components into 'lessons, structures, extensions, or totalities designed to illustrate . . . the author's prowess in representation', which according to Said is also opposed to Islamic tradition, but which in its Western translation is too easily associated with a tradition of 'textuality' – itself emotionally and intellectually based on a metaphor from scripture.

In *Midnight's Children* the two primary storytellers were characterised by their ties to the earthly and the bodily – Tai, the unwashed labourer, and Padma, the dung goddess. In *Shame* Rushdie reintroduces the image of the storyteller in the form of the singer of genealogies, the matronly Bariamma, 'the blind old lady [who] recounted the family tales' (p. 78). They are tales associated from the start with the genealogies of Holy Books, and thus wrestle throughout the narrative with the 'fairy tale' undertones implied by the book's division into discrete and (on the face of it) secular parables of recent Pakistani history.

On the level of the Quranic parody (which is, after all, only one of *Shame*'s levels) the tale of the whole nation is therefore no longer autochthonous and plebeian but bequeathed: a tablet, fixed in heaven, prescribing nationhood from above, in much the way the historical Zia did when, according to Tariq Ali, he 'informed a bewildered nation that he had been overpowered by a dream in which a voice (presumably that of the Almighty) had suggested that elections were un-Islamic'.[24] Thus, the function of Bariamma as a storyteller is much more instrumentally tied to the political needs of the nation than Padma's had been, and possesses qualities that explicitly echo those of the *Quran*:

> Her stories were the glue that held the clan together, binding the generations in webs of whispered secrets. Her story altered, at first, in the retelling, but finally it settled down, and after that

nobody, neither teller nor listener, would tolerate any deviation from the hallowed, sacred text. (*Shame*, p. 79)

In brief passages like this one finds both a thematic reference to Islamic doctrine and its opposite. But as we have been saying, *Shame* more typically relies for this kind of message on the meanings implicit in its own style, as if to suggest the covert operation necessary for authors who complain under regimes of terror. In this sense, *Shame*'s lack of linearity reproduces a stylistic feature of the *Quran* itself. As Norman O. Brown has argued:

> The *Quran* is not like the Bible, historical, running from Genesis to Apocalypse. The Koran is altogether apocalyptic. The Koran backs off from that linear organization of time, revelation, and history which became the backbone of orthodox Christianity. . . .
> The rejection of linearity involves a rejection of narrative.[25]

We remember that Padma's earlier complaints about Saleem's non-narrative style showed her supposed lack of complexity and subtlety. There she represented the unreflective continuity of tradition, and its desire for linear narrative. In the *Quran*, on the other hand, tradition is radically non-narrative. In a very compressed way, Rushdie has therefore hit upon a method not only of mimicking (and mocking) the literary icon which symbolises for him so much in political life that he detests, but at the same time of adopting that literature's very logic for his own purposes. For the fund of Quranic formulae he draws on implies not only anonymity and acausality but historical repetition: precisely the lesson he promotes in his reading of the Pakistani tragedy.

To put it another way, the chaotic tumbling of history forward through its myriad phases, captured so well in *Midnight's Children* in the 'Public Announcements', becomes in *Shame* a fixed stock of elements which the storyteller retells in more or less arbitrary recombinations, and with frightening emotional detachment:

> [The family tales] were lurid affairs, featuring divorces, bankruptcies, droughts, cheating friends, child mortality, diseases of the breast, men cut down in their prime, failed hopes, lost beauty, women who grew obscenely fat, smuggling deals, opium – talking poets, pining virgins, curses, typhoid, bandits,

homosexuality, sterility, frigidity, rape, the high price of food, gamblers, drinks, murderers, suicides and God. (*Shame*, p. 79)

The seeds of this view of historical fixity are already present in *Midnight's Children* but arise in a different context. The motif there of the public and the private is seen especially in Saleem's effort to contain India's sprawling history within his own person ('I am the sum total of everything that went before me . . . ' (*MC*, p. 370). This is on one level a recognition in miniature of India's own responsibility for itself in the post-independence period. The point about *Shame* is that it codifies this microcosmic 'I' on a stylistic level in what Norman O. Brown calls the *totum simul*. Here the narrative in each of its parts contains everything at once and, more radically than Saleem (the one who contains all), eliminates any notion of progress.

This is, *mutatis mutandis*, precisely the method of the *Quran* which has what Brown calls an 'apocalyptic or eschatological style . . . simultaneous totality; the whole in every part'. According to Brown, such a work has 'infinite aspects, because each of them, and any moment of it, contains the totality of the work'.[26] Just as the individual fairy tales – the tale of Mahmoud, the tale of Babar – recapitulate the moral lesson counselling against religious sectarianism and false nationalism, certain passages *within* the tales recapitulate the whole book. One example occurs on the very first page of *Shame*, where Omar's grandfather is on his deathbed:

> During his last delirium he embarked on a ceaseless and largely incomprehensible monologue amidst whose turbid peregrinations the household servants could make out long passages of obscenity, oaths and curses of a ferocity that made the air boil violently around his bed. In this peroration the embittered old recluse rehearsed his lifelong hatred for his home town, now calling down demons to destroy the clutter of low, dun-coloured, 'higgling and piggling' edifices around the bazaar, now annihilating with his death-encrusted words the cool whitewashed smugness of the Cantonment district. (*Shame*, pp. 3–4)

In this single passage at the story's opening, old Shakil systematically announces all the major features of *Shame*: its 'turbid peregrinations', its storyteller whose dismissal of the outside world has made his speech like a 'monologue', its tale told *to* rather than *by* servants, while being filled with popular verbal forms ('obscenity, oaths, curses'), and its renunciation of the native country in the form of a 'lifelong hatred for his home town', seen as a meeting place of Pakistani commoners ('bazaar') and English sahibs ('Cantonment').[27]

Naturally, this creates a sense in which the story is already written. Like the *Quran* long ago transcribed from the words of Allah, it is indelibly carved into the texture of Pakistan's dismal history – all motive, background and development are suspended, and time has little meaning. To take only one example suggesting this apocalyptic mood, the narrator at one point tries to check himself from jumping ahead, but implies as he does so, that it is impossible: '[E]nds must not be permitted to precede beginnings and middles. . . . This is precisely the sort of unhelpful advice of which storytellers must take no notice whatsoever' (*Shame*, p. 16).

Thus the narrative is filled with passages that do not so much foreshadow events as establish the simultaneity of present and past:

> On my way back to the story, I pass Omar Khayyam Shakil, my sidelined hero, who is waiting patiently for me to get to the point at which his future bride, poor Sufiya Zinobia, can enter the narrative. (*MC*, p. 73)

For the passages that keep forcing their way into the beginning from the end are already contained in the beginning: the bed old Shakil dies on on page one is the bed on which Omar is born and upon which Sufiya (Omar's wife) murders him before perishing in a nuclear blast in the book's final paragraph.

This kind of critical shorthand characterises Rushdie's imagery of the 'palimpsest' in which national leaders, in order to legitimise their illegitimacy, falsify the record in much the same way that the ancients covered over old stories with a fresh layer of wax. As in this figure, Rushdie often relies on a relentless punning, as in his assertion that he is 'dealing with a past that refuses to be suppressed' as though insisting that the truth about Pakistan by acts like his own would eventually be known and condemned by others. Of course, the phrase also means that feudal anachronisms continue to be 'modern' there – an idea contained, for example, in *Shame*'s Section IV entitled 'In the Fifteenth Century', a joke made possible by Rushdie's use of the Hegiran calendar (which dates from the flight of Muhammad in the early seventh century, the famous 'Hegira') rather than the Julian calendar.

Prefigurement and microcosmic encapsulation, like the apocalyptic narrative, are also suggested by purely stylistic devices. One of these Rushdie playfully calls the 'Sanskrit Mantra', the recitation of key words whose significance is never explained but whose repetition gives the appearance of special meaning. The words 'tilyer', 'monkey' and 'Himalaya', for example, appear in contexts that appear to have no relation to one another and so create the impression that the later parts of the book are in some way arrested in the time of the former, tying together disjunct movements of the book on a sacred and unconscious level. It is perfectly in keeping with Rushdie's irreverent treatment of religion that Sanskrit is the sacred language, not of the *Quran*, but of the Aryan *Vedas*, and that the concept of the mantra is alien to the fiercely proselytising and monotheistic religion of Islam.

The kinds of orality at odds in the transition from *Midnight's Children* to *Shame* represent different facets of the same political pessimism. In *Shame*, apparent invention and open-endedness are really just a kind of patterning, and provide the elements for a repetitious plot of tyranny, demagogy and death – the same old story. Thus the tale-teller Bariamma recounts the saga of the Hyder family in a distorted 'Quranic time':

> But neither Raza nor Bilquis could have known that their story had scarcely begun, that it would be the juiciest and goriest of all the juicygory sagas, and that, in time to come, it would always begin with the following sentence (which in the family's opinion, contained all the right resonances for opening of such a narrative): 'It was the day on which the only son of the future President Raza Hyder was going to be reincarnated'. (*Shame*, pp. 79–80)

Pakistani history is in this way frozen into formulaic patterns that it would be 'gross sacrilege to alter' (p. 81). The murderous career of Raza Hyder is a merely typical situation in a recurring cycle of despotism, recorded in an act of unalterable prophecy.[28]

The sentence with which the 'juicygory' saga must always begin is a political prophecy whose outcome is assured not so much by providence as by Raza's predictable dictatorial skills. And, of course, the inheritance of Raza is shown here to rely on the grossly inappropriate Hindu concept of 'reincarnation'.

It would be wrong, however, to see the book entirely through the framework of this mock-*Quran*. For, as Anthony Barnett has pointed out, one of its most characteristic features is its use of the 'demotic'. 'The novel', he observes, 'gossips and repeats what is already said by those peasants, who are not, after all, completely mute.'[29] But just as Rushdie heightened and made conscious the age-old affiliations of novel and nation, so he employs the demotic for very local and specific purposes. What Barnett did not recognise, for example, is that the demotic itself refers not only to popular but *hieratic* speech – not only folk tale but Holy Book.

The most obvious, but not the only, expression of the two-sided character of Rushdie's demotic prose is the recurrent swearing, oaths and curses throughout the novel which are simultaneously informal and sacral. He links the two in the common epithet 'I shit on the *Quran*', expressing the irreverence that gives the curse its shock value when uttered by certain of his Pakistani characters. Once again, but more indirectly, Rushdie restates a central theme found already in *Midnight's Children* when he found Padma to be complicit in perpetuating the mythology of the primordial 'nation'. For in a discussion of the dichotomy betwen Epicureanism and Puritanism embodied in the revolutionary figures of Danton and Robespierre, he argues that the 'people' are like Robespierre who 'distrust[s] fun' (*Shame*, p. 265).

If the novel means anything, it is that 'popular' authority is hardly that which leads politically to the Enlightenment values of 'liberty, equality and fraternity' which he mentions by name in the book and which he says he 'recommends highly'. Nevertheless, the novel's ambiguities – its intentionally 'parabolic' aura – would be impossible without the counter-balance of a certain trust in the ability of people (like *Midnight's Children*'s Padma) to resist the political nightmare in which we live. Here the scope of this resistance is predictably verbal – a blasphemous or obscene unruliness expressed above all in marginal or 'nonliterary' genres, in informalities and in general irreverence. In this sense, a degree of showmanship for its own sake takes on the political significance

of *anti-authoritarianism*, as in this speech of the wronged cousin
Mir Harappa in the act of plundering Iskander's home before the
calmly knitting figure of Iskander's wife:

> Sisterfucking bastard spawn of corpse-eating vultures. Does
> he think he can insult me in public and get away with it?
> Who is the elder, me or that sucker of shit from the rectums
> of diseased donkeys?
>
> Who is the bigger landowner, me or him with his six
> inches of land on which even the lice cannot grow fat? You
> tell me who is king in these parts. Tell him who can do what
> he likes around here, and that he should come crawling to kiss
> my feet like a murdering rapist of his own grandmother and
> beg for pardon. The nibbler of a crow's left nipple. . . . (*Shame*,
> p. 102)

Here, Rushdie takes this distinctive cultural talent for verbal
abuse – so foreign to the relatively unimaginative and somehow
more vicious (even if more reserved) swearing of the Anglo-Saxon
world – and connects it thematically to his satirical barrage against
the contradictory populism of the Islamic revival in its Pakistani
form. If a passing reference to the European Enlightenment
had seemed, along with mention of Khomeini and Zia, like a
preference for the 'freer' West, in steps this tenuous balance in
the shape of a beloved freedom of popular expression especially
characteristic of the East. He revives again the point about the
complexities of imperialism as a mutually conditioning relationship. The mockery of national fiction in *Shame* was conceived,
after all, by an author who (as Rushdie says) had been 'borne
across'; his Pakistan is a translated one. By the overgrafting of
ironic contemporary sources, the primary intention is to destroy
any coherence his imagination might have given the country by
adopting a formal attitude that makes every statement capable of
being at the same time withdrawn.

Once again the key to these intentions arises in a stylistic
comment he makes midway through the book: 'to unlock a
society, look at its untranslatable words' (p. 111). Aside from
Sharam (ineffectually rendered in the book's title), the only untranslatable word featured is *takallouf*, which he defines as 'a species
of compulsory irony which insists for the sake of good form on
being taken literally'. In a work in which the act of inviting the

English to a dinner party (a social gaffe) is referred to as a 'solecism' (p. 8), *takallouf* can be seen as *Shame*'s central literary principle, a kind of emblem for the entire book, referring both to Rushdie's inability to view his land with anything but irony and the compulsory dishonesty of any official proclamation emanating from Islamabad, and (finally) the press reports that people take literally only 'for the sake of good form', saying privately to themselves, 'a fairy tale'.

POLITICS AND THE FAIRY TALE

Throughout *Shame*, the national 'essence' of the immemorial past – the stately, feudal, monarchical culture on the one hand, and the traditional popular one on the other – is real only in an extremely contemporary and utilitarian form. The fairy tale is here riddled with the evidence of 'current events': 'In the remote border town of Q, which when seen from the air resembles nothing so much as an ill-proportioned dumbbell, there once lived . . . .' It is an opening that is at once formulaic and updated, a statement likely to be made only by one accustomed to travel by airplane ('seen from the air'). Similarly, in the fairy tale dialogue one is made to hear the echoes of an on-the-spot interview, or in the narrative digressions, an echo of the interruptive 'newsflash'.

Rushdie evokes the fairy tale rather than some other demotic form because of the meanings associated with it in the minds of its Western readers. It is, first of all, the genre of subversives – the covert satirist operating under conditions of intense repression. It suggests the author's right to castigate his government and to refuse it as his own. On the other hand, the origins of the fairy tale are closely bound up with the whole process of European nation-forming in suggestive ways.

According to some accounts, the fairy tale is a moralising, literary and upper-class deformation of the folk tale, an earlier oral form.[30] While the folk tale was communal, traditional, oral and public, the fairy tale was individual, innovative, written and private – a transcription of the earlier tales by first Renaissance, and later Romantic, anthologists who, in the words of Jack Zipes, 'obliterated the original folk perspective and reinterpreted the experience of the people for them.'[31] The act of setting the tales

in a written form involved a domestication of their content, especially evident in the context of European Romanticism where 'folk
tales were rewritten and made into didactic fairy tales for children
so that they would not be harmed by the violence, crudity and
fantastic exaggeration of the originals'.[32]

Although this European process may not apply in all particulars
to the South Asian tradition, the ideological shift implicit in the
'literari-faction' of folk tales applies here. The urge of the literary
intellectuals to appropriate the tales in the Romantic period did
not only grow out of a desire to co-opt a potentially threatening
cultural movement from below, but was an active response to
Herder's view of language as the inalienable essence of self and
nation. As Eric Leed has pointed out, 'an entire generation of
nationalistic, bourgeois intellectuals equipped with this concep-
tion of language, poetry, and the nation set about "discovering
the people" '.[33]

The delicate mendacity of this transformation from the authentic
to the literary, 'folk' is something we mentioned above as being
characteristic (in Fanon's arguments, for example) of the cosmopolitan colonial writer. In fact, the process illuminates the paradox
of bourgeois development in Europe, simultaneously symbolised
by the building of nations and the construction of 'free individuals' – on both counts alien to the folk tradition from which they
borrowed. Leed points out that the written tradition amounted to
a partisan declaration of individuality:

> When the basic social unit came to be regarded as the inde-
> pendent individual, social relationships and – more important
> for us – communicative relations, had to be judged in new
> ethical terms. The domain of letters was the domain of freedom,
> that impersonal and empty space, that neutral matrix in which
> individuals formed their own judgments.[34]

It is not surprising that the shift involved hostility to popular
tradition. Indeed, as Leed points out, Roman Jakobsen, an influential researcher in this area, saw the collectivity as a 'censor'
of the individual performer, much as in Rushdie's view of the
people who 'distrust fun', and whose consensus (in its Islamic
form, *ijma*) allows one to speak of Quranic rigidity as a 'popular'
form of expression. In contrast, 'the writer of texts was inherently
different from the oral poet. By virtue of the fixity granted his work

by his medium, the writer could, if he chose to do so, create in opposition to his cultural setting'.[35] In other words, the ideological 'tag' of the genre 'fairy tale' is from the start laden with the idea of 'freedom' in a specifically middle-class sense, accompanied by notions of the 'imagination' and the solitary artist – untroubled by government decrees or by the fickle moods of the 'common herd'.

As the associations develop in the postwar period, the new problem of what Marshall MacLuhan and Walter Ong call the 'secondary orality' of the technological media blurs the focus, causing a rupture in the concepts of 'freedom' and the 'imagination'. The power of Rushdie's *Shame* is that it engages, sometimes very consciously, this entire network of political–cultural dilemmas – sometimes tracing, sometimes erasing, their contours. While he shares these concerns, his response is significantly different. Although he agrees that the fairy tale is no means of protest against a Western-inspired 'culture industry', he likes that culture industry to the degree that it implies a certain ethical and artistic flexibility that is enhanced by its contact with the archaic culture of the contemporary Islamic world, arrested at a pre-Enlightenment stage. He does not, therefore, portray Pakistan's failure as the result of its excessive 'reason' in the Enlightenment sense, but just the opposite – its pseudo-religious, feudal despotism. It is easier to see, then, the use of this tradition in *Shame*. The proverbial kings and soldiers of the fairy tale are there made to seem like mediaeval leftovers in a modern world, while their modernity lies in their very inability to make us envy them, which the heroes of most traditional fairy tales inevitably do.

In this sense, the élite or upper-class features of the fairy tale capture the despotism of *Shame*'s historical subjects. A 'privately designed text',

> it depended on the technological development of printing and the publishing industry . . . [which] excluded the common people and addressed the concerns of the upper classes. It was enlarged, ornamented and filled with figures and themes which would appeal to and further the aesthetic tastes of an élite class.[36]

Freedom of the individual is, of course, inevitably raised by the modern state. It is, in fact, the central ironic argument of *Shame* that the process supposedly represented by Pakistan's escape from European control had the accidental effect of exiling it from the rights and protections developed on the European continent in the late eighteenth and early nineteenth centuries – the period of European nationalism. As a story told from within the ruling chambers, *Shame* particularly diagnoses the nation according to this, its executive and political function.

It is true that the British and American share of blame in the barbarism of Pakistan's generals is alluded to – for example, in the story about Colonel Arthur Greenfield's library and its 'hypnosis' textbooks, or the unflattering references there to the United States Information Agency and the British Council; but more commonly in *Shame* it takes the form of old-fashioned authoritarianism of the militaristic–feudal type, living, as it were, on its own steam, plodding along with a cruder but effective means of 'hypnosis': say, in the official *pronunciamentos* intended to keep thought within proper bounds, as we see when we learn that the initials of the Chief Martial Law Administrator (CMLA) are popularly thought to stand for 'Cancel My Last Announcement'; or when we learn about the 'hearing problem' of the Pakistani population, whose radios broadcast things which could not possibly be true; or the censorship that was so thorough that some things were not only left unsaid, but were 'not permitted to be true'. Once again, we are dealing not with voluntary consent but forced submission (which is only fitting, as Rushdie loves to mention) in a society whose official religion takes its name from the word 'submission'.

All of this is significant because of where this kind of double-barrelled parody leads him when confronting the problem of modernity itself. Popular culture is, it seems, liberating. At one point, for example, as Raza arrives triumphantly in Quetta to begin the extermination of the Baluchis, he mistakes the crowd assembled at the railway station for his reception party. It turns out that they have come to greet several movie starlettes in the adjacent car. It is inevitable that we see the movie starlettes as welcome relief from Raza's Islamic strictures against the indulgences of popular entertainment. At another point, on the other end of the political spectrum, Raza's political antagonist, the Baluchi rebel Babar Shakil, falls in love with a popular singer whom he listens to on an old transistor radio and in this way resists the backwardness of this comrades who regularly copulate with sheep.

SHAME AS POSTMODERN ORAL TALE

Rushdie's use of 'shadow' genres was more than a vehicle for satirising the social forces they implicitly represented. They served also, although in a different way from *Midnight's Children*, to break the narrative 'spell' of the self-confident fictional world of the modernist novel. This effort relied on devices of discontinuity and fragmentation that many have found to be the defining stylistic features of postmodernism, particularly as pastiche and as the mimicry of various local jargons, social masks and commercial spiels. Rushdie's written orality and his formalistic rendering of the East–West conflict (and the blurred boundaries between a colonising and a decolonising consciousness) bears on this issue and calls for a distinction between types of postmodernism that has not really been made in Third-World literary studies. The technique of formal juxtaposition itself, after all, suggests the kind of illusory unity resulting from European conquest: disjunct localities commonly pictured as beads on a string, without the string.[37]

The term 'postmodernism' must be seen as a term used by writers who seek to account for world culture without leaving the accustomed terrain of home. It represents a kind of bad conscience, allegorically describing the decline in Western dominance as a crisis in European art. It is not that recent Western cultural theory has always restricted itself to the aesthetic dimensions of the problem, or even confined itself to the movements of the European and North American avant-garde. But while it is recognised (by Andreas Huyssen, Craig Owens, Jean-Francois Lyotard and many others) that aesthetic postmodernism has something to do with the forced recognition of the cultural 'other', the interest remains in the reactions to this recognition in dominant culture, and so reintroduces ethnocentrism through the back door. In an unreflective way, one speaks of 'post-industrial society', simply because industry has moved to South Korea, Taiwan, Guatemala and the Philippines.

What strikes one in the discourse of postmodernism is the aesthetic allegories of freedom and tyranny reminiscent of Rushdie's use of genres as ideological flags. Hal Foster, for example, writes that 'postmodernist art is poised, at least initially, against a modernism become monolithic in its self-referentiality, and official in its autonomy'. The allegorical reference here to the triumph of the modern state and its powerful bureaucratic apparatuses is hard to miss, although it is sublimated rather than illuminated by its aesthetic outer garments. By limiting the discussion to European and North American art, those who try to locate an 'oppositional' postmodernism are really talking about a revolution in sensibility that has very little to do with the real conflicts occurring in the world. Thus, for Jean-François Lyotard, recognition of the 'other amounts to a mode of non-binary thought – a recognition of 'difference'. These approaches ultimately conceal, although perhaps not intentionally, the character of the postmodern world as one in which the European way of life loses its confident superiority before the chorus of combative Third-World nationalisms, speaking with a cultural vigour and a sense of the future that seemingly throw Europe back into a grim nostalgia.

Rushdie and other cosmopolitan Third-World writers have engaged current political issues with a sense of human tragedy and protest that is anomolous in these circles. The hidden side of postmodern discourse lies precisely in a conflict of attitudes between writers on both sides of the imperial process. Rushdie is especially interesting in this regard because he represents a transitional moment where 'native' or local culture seems to be rendered meaningless by a communications network that effortlessly crosses borders and keeps an infinite stock of *past* artistic styles and local practices (in the form of old Hollywood movies, say, or of current documentaries of primitive societies) perpetually in the *present* and available for use. We have seen how important international communications are to Rushdie and how they are tied to the efforts of writers from the former colonies to make themselves heard in a world of 'tv series and Readers Digest culture' which seem to make their concerns distant curiosities to audiences within dominant cultures. While Rushdie remains uncharacteristically bi-partisan in his fiction (a feature that his journalism doesn't have), he does not accept as final the anonymity of entire populations and the permeation of private language by commercial codes, perhaps because, as a former ad writer himself, he knows their tricks.

On the contrary, although he refuses to create compensatory images that give the impression of destroying regimes like Pakistan's by doing so in a safe world of the imagination, all his writing is dedicated to recovering individual expression, and to weakening the power that various politicians as 'salespersons' hold over us. One can see this especially in his parody which is not 'amputated of the satiric impulse' and 'devoid of laughter', as Jameson has asserted all postmodern fiction is (and in this Rushdie is joined by the outlooks of Grass, Vargas Llosa and García Márquez).[38] It is this aspect of his writing that shows, despite his pessimistic projections, that he believes in such old-fashioned things as morality and 'humanity' as values which have not been totally destroyed. Yet the formal similarities of his work with postmodern trends as a whole – its very definite place in the cosmopolitan culture of the last two decades – suggest not so much an exception to, as a different type of, postmodern writing.

There is too much 'real history' in Rushdie's work, juxtaposed with a highly personal, subjective and often humorous account of the effect of those real historical events on people who, while they are unable to master history's flow, make the events meaningful by coming to understand their human cost.[39] The following contrasts may suggest the revisionist spirit with which Rushdie (and others) enters the 'postmodern' scene.

Postmodernists	*Third-World cosmopolitans*
1. Pastiche	Digressions and juxtapositions of the oral storyteller.
2. Humourless parody, a feeling of political and cognitive impotence	Humorous parody of current and identifiable political villains
3. Use of media images designed to help us forget, to create historical amnesia.	Novel as 'history of the present' – a vehicle of information conveying the urgency of the historical record for those in dominant culture.
4. Feeling that art suffers from the realisation of its marginality; the *angst* of discovering that it is not autonomous but part of 'mass culture'.	Feeling that art glories in the realisation of its *functional* role in political and social life.

5. Nostalgia; *le mode rétro*.	Tradition; popular roots.
6. 'Quotes' popular culture, and embraces it cynically.	'Quotes' high culture (epic, holy book, national legend), and popularises it.

Concern with the ideology of nationalism as an expression of state violence brings us to a quality of the present condition that is submerged in most accounts of post-modernism – namely, the technologising of repression. Here the fragmented individual is quite literally the product of an active repressive apparatus rather than the corollary of a general, unconscious mood.[40] These writers, haunted by the memory of Fascism and depressed by the elusiveness of popular forms of government in the developing world, have found fictional forms that place them in an international avant-garde, and outside the company of pure 'English', 'German' or 'Latin American' literatures, or the study of the so-called 'Commonweath'. For this reason, despite Rushdie's highly subtle and intricate literary machinery, he has been able to give to more people than ever before in the West the issues of Pakistan – an imagined Pakistan, perhaps, and only one version, but one replete with a sense of its history and territorial contexts.

In fact, it is only in the sense of this strange postmodern consciousness that Rushdie, a Bombay Muslim who has lived in England since the age of 14, a writer whose family moved to Pakistan only slightly more than ten years ago, can be called a 'Pakistani' writer. Just for this reason, *Shame* is an extraordinary document: for it reveals a critique so completely 'felt' that it could only have come from a native, and yet so imbued with English points of reference that it could not possibly have. Thus, *takallouf*: a painful and involuntary distancing from any position not immediately transferrable to issues of style, that perpetual flight from a fixed national and ideological identity that has become the trademark of the humane cosmopolitan writer from the Third World.

6

Pitting Levity against Gravity

Nous en avons fini, du combat contre l'exil. Nôs taches sont aujourd'hui d'insertion. Non plus la généralité prodigieuse du cri, mais l'ingrat recensement du détail du pays.

Edouard Glissant[1]

In the poem *'Shikwah'* ('Complaint') from a collection published in 1908, the great Urdu poet Muhammad Iqbal once accused God of infidelity. That fact is interesting to consider in the aftermath of *The Satanic Verses* scandal. The rage of Islam against the book, and the consequent rage against Islam fuelled by the scandal itself, make it hard to understand how a poet generally taken to be the spiritual founder of Pakistan could say this and live.[2] For he catalogues in that poem all that Muslims have done for God over the centuries, and points out that God has nevertheless neglected them, and allowed the Muslim world to be destroyed. In one of its more startling passages, Iqbal exlaims: 'At times You have pleased us, at other times / (it is not to be said), You are a whore.'

The line of most Western commentators, unaware of examples like these, has been that 'intolerance' is the written law of the undifferentiated Muslim heart. But that is a position that does not appreciate the diversity with which Islam (like most religions) is actually assimilated and expressed. Writers as sensitive to the colonial question as Eqbal Ahmad, Ibrahim Abu-Lughod and Edward Said have condemned the 'bigoted violence' against Rushdie and his book, and pointed out that the violence was 'antithetical to Islamic traditions'.[3] But it was a practical, and not merely a theological, matter that brought tens of thousands of British Asians into the streets to protest about the novel, and made thousands more risk (and in some cases lose) their lives in rioting in India and Pakistan. They were tired of seeing one more orgy of vilification in the Western press.

As very few pointed out in the frenzy of late February 1989, this extreme response had everything to do with Rushdie's special position as an 'insider/outsider' – a position this study has tried to examine at some length. If Rushdie had not already been known throughout the subcontinent and Middle East as a best-selling novelist who had managed to popularise real Indian history and customs for a mass Western reading public, his opinions would not have mattered as much. His revisions of the historical and mythical narratives of Islam, in other words, were the work of one who knew all the pressure points and who went about pressing them. In the end, *The Satanic Verses* is not simply blasphemous but a systematic attempt to unravel the religion from within.

Rushdie could certainly control (if not predict) the way the novel would scandalise orthodox Muslims. Unlike *Midnight's Children* with its suggestion that the inspirational founder of Pakistan should not be Muhammad but rather Buddha, sitting glassy-eyed and stupid under a tree in Gaya; or *Shame*, with its suggestion that Pakistan's *Quranic* 'recital' was indistinguishable from the rantings of the military, the similar irreverences of *The Satanic Verses* are flagged in the title itself, and therefore much more obvious. Anyone reading the table of contents alone, with chapter headings such as 'Ayesha' and 'Mahound', could see that the novel was a 500-page parody of Muhammad's life. But it is probably not true that Rushdie foresaw the way *The Satanic Verses* would be manipulated by the Western press. Given Rushdie's adherence to the principle of satiric 'equal time', it must have been dismaying to him to see the novel made into a fable of Western freedom vs. Oriental fanaticism.

At some level, the issue for the protestors had not only been the novel's transgressions of the *Quran* and the Prophet, but a recognition that the banner of 'secularism' has for more than a century been the standard of a Westernised elite eager to 'vend [its] Islam wares in the West'.[4] Rushdie was not simply ridiculing the mimic men and mimic women of empire who happened to be hiding behind Islamic garb, but also the programmes of change encoded within the contradictory fears, hatreds and aspirations of the oppressed as they actually exist. Syed Shahabuddin, the Indian minister responsible for having the novel banned in India, had a point when he spoke of *The Satanic Verses* as 'literary colonialism'.

The West has, he argued, not yet 'laid the ghost of the Crusaders to rest', and although Rushdie had not joined its ranks, he was sufficiently unaware of its existence to avoid being used by it. Literary colonialism had become a campaign carried out 'in the name of freedom and democracy . . . under the deafening and superb orchestration of [the] liberal band'.[5]

It is good to remember, at any rate, that ordinary lower-class Muslims in India and Pakistan – as well as in the English cities of Bradford, Birmingham and London – had attacked *The Satanic Verses* long before the Ayatollah Khomeini entered the scene to capture the headlines, and place the entire affair in the framework of an easier and more convenient demonology. While the conflict soon became the familiar morality play featuring high-level confrontations between Iranian 'terrorism' and English respect for law, there had been from the start a much more popular component among the protesting faithful, who had nothing material to gain from demonstrating their outrage (unlike the Ayatollah or Shahabuddin, for example), and who had nothing to lose but their faith. It is important not to forget that. Aziz Al-Azmeh, in a somewhat different response to the book, explained that 'in many third-world countries, *The Satanic Verses* is characterised as the work of a self-hater eager to ingratiate himself with the coloniser simply because the novel challenges the most conservative instincts of those groups claiming Muslim "nativism" '.[6] This characterisation of Rushdie is unfair, I think. But it comes close to locating the class resentments that are simmering beneath the surface of an affair that has persistently been seen in religious terms alone.

To betray a religion one has first to be a real part of it. As an 'England-returned' student during brief stints in Pakistan where his family had moved from Bombay in 1964, Rushdie was living (like his character Gibreel) a 'childhood of blasphemy'. Opposed to his family's move, and resentful of the new suroundings on his extended visits home, Rushdie early on got a reputation for troublemaking. Rumour had it that he liked to draw the Arabic script for 'Allah' so that it resembled the figure of a naked woman. Rushdie did not just pick up the outward gestures and moods of Islam passively while growing up in Bombay, but conducted a full-scale study of its history while at Cambridge. The hold of Islamic thinking on his work is deeper than might be suggested by a scattering of allusions.

His very first unfinished novel, after all, was about a Muslim holy man (the novel that later became *Midnight's Children*), and from that point his career progressed through the Sufi mysticism of *Grimus* and the textual apostasy of *Shame*. Much of the plotting of the earlier novels depends on key events in the life of Muhammad, who like Saleem Sinai was an orphan, who like Raza Hyder had a daughter but no sons to survive him, and who like Flapping Eagle escaped repression by fleeing to Abyssinia. Despite all the attention given *The Satanic Verses*, it has not been seen how deeply it takes the central subjects of Rushdie's fiction (cultural hybridity, migrant consciousness) and finds their essence in Islam itself – as, for example, in his fictional Mecca ('Jahilia') which is said to be inhabited by those who 'have miraculously made permanance out of mutability', for whom 'journeying itself was home', and who live 'at the intersection of the caravan routes'.[7]

Rushdie, then, is a renegade only in the sense that Muhammad was to the pagan Meccans and the Jews of Medina. *The Satanic Verses* poses as a revelation of a refurbished Islam based on the flawed humanity of the Prophet. In an interview with the Indian magazine *Sunday*, Rushdie called Muhammad the 'only prophet who exists even remotely inside history'.[8] In response to the protests against the novel in England, he later developed this point:

> Muhammad ibn Abdallah, one of the great geniuses of world history, a successful businessman, victorious general, and sophisticated statesman as well as a prophet, insisted throughout his life on his simple humanity. There are no contemporary portraits of him because he feared that, if any were made, people would worship the portraits. He was only the messenger; it was the message that should be revered.[9]

Rushdie takes the chance of portraying the Prophet here (knowing it is taboo), and of placing him back into history, because the letter of the law is today being observed without reverence for the original message. To challenge the 'handful of extremists [who] are defining Islam', he therefore needs to break the law.[10] As the reference to the Iqbal poem above shows, there has traditionally been less tolerance towards attempts to humanise Muhammad or historicise the *Quran* than to attack God himself. The way Rushdie destroys this idol-worship is by assuming the gall to place himself at the Prophet's level. Thus, as history records, Muhammad was about forty years old when his revelations began; so now is Rushdie, and so is his character, Gibreel Farishta. Like Rushdie, Muhammad was not only a seer, but a social agitator, substituting religious brotherhood for the tribal identities of the Arab peoples; and his attack on pagan worship was a direct threat to the commercial enterprise set up around the pilgrimage to the pagan Kaaba, just as Rushdie in the novel continues the critique developed in *Midnight's Children* where religion was portrayed as 'a good business arrangement'.

In the end, though, the novel cannot be seen through the distorting images of the protests or what the media made of them since they overestimate the Islamic themes of a novel that is, after all, primarily about a very secular England. The book has to be seen against the background of Rushdie's career.

RUSHDIE AND THE BLACK COMMUNITIES OF BRITAIN

Among Rushdie's novels, only *The Satanic Verses* does not end in oblivion. The countries of the earlier work had been countries 'of the mind'; they could be thought of in terms of apocalypse because they were the ones left behind. But forced to take a stand abroad in the England of *The Satanic Verses*, the immigrant is left with nothing but survival.

At first sight, then, the novel looks more oppositional – more a product of that art of communal resistance suppressed in the earlier work – simply because its survival is won at the expense of English institutions: the British bobby, the BBC newscaster, and the government of a Prime Minister congenially referred to as 'Mrs Torture' and 'Maggie the Bitch'. If the black communities are given the same savage scrutiny – if Asian middle-class hostel owners bilk their West Indian tenants, complain of being stuck in a country 'full of Jews and strangers who lump [them] in with the negroes', or who can think of the English only in the bigoted terms of the mad barber of Fleet Street, with a stiff upper lip on the outside but a secret obsession for kinky sex and death – a mood of specifically anti-institutional anger remains, and one that is not altogether cancelled by the ironies of the earlier work. Following Fanon's criteria, we are not surprised to see this slightly new perspective produce subtle shifts in the narrative. Although 'translating' just as heavily from a borrowed Islamic tradition, the novel no longer simply targets that tradition for rebuke; as a part of what makes the new immigrant different from the English, it is something that can be learned from, even emulated, at the cultural level. Because here Rushdie is dealing with a life not only remembered and longed-for but experienced first-hand. England is where Rushdie lives (not India or Pakistan), and so the immediacy of the account takes us away from those snapshots of emotion, and those distanced descriptions of lives actually lived, that fill the pages of the earlier novels. Those works were essentially thinking pieces whose only really vivid human interactions took place where the personal narrator spoke directly to the reader; the plotting of the characters was essentially an orchestration of parodic vignettes that collectively made up an argument. By contrast, the metafictional strategies of *The Satanic Verses* are not nearly so pronounced; the characters are for the first time people living in the world, acting out their lives in a story of their own. The story is not *about* events, but in them.

A good part of the intellectual background of the novel had been sketched out in an essay Rushdie wrote in 1984, a year of saturation Orwell coverage in the British press. In 'Outside the Whale' he had taken Orwell to task for failing to account in theory for what Orwell himself had done so well in practice – namely, take on the politicians in fiction. The 'logic of retreat' of Orwell's late work was, however, cast against the background of a much larger contemporary drama. Recent British television and film had allowed 'the British Raj, after three and half decades in retirement, [to make] a sort of comeback'.[11] Singling out films such as *Gandhi*, *Octopussy* and *A Passage to India*, and television serials like *The Far Pavilions* and *Jewel in the Crown*, he concluded that 'Raj revisionism, exemplified by the huge success of these fictions, is the artistic counterpart to the rise of conservative ideologies in modern Britain', among them the government's increasingly hostile and restrictive anti-immigration laws, the growth of the National Front, and the 'feel-good' ideology of empire in the speeches of Margaret Thatcher, depressingly demonstrated in the war with Argentina over the Falklands (Malvinas) Islands.

In another essay written a year earlier for *New Society*, Rushdie had taken on the question of racism itself: 'Britain is undergoing the critical phase of its post-colonial period. This crisis is not simply economic or political. It is a crisis of the whole culture, of the society's entire sense of itself.'[12] It was the postwar immigrations that had given the imperial pose new life:

> The British authorities, being no longer capable of exporting governments, have chosen instead to import a new empire, a new community of subject peoples of whom they can think, and with whom they can deal, in very much the same way as their predecessors thought of and dealt with 'the fluttered folk and wild', the 'new-caught sullen peoples, half-devil and half-child'.[13]

Noting 'the huge, undiminished appetite of white Britons for . . . the Great Pink Age', he went on to consider the unusually varied 'vocabulary of abuse' in the English language itself (wog, frog, kraut, paky), the way the word 'immigrant' in England's public debate invariably means 'black immigrant', and Margaret Thatcher's use of 'we' in a speech recalling the days when England ruled one quarter of the world – a 'we' that naturally excluded England's two million formerly colonised peoples.

The novel, however, does not develop these polemical observations. It sets out instead to capture the immigrants' dream-like disorientation, their multiform, plural 'union-by-hybridization' (*SV*, p. 319). *The Satanic Verses* is the most ambitious novel yet published to deal with the immigrant experience in Britain, but it is not by any means the first. Both its originality and its departures are visible only in terms of the enormously varied work that came before it, especially in the postwar period. These include the novels of the West Indian diaspora of the 1940s and 1950s – Samuel Selvon's *The Lonely Londoners*, Edward Braithwaite's *To Sir with Love*, George Lamming's *The Emigrants* and many others.[14] G. V. Desani's *All about H. Hatterr*, as we have already said, had been published as early as 1948. Even in the first postwar generation, novels such as these were operating within a larger milieu of union activism, community organising and the founding of the first black publishing houses, all of which were to lead in the 1970s and 1980s to an ever more vocal and visible movement exemplified today by the

novels of Caryl Phillips, the poetry of Grace Nichols and
Linton Kwesi Johnson, the plays of Mustapha Matura and
the films of Menelik Shabazz.[15] 'Blacks' had, after all, been a
presence in Britain for centuries as African musicians in the
court of Henry VII, as Indian servants or *ayahs* accompanying
returning colonial nabobs, or as sea-going *lascars* settling in the
port towns of Cardiff, Bristol and Liverpool. The sudden increase
in the numbers of blacks coming to a labour-starved England
following the Second World War – from the West Indies, the
Punjab, Pakistan, Africa and elsewhere – made a self-consciously
'British' community of the 1970s and 1980s possible. As *Race
and Class* editor A. Sivanandan put it, they became 'a people
for a class' with a 'legacy of holism [that] made our politics
black'.[16]

Although intellectually and politically, Rushdie does not share
these views of Sivanandan, he remains sympathetic to many of
them, and has in fact lent his support through jacket blurbs and
introductions to some of the books that document the emergent
black communities.[17] He is, however, simply not a part of that
movement which, in a military metaphor, has called itself the
artistic 'frontline'. The circles in which he travels are much
closer to those of playwright and screenwriter Hanif Kureishi,
whose *My Beautiful Laundrette* and *Sammy and Rosie Get Laid* have
enjoyed the same international acclaim as Rushdie's novels, and
which typically concern themselves with middle-class Asians
who own small businesses and have influential relatives from
the home country visiting an England that has come to look,
as Kureishi once put it, 'very much like a Third World country'.
The contrast between this kind of focus and that, say, of
Bombay-born British author Farrukh Dhondy, is startling. A
member of the British Black Panthers in his teens, a former
teacher in the East End, and currently director of program-
ming for Channel 4, the alternative television station, Dhondy
is only one of several current writers (and perhaps the best)
to look at the very different world of Southall streetlife and
the working-class Asian youths of the housing estates. In other
words, as we have been saying, the differences are not the result
of simple place or privilege – the fact, for example, that the Asian
communities themselves tend to be more middle-class than the
West Indian – it is a difference expressed in a larger political
aesthetic.

'Pitting levity against gravity' is a phrase that helps explain this difference. Taken from the novel's opening pages (in a procedure that is typical of Rushdie's methods), the phrase embeds within a passing comment important clues to his narrative strategy. Staring in the face of misery, and with serious doubts about the future of the human race, Rushdie insists on the comic. The first thing to strike any reader of Rushdie is that, while engaged and pedagogical, his novels are simply funny. At the same time, the phrase echoes the idea that the 'weightlessness' of the migrant sensibility is universal – both in the sociological sense of the effects postwar immigrations and mass media have had on our collective thinking, and in another sense. He is, in other words, attacking the creation of a racial or ethnic 'other' by suggesting that we are all, in a way, migrants because we have all migrated to earth from our home 'out there'. These religious imaginings, not entirely metaphorical, are an important component of what he means by 'defying gravity', and are borne out by the mystical overtones of the word 'levity' which he later confuses intentionally with 'levitation'. As we learn almost from the very first page, *The Satanic Verses* is not (like the earlier novels) a rational critique of religious charlatanism by a Westernised Bombay Muslim. Now set in the West itself, it is rather a novel whose questions are essentially religious, and which takes its imagery from Islam in a much more positive sense than previously. Cast into an alien territory that very often seems like hell, the immigrant is thrust into a mental framework of questioning at all levels. *The Satanic Verses* is an immigrant theodicy.

Like his penchant for blasphemy, Rushdie's theodicy is in part formed under the shadow of Iqbal, the Milton of Urdu poetry. Already familiar with the work of Ghalib, Iqbal and Faiz, Rushdie almost certainly knew Iqbal's *'Jibreel-O-Iblees'* ('Gabriel and Satan'), a dialogue between the Archangel and the Prince of Darkness on the nature of repentance and forgiveness.[18] After a lengthy debate in which Satan explains why he is happy to remain in his fallen state, he triumphantly points out that God is so occupied and discomforted by him that it is all God thinks of. His victory is that he disrupts the serenity and the wholeness of God Himself, as he puts it in the poem's punchline: 'I prick the heart of the Absolute like a thorn'.

REBIRTH, DISSENT AND THE THEORY OF
ACQUIRED CHARACTERISTICS

The theodicy is at once, and usually in combination, played out at three levels. The first level is introduced in the book's title, which contains the principle of organisation for the entire novel. It alludes to an incident recorded by the ninth-century Arab historian Al-Tabari, in which the Prophet at first sanctioned, and later deemed corrupt, certain verses of the *Quran* that he believed had originated not from Allah but from the devil. As the novel explains, it was an act of religious tolerance and openness to alien intrusions that accounted for Muhammad's first satanic inspirations. Historically, the popular devotion among the pagan Meccans for the female deities Al-Lat, Al-Uzza and Al-Manat had prevented the peaceful expansion of Islam in its crucial early period; as a consequence, Muhammad at first believed it was God's will that their worship be permitted within the limits of Islamic doctrine. This concession, although apparently blasphemous (since Islam was nothing if not the discovery by the Meccans of the one true God), nevertheless ensured the new religion's success.

The novel is not really about these 'satanic verses', however. Much like *Shame*, it projects itself as a rival *Quran* with Rushdie as its prophet and the devil as its supernatural voice: '[God] moves in mysterious ways: men say. Small wonder then, that women have turned to me' (*SV*, 95). Or perhaps it is not the devil but only what the parasitical self-servers within the Faith call the devil by invoking God 'to justify the unjustifiable'. In this fertile indecision, this apotheosis of self-questioning, the counter-*Quran* of the novel finds its theology. To ask 'Is my sense of right divine, or only a form of arrogance?' is to subscribe to the religion of doubt that Rushdie would like to see expand and flourish. Rushdie, then, takes on the features both of the Prophet and of Salman Al-Farisi, the Persian scribe to whom by legend Muhammad dictated the *Quran*. In the apocryphal passages of the *Satanic Verses*, this new Salman wilfully alters the words of his apparently unsuspecting (and illiterate) master. The novel thus floods into, overlaps with and creates anew the 'satanic verses' of tradition, although only in a world, as it argues, in which the supreme deity is both devil and God at once – both *'Ooparvala* . . . the Fellow Upstairs' and *'Neechayvala*, the Guy from Underneath' (*SV*, p. 318).

Already familiar in the double characters of the earlier

novels (Flapping Eagle and Grimus, Saleem and Shiva, Raza and Iskander), this twinning of opposites repeats itself in the heroes of *The Satanic Verses*, who are two famous Indian film and television stars recently relocated to England – Gibreel Farishta and Saladin Chamcha. The syncretism, however, is if anything more complex and more brilliant. The foreign vocabulary that dots the narrative has been meticulously gathered from Turkish, Persian, Egyptian, Indian and Arabian sources; it is not simply the Hindi, Urdu and Arabic that one growing up in Bombay might naturally come across. This linguistic polymorphism seems to realise what *Shame* only promised: the feeling of a genuine pan-Islam, especially of its non-Arabic peoples. Similarly, while a good deal has been written in reviews about the Islamic dimensions of the novel, the elaborate Indianness of the book has been forgotten. As much as *Midnight's Children* this is a book about India, especially the India of Bombay as seen by those who have just left it.

The clearest example of this lies in the contemporary identity of Gibreel Farishta, who in addition to all his other identities is meant to represent the great Bombay film idol, Amitabh Bachan.[19] The premier star of the Indian screen from the late 1960s until the early 1980s, Bachan also happened to be the product of the prestigious Doon School (the Indian Eton or Harrow), classmate of Sanjay Gandhi, a personal friend of the Nehru family, and later an elected member of Congress from Allahabad. Exactly as Rushdie describes in the book, Bachan became seriously ill in the early 1980s after a freak injury suffered while shooting a film. Like Gibreel he lingered between life and death for weeks as all of India held its breath, and Indira Gandhi cancelled scheduled visits abroad to fly to his bedside in Bombay. Similarly, the so-called 'theologicals' that Gibreel starred in are an actual genre in the Hindi cinema, especially popular in the Hindu south of India, and popularised recently by the actor N. T. Rama Rao, who is mentioned by name in the novel (although these films are called 'mythologicals' not 'theologicals' and Bachan did not star in them). Obviously, such films are drawn from Hindu, not Muslim, sources, since to represent the Prophet visually is taboo. As Firoze Rangoonwalla points out, however, 'the costume and fantasy films are often given a Muslim base to act as a countering influence and a way of catering to that section of the big Indian audience'.[20]

The syncretism can be seen also in the novel's startling

opening passage, where Gibreel and Chamcha tumble from the heavens in a great free-fall onto the shores of England, after the jumbo jet in which they were travelling is blown to pieces by Sikh terrorists. Plummeting together through the 'almost-infinity of the almost-dawn' these 'two real, full-grown, living men' rush towards their destinies in 'the great, rotting, beautiful, snow-white, illuminated city, Mahagonny, Babylon . . . Proper London, capital of Vilayet' (p. 4). Jesting with Chamcha as he falls, flapping his arms and assuming foetal postures in mid-air – 'pitting levity against gravity' – Gibreel is strangely ecstatic, for he realises joyfully in the novel's opening lines the religious component of the novel's tripartite theodicy: 'to be born again . . . first you have to die'. Naturally by this point we can only take these words as a collapsing together of Hindu reincarnation (strengthened by the Hindi film allusions in this predominantly Muslim imaginative terrain) and the metaphorical 'rebirth' that recent converts to Islam or Christianity speak of. Echoed repeatedly throughout the book, those hopeful lines build slowly to the triumphant conclusion that 'evil is never total, that its victory, no matter how overwhelming, is never absolute' (p. 467).

Taking its lead from the title, the scene of course re-enacts Shaitan's fall, which is cast here in the form of big-name celebrities from India being cut down to size in the alluring and indifferent Britain, where doctors and professors become publicans and janitors overnight. But the downward motion, as in the often adversity-filled life of the Prophet, is only a preparation for their ascension into heaven. As fall, the scene evokes the 'mutation' of the immigrants themselves, a change involving the 'debris of the soul, broken memories, sloughed-off selves, severed mother-tongues, violated privacies, untranslatable jokes [and] . . . extinguished futures' (p. 4); as ascension, the new self, if any remains after the painful transformation. Here Rushdie plays with another allegorical level – the scientific – and asks whether the immigrant is contending with the barbarous survival strategies of 'natural selection', pitting a British master race against an inferior (tinted colonial) one; or whether, in a quite different option, the immigrants can give new life to the theories of Lamarck by consciously adopting the characteristics that their new environment demands; or (in the worst of the alternatives) they are merely the laboratory animals of a new technological 'creationism' – the playthings of a group of Western fanatics who through eugenics want to concoct a species of their own liking.

It is in this spirit that the many-levelled architecture of the novel works by reflecting each level off the other levels like the inverted images in a broken mirror: Gibreel is the angel Gibreel (the one who announces to the Prophet his mission, the biblical Gabriel) as well as that even better-known angel thrust out of heaven for daring to dissent – his heraldic brother, Shaitan (Satan). Ayesha – historically the favourite wife of Muhammad – is in the Titlipur dream-sequences also the Moses of Exodus, Gandhi on his famous march to the salt sea, the Ayatollah Khomeini's idea of the abominable Al-Lat, and Chamcha's lover Pamela; Jahilia is the spiritual state of immigration, the bad capital of corrupt pagan Mecca, the good (bad) capital of post-*hegira* Islam, and London. Examples like this could be compounded throughout the novel: images of a single troubled mind freely associating.

Just as in the slogan of rebirth above, another slogan rings throughout the book, bringing us to the political level of the theodicy – 'to will is to dissent'. Shaitan and Gibreel therefore belong together, for both can be seen to merge in tradition (both apocryphal and canonical) in the sense that both intercede with and ultimately affect the utterances of Muhammad. For in the tormented mind of Gibreel (who becomes certifiably insane after arriving in England) Muhammad is cast in the role of 'Mahound', an abusive name for Muhammad used by medieval European scholars who liked to portray the prophet as a crazed charlatan. In this sense, Rushdie's use of the term is precisely right and proper as an inevitable inversion of his own intentions: the act of turning 'insults into strengths' (*SV*, p. 93). At the same time, it is natural that Muslims would despise the book for its relativity and for reducing the prophetic legend to a psychological truth. All three identities – prophet, evil spirit and God's messenger – are assumed by Gibreel Farishta, who comes to London to blow the trumpet of doom in yet another incarnation: Azraeel, the exterminating Angel.

What we have in these images is more than an attempt to capture the immigrant's confused identity, or even an attempt to elaborate the by-now familiar point that the oppressed, simply because they are oppressed, are not necessarily 'angelic'. Beyond all the layerings of religious paranoia at the psychic level, what we have is a grotesque imaging of racist fantasies. For it is the

British 'mainstream' that ascribes to the black newcomers a devil's role. Thus shortly after being washed up on the shore of England after his miraculous fall, Chamcha begins to sprout horns, grow goat hooves and display an immense erection. As his name implies, Chamcha had considered himself the perfectly acculturated Indian Englishman; he wears a bowler hat and pin-stripe suit and walks with fastidious carriage. No matter, though, since being (as Rushdie puts it) 'of the tinted persuasion', he embodies in the eyes of the police (who come to arrest him for entering the country illegally!) all the appropriate slanders levelled at the 'black beasts' in their midst: they are brutish, oversexed, unclean and (as the goatish incarnation implies) tragic. Later in the novel, as his bestial transformations progress, the black communities marvel at his Luciferian snortings and sulphurous breath, finally taking him as their own. Opposition to British hegemony within the black community takes the form of accepting the devil's role assigned to them by Britain, not passively but as a means of resistance. They show their defiance by fighting back in a distorted way appropriate to their commercialised surroundings – that is, with a fad, with pop tribal badges in the form of fluorescent halos and cheap clip-on devil's horns.

With the usual faithfulness to his sources, Rushdie closely interweaves the details of tradition into his modern rendering of politico-religious mission. Because Gibreel appears in both Bible and *Quran* as counsellor to the Prophet and inspirer of Moses, he 'became the guarantee of the coherence of Islam and the two older religions'.[21] The syncretic reference is repeated in the figure of the scribe Salman Al-Farisi, who first converted to Christianity, later travelled to Syria and Central Arabia in search of the Prophet, and was later still sold as a slave to a Jew. Both his obvious allusions to Rushdie himself and his Persian nationality perversely suggest the extremist brand of Shiite Islam in contemporary Iran, which Rushdie dislikes and which he describes briefly in the novel in a short section dealing with the exile of Khomeini in London before the Iranian revolution. As a contrast, Rushdie's secular attractions to the more artistic and personal brand of Islam found in Sufism is indirectly referred to in his use of Salman, who by tradition is said to be one of Sufism's founders.[22] As for Shaitan, the correspondences are even more elaborate. It is popularly thought that every poet requires a shaitan to inspire him, and that every person is 'attended by an angel and a shaitan who urge him to good and evil deeds respectively'.[23]

Gibreel and Chamcha, then, are the polarities of the novel – one, the self-anointed angelic/prophetic presence who hears infernal voices; the other, the 'good' immigrant turned Shaitan in the English metropolis. The narrative deliberately confuses the supernatural and the everyday precisely by switching rapidly between these characters' psychic imaginings and their normal activities as *actors* – that is, masters of disguise 'like much-metamorphosed Vishnu' (*SV*, p. 17). When, for example, in the second chapter, we suddenly find ourselves without explanation in eighth-century Mecca during the early days of Islam (although it is a parable whose characters have recognisable counterparts in the story proper) we do not yet know what we later learn: that it is not an historical flashback but the (imagined? dreamed?) contemporary set of a popular religious film being directed by Gibreel, whose career has floundered after coming to England and who is trying to make a comeback. There are two such stories taking up several chapters of the book. One dealing with 'Jahilia' (literally 'ignorance' and Islam's term of abuse for pre-Islamic Arabia) features the Prophet 'Mahound' – a story that introduces us to the scribe Salman and the court satirist Baal of which more later. The other is set in contemporary India, and involves the march of a small band of Muslim faithful to the shores of the Arabian Sea, the waters of which are made to part so that the pilgrims can walk unhindered to Mecca. The narrative rationale for these digressions is found in Gibreel's former status as a screen idol in India. His was a

> unique career incarnating, with absolute conviction, the countless deities of the subcontinent in the popular genre movies known as 'theologicals' . . . . For over a decade and a half he had represented, to hundreds of millions of believers in that country – in which, to this day, the human population outnumbers the divine by less than three to one – the most acceptable, and instantly recognizable, face of the Supreme. (*SV*, p. 16)

We have, in other words, a motive for the lengthy narrative shifts in the mind of Gibreel himself, who recasts the characters of the novel into a context appropriate to his own tormented psychology, and who, as if in a vision, 'dreams' the Jahilia and Arabian Sea episodes as part of his mission to bring religion to the irreligious land of Vilayet (England). He had, it is said, 'played too many of those winged figures for his own good'. On the other hand, and at the same time as events portrayed in the popular cinema, these moments of high religious significance for Muslims are being trivialised in just the way that everything meaningful is trivialised by the vulgar market mentality of capitalist England.

Chamcha's acting career demonstrates this vulgarisation even more clearly for he had flourished as the 'Man of a Thousand Voices and Voice', an actor whose talent for voice-overs was used in television commercials to make such things as garlic crisps, baked beans and frozen peas seem more appealing. In an even more embarrassing case of salesmanship, he becomes the star of a popular children's television programme *The Aliens Show*.

> It was a situation comedy about a group of extraterrestrials ranging from cute to psycho, from animal to vegetable, and also mineral, because it featured an artistic space-rock that could quarry itself for its raw material, and then regenerate itself in time for the next week's episode; this rock was named Pygmalien . . . and there was a team of Venusian hip-hoppers and subway spray-painters and soul-brothers who called themselves the Alien Nation . . . The stars of the show, its Kermit and Miss Piggy, were the very fashionable, slinkily attired, stunningly hairstyled duo, Maxim and Mamma Alien, who yearned to be – what else? – television personalities. They were played by Saladin Chamcha and Mimi Mamoulian. (*SV*, p. 62)

If the theme of 'rebirth' applies here in obvious ways, the much more dangerous transformation of species to species is ever present as a threat. 'Creationism' as the West's own peculiar brand of religious demagogy is from the start allied with a spurious 'science' that challenges the more hopeful Lamarckianism of the true alien immigrants. Thus, on the plane to London, before the hijacking that eventually leads to his and Gibreel's miraculous fall, Chamcha meets an American 'creationist' by the name of Eugene Dumsday (eugenics, doomsday). A grating Christian lunatic and sworn enemy of Charles Darwin, he theorises that the ills of postmodern drug-and-sex culture are due to the pernicious influence of natural selection theories. As such, he introduces into the narrative the merging of 'advanced' Western technology and the West's frightful backwardness, a backwardness intensified by a assurance of superiority and the technological means to realise its ethnocentric vision.

In this vein, Chamcha, adrift in London, comes to appreciate the specifically mental eugenics at work on the inhabitants of a television culture:

> It seemed to him, as he idled across the channels, that the box was full of freaks: there were mutants – 'Mutts' – on *Dr Who*, bizarre creatures who appeared to have been crossbred with different types of industrial machinery: forage harvesters, grabbers, donkeys, jackhammers, saws, and whose cruel priest-chieftains were called *Mutilasians* ... Lycanthropy was on the increase in the Scottish Highlands. The genetic possibility of centaurs was being seriously discussed ... on *Gardeners' World* he was shown how to achieve a 'chimeran graft' ... a chimera with roots, firmly planted in and growing vigorously out of a piece of English earth .. he, too, could cohere, send down roots, survive. Amid all the televisual images of hybrid tragedies – the uselessness of mermen, the failures of plastic surgery, the Esperanto-like vacuity of much modern art, the Coca-Colonization of the planet – he was given this one gift. It was enough. (*SV*, pp. 405–6)

As Rushdie later shows, however, the crossbreeding of market and media produces an inhuman blob, as faceless as it is powerful. Chamcha's humanist resolve after his bout with television is everywhere challenged by the various antagonists he meets in real-life London. As the police raid a black nightclub, the television news cameras are said to stand aloof from the 'disordered shadow-lands' where people are being beaten, behind the protective wall of 'men in riot helmets, carrying shields'. Although the reporters speak gravely under the Klieg lights, the fact is that 'a camera requires law, order, the thin blue line. Seeking to preserve itself, it remains behind the shielding wall, observing the shadow-lands from afar, and of course from above: that is, it chooses sides' (pp. 454–5).

Similarly, when faced with having to beg for his job back on *The Aliens Show*, Chamcha is told by producer Hal Valance that ethnic shows no longer sell. Valance is one of Rushdie's funniest and cruellest creations – the monstrous embodiment of the capitalist ad-man, the spawn of a society with throwaway ethics: 'With Hal, all explanations were *post facto* rationalization. He was strictly a seat of the pants man, who took for his motto the advice given by Deep Throat to Bob Woodward: *Follow the money*' (p. 265). Systematically eliminating all the blacks from this commercials because the commercials 'researched better' that way, he has a nose for the winds of change in the authoritarian populist climate of Thatcher's Britain. As he explains, 'I love this fucking country. That's why I'm going to sell it to the whole goddamn world, Japan, America, fucking Argentina. I'm going to sell the arse off it. That's what I've been selling all my fucking life: the fucking nation. The *flag*' (p. 268). In a typical reversal, the sentiments echo those of the neo-colonial elite satirised in the Third-World novels, and which are referred to earlier in the narrative in a reference to Sanjay Gandhi 'the airline pilot [who] flew back from the European conference chambers in which he had been negotiating the sale of the Indian economy to various transnational conglomerates.'[24]

The novel's essential anger is evoked by the ugliness of characterisations like these, which as usual are localised and theoretically accounted for in the specific monstrosity that Western capitalism has created. As one of the characters at one point explains, 'I . . . am conversant with postmodernist critiques of the West, e.g. that we have here a society capable only of pastiche: a "flattened" world' (p. 261), or later: 'in this century history stopped paying attention to the old psychological orientation of reality. I mean, these days, character isn't destiny any more. Economics is destiny. Ideology is destiny. Bombs are destiny' (p. 432). At the fissure between old and new worlds, the immigrant consciousness rebels against this nightmare of the pre-fab soul – especially the older generation which has too many memories of a life in which family and community still mattered, even in the urban centres. The youth are caught between the attractions of subcultural style – the 'liberation' of punk hairdos and 'two-tone' music clubs (which gives the West a friendly face) – and an even more violent rejection, since as youth it is primarily they who are the targets of police harassment for having dark skins.

The repressive apparatus of the British state is therefore

pictured relentlessly in the novel: Chamcha is beaten senseless by police officers in the back of a black maria, and forced to eat his own faeces; in the wake of mysterious serial killings, a black community activist is framed and, in the ensuing protests, a reign of official terror descends upon 'Brickhall' (Brixton, Southall, 'Brick Lane'): 'black youths hauled swiftly into unmarked cars and vans belonging to the special patrol groups and flung out, equally discreetly, covered in cuts and bruises' (p. 451). In this, as in other passages, the three motifs of immigration converge: the repressive science of 'creationist' racism in the sense that the freakish transformation of Chamcha – who despite his meticulous training to be English has been branded with the 'blacks' (even as he insists 'You're not my people. I've spent half my life trying to get away from you') – is viewed by his friends in Brickhall as the horrible outcome of vicious medical experiments performed on him while held in detention, a view everyone willingly believes remembering 'intra-vaginal inspections [upon entry into Britain], Depoprovera scandals, unauthorised post-partum sterilisations, and, further back, the knowledge of Third World drug-dumping' (p. 252).

Of course, in this case as in others, the victims believe what is reasonable but not real. Chamcha's bestialisation is not the crude work of scalpel and injection, but the no less dangerous work of organised bigotry. The inaccuracy, even the tragedy, of their mistake suggests for Rushdie the limitations of resistance, and he clarifies the point by reasserting the religious level of his allegory. For the scene briefly alludes to the Jahilia episode in which Jahilia, like immigrant London, is described as 'a city visible but unseen', which in turn reverberates with the Chamcha passage in the statement that one believes what one 'is prepared to look at'. The acceptance of a devil's role, under the pressure of an awareness that they are 'invisible', humanly speaking, leads the black communities to the empowering myth of a 'dream-devil', their own loyal Azraeel, whose vengeance is sweet even if it is blind. The problem is that their exterminating angel happens to be a deranged serial killer, whom the police want to believe is black, but who in fact has nothing to do with the black community. Sadly, 'the browns-and-blacks found themselves cheering, in their sleep, this what-else-after-all-but-Black-man, maybe a little twisted up by fate class race history, all that, but getting off his behind, bad and mad, to kick a little ass' (p. 324).

'To will is to dissent' – it is what separates humans from the angels. But unless the forms of dissent escape the polarisations of race, they compound the injuries. Rushdie's characteristic middle-ground is therefore located in what he considers to be the totality of English race relations. It cannot be total unless one factors in the part of the equation erased in black urban resistance:

> [England's] hospitality – yes! – in spite of immigration laws, and his own recent experience, he still insisted on the truth of that: an imperfect welcome, true, one capable of bigotry, but a real thing, nonetheless, as was attested by . . . the annual reunion, in Wembley, a stone's throw from the great stadium surrounded by imperial echoes – Empire Way, the Empire Pool – of more than a hundred delegates, all tracing their ancestry back to a single, small Goan village. (*SV*, p. 398)

This conjuration of a general guilt is the by-now familiar feature of Rushdie's fictional mood, which pulls back from the politics of conjuncture – specific responses to specific practices. The hegemonic and the subaltern are for him equally 'human'. Thus in an England that has recently seen the deportation and marginalisation of Asian and West Indian families, a press campaign directed against 'muggers' and the 'dole', he balances the politics of blame by evoking the vulnerability of white Britain. Just as in Derek Walcott's argument about the 'filial impulse' of violent rejection, he suggests that simple slogans of anger directed against the British state give away too much; they imply that official Britain and its 'mainstream' have more control and more self-assurance than they actually do. Thus, in one of many explanatory digressions, we find the story of an elderly British woman named Rosa Diamond, whose sole moment of pleasure in a long life – the memory that kept her going – was an affair she had with an Argentinian gaucho. Although he never mentions it, Rushdie obviously chooses Argentina as Rosa's mental refuge because of the dissonance the idea of 'Argentina' is bound to have in a country still high from its imperial adventures in the Falklands. At the personal level, Argentina (like the Caribbean and South Asia) has what England covets. As the gaucho puts it: 'Are you such exotics in your cold England? . . . señora, I don't think so. Crammed into that coffin of an island, you must find wider horizons to express these secret selves'. Rosa herself sadly concludes: 'passion was an eccentricity of other races' (p. 146).

In other ways, though, Rushdie comes to terms here for the first time with the escapism of his earlier work. The well-worked theme of writer as collaborator has matured into something more realistic. Hanging so much on the attractions of Western 'freedom' in the other novels, he sees in the British context some of the hollowness of its actual practice. It is, for example, a joke at his own expense when, in the Jahilia episode, he finds himself the offspring of both Salman the scribe and Baal the satirist. As the chapters explain, Salman was a reprobate who was both bold and cowardly – who without programme or conviction (only a kind of contrariness) dared to ignore the sacred words dictated to him by Mahound, and instead created his own. Baal, on the other hand, was the Jahilian Grandee's court hireling; he had been given a particular job, which was to satirise the village poor, the water-carriers and the homeless – to exercise, on behalf of the state, the 'art of metrical slander' (p. 98). Being the proud and arrogant poet that he is, he at first protests, saying 'It isn't right for the artist to become the servant of the state', at which point the Grandee observes that his only other option is to be the paid poet of professional assassins. Caught in that particular market/state dichotomy, Baal is forced to see the vanity of staying pure:

> Now that he had abdicated all public platforms, his verses were full of loss. . . . Figures walked away from him in his odes, and the more passionately he called out to them the faster they moved . . . his language [was] too abstract, his imagery too fluid, his metre too inconstant. It led him to create chimeras of form, lionhead goatbodied serpenttailed impossibilities whose shapes felt obliged to change the moment they were set, so that the demotic forced its way into lines of classical purity and images of love were constantly degraded by the intrusion of elements of farce. (*SV*, p. 370)

Since *Grimus* at least, Rushdie has known that 'the public platform' was where writers ought to be, and in Baal's desperation we sense some of Fanon's observations on the rejection of farce among the Algerian storytellers under the impact of their own social upheavel. *The Satanic Verses* in fact problematises the colonial writer's metropolitan half, which is why for the first time Rushdie actually quotes approvingly, Gramsci and Fanon in the novel itself.

The hostile reception of the novel by Muslims has crowded out the legitimate anger that Britain's black communities as a whole – especially the Caribbean – might have had if given the chance. The book's characterisations of West Indians (like its characterisation of women) are often embarrassing and offensive. Although very much at home in the up-market publishing sphere, Rushdie nevertheless plays the role of court satirist too well. Some random examples might include the Sikh 'terrorist' Tavleen, who reveals beneath her gown a string of grenades bobbing like 'fatal breasts'; the comically stupid and overweight Afro-Caribbean community activist, Uhuru, given the last name 'Simba' after Tarzan's elephant; the clownish West Indian Underground employees speaking dialect as though it were fit for low comedy; the happy prostitutes of the Jahilia bordello who find pleasure in pretending they are the Grandee's harem for their fantasising clients, and who want their favourites to 'be the boss'; the West Indian lawyer Hanif, who is said to 'affect' a Trinidadian accent; Allie Cone, Pamela, Mishal, Rekha – the main characters' wives and lovers – all obsessed with childbearing or suicide at the loss of their men.

At one point, Rushdie's parody of 'dub' poetry (clever as it is) is misplaced and self-revealing. Its master is the repulsive Pinkwalla, a monstrous seven-foot tall albino, an 'East-India-man from the West Indies', a 'white black man', who entertains the customers of his Club Hot Wax with pseudo-radical raps: 'Now - mi - feel - indignation - when - dem - make - insinuation - we - no - part - a - de - nation - an - mi - make - proclamation - a - de - true - situation - how - we - make - contribution - since - de - Rome - Occupation' (p. 292). The humour is hollow and out of touch. Anyone familiar with the 'dub' poetry of Michael Smith, say, or Jean Binta Breeze – whose extraordinary images of cultural encirclement have given them an underground following on three continents – would know that far from being a kind of proxy politics or masturbatory venting of rage, their work has often been able to reach and affect the immigrant working classes. One thinks, for example, of Linton Kwesi Johnson's poem commemorating the arrest and frame-up of the trade unionist George Lindo, or of Michael Smith's 'Mi Cyaan Believe It' about the 'mad 'ouse' of black city life. Rushdie, however, places poets like these on the same parodic scale as *Midnight's Children's* Cyrus, the guru sham. Rushdie does not seem to understand what others closer to the crucible of British expulsion/acculturation understand. In the words of Paul Gilroy in this study of the expressive black cultures of Britain:

> Black expressive cultures affirm while they protest. . . . Here, non-European traditional elements, mediated by the histories of Afro-American and the Caribbean, have contributed to the formation of new and distinct black cultures amidst the deca-dent peculiarities of the Welsh, Irish, Scots and English. These non-European elements must be noted and their distinctive resonance accounted for.[25]

That inability to protest and affirm at the same time, that peculiar attraction–repulsion complex with regard to the 'heroic narratives' of 'the people' as it has been elaborated in the discourses of decolonisation has consistently led in Rushdie's work to an aesthetic double-bind: an encyclopaedic frenzy, a narrative canvas packed with the colours and gestures of human 'stuff', and yet set within a horrifying narrative closure. The organic text, cleverly encircling a linear history of 'progress', consistently stifles the open-endedness of what Bakhtin called the 'still-unfolding present' and holds it captive within the structures of its own '*takallouf*'.

I have been trying to show both the advantages and the limitations of this kind of writing. Despite his interventions into the cloistered West and its book markets, Rushdie has been conditioned by them too. Despite the fresh thinking about national form, about a new homelessness that is also a worldliness, about a double-edged post-colonial responsibility, *The Satanic Verses* shows how strangely detached and insensitive the logic of cosmopolitan 'universality' can be. It may be, as he says, that 'bigotry is not only a function of power', but it does not seem adequate to argue in the particular immigration/acculturation complex of contem-porary Britain that the central issue is one of 'human evil'. The means of distributing that evil are obviously very unequal, and the violence that comes from defending one's identity or livelihood as opposed to one's privileges is not the same.

By bringing to the surface for discussion all the interlocking debates of decolonisation, Rushdie, more than anyone else writing in English, has made English literary tradition international. And he has done this precisely by dramatising the totality of the components that make up that tradition – including those colonies and minorities until now referred to only from the safety of the 'centre'. But by doing so, he has also taken on another kind of responsibility, which is to the decolonisation struggles he interprets (and translates) for a Western reading public. The fulness and complexity of their collective visions are often foreshortened in the personal filter of Rushdie's fiction.

One only has to think, for example, of how Fanon – trained in the France of Sartre and Césaire, and the writer of a captivating and hallucinatory prose – was not, as one might expect in the company of Rushdie's Third-World postmodernism, an advocate of a literature of polemic. On the contrary – and in keeping with the (somewhat condescending) thrust of the *Satanic Verses'* reprimands against the actual forms of black British protest – his position was that 'stinging denunciations' are too easily welcomed by the occupying powers who recognise in them a form of catharsis.[26] And one could point also to Cabral, who as Basil Davidson points out, had 'no illusions about the incapacity of nationalism, as such, to solve the basic problems of post-colonial development'. What they did know, and insist on, was the necessity of national struggle. That is a point of view Rushdie shares in theory, but which he cannot bring himself to fictionalise. And it is in that sense that Bakhtin spoke of a 'laughter of all the people' as opposed to the 'negative and formal parody of modern times', and that Gramsci spoke of 'a new conformism from below [permitting] new possibilities of self-discipline, or perhaps of liberty that is also individual'.[27]

'Discipline', 'organisation', 'people' – these are words that the cosmopolitan sensibility refuses to take seriously. We get a sense in their work of the comic, but not of the comedic, which is so lively in the very unfunny work of some of the writers mentioned above – Roque Dalton, June Jordan, Obi Egbuna, with their imaginations of a future, and their portrayal of political activity as being at the heart of personal experience. We get protest, but not affirmation, except in the most abstractly 'human' sense. That is something, and it is perhaps even necessary as a mediation. For the greatest problem is still being unable to conceive of the colonial as even having a voice that matters.

Notes

Notes to Chapter 1: National Fictions, Fictional Nations

1. Quoted in Peter Worsley, *The Third World* (Chicago, Ill.: University of Chicago Press, 1964) p. 5.
2. Raymond Williams, *The Year 2000* (New York: Pantheon Books, 1983).
3. Armand Mattelart, 'Introduction', *Communications and Class Struggle*, vol. 2 (New York: International General, 1983) p. 57.
4. Paul Ricoeur, 'Civilization and National Cultures', in his *History and Truth* (Evanston, Ill.: Northwestern University Press, 1965) pp. 276–7.
5. Hugh Seton-Watson, *Nations and States: An Enquiry into the Origins of Nations and the Politics of Nationalism* (Boulder, Col.: Westview Press, 1977) p. 5.
6. See, for example, Frederic Jameson's 'Third-World Literature in the Era of Multinational Capital', *Social Text*, vol. 15 (Fall 1986) pp. 65–88. This chapter was written before Jameson's piece, which appeared following a conference on 'The Challenge of Third World Culture' at Duke University in September 1986 at which sections of the present chapter were delivered. See also the response to his essay by Aijaz Ahmad, 'Jameson's Rhetoric of Otherness and the "National Allegory" ', *Social Text*, vol. 17 (Fall 1987) pp. 3–25.
7. See Benedict Anderson's *Imagined Comunities* (1983); Ali Mazrui's *Cultural Engineering and Nation-forming* (1972); as well as the introductory chapters of overviews on so-called 'Commonwealth' literature, Bruce King's *The New English Literatures* (1980). For a work not restricted either to English or Third-World contexts, see H. Ernest Lewald's anthology *The Cry of Home* (1972).
8. Examples might include Edward Said, Ariel Dorfman, Amiri Baraka, Homi Bhabha, Abdul JanMohamed, Cornell West and others.
9. Gordon Lewis, *Slavery, Imperialism, and Freedom: Studies in English Radical Thought* (New York and London: Monthly Review Press, 1978) p. 304. For the French tradition, see Barbara Harlow's *Resistance Literature* (New York and London: Methuen, 1987) p. 27, with its discussions of France-based North African writers such as Mehdi Charef, Driss Chraibi and Rachid Boudjedra.
10. Salman Rushdie, 'The Empire Writes Back with a Vengeance', *The Times*, 3 July 1982, p. 8.
11. Ariel Dorfman, *The Empire's Old Clothes* (New York: Pantheon Books, 1983) p. 9.
12. For the purposes of this study, by far the best works on the nation are Benedict Anderson, *Imagined Communities: Reflections on the Origin and Spread of Nationalism* (London: Verso and New Left Books, 1983);

Samir Amin, *Class and Nation*, trans. Susan Kaplow (New York and London: Monthly Review Press, 1980); Anouar Abdel-Malek, *Nation and Revolution*, (vol. 2 of *Social Dialectics*) (Albany, N.Y.: State University of New York Press, 1981); Tom Nairn, *The Break-up of Britain: Crisis and Neo-nationalism* (London: New Left Books, 1977); Worsley, *The Third World*; and Seton-Watson, *Nations and States* – particularly Anderson, Worsley, Nairn and Abdel-Malek.

13. Anderson, *Imagined Communities*, p. 12.
14. See Elie Kedourie, *Nationalism* (London: Hutchinson, 1960 p. 63: ' "Only one language", says Schleirmacher, "is firmly implanted in an individual. . . . For every language is a particular mode of thought and what is cogitated in one language can never be repeated in the same way in another . . . ".' This was the philosophical foundation in Germany for a much broader social movement described by José Carlos Mariátegui citing Francesco de Sanctis: 'In the history of the West, the flowering of national literatures coincided with the political affirmation of the nation. It formed part of the movement which, through the Reformation and the Renaissance, created the ideological and spiritual factors of the liberal revolution and the capitalist order.' *Seven Interpretive Essays on Peruvian Reality*, trans. Marjory Urquidi (Austin, Tx. and London: University of Texas Press, 1971) p. 183.
15. The phrase is Anderson's. See also Anthony Barnett, 'Salman Rushdie: a Review Article', *Race and Class* (Winter 1985) p. 94: 'The novel as a literary form, like the newspaper, was one of the conductors of and remains part of, the essential chorus for the rise of nations and nationalism.'
16. The phrase is Anderson's.
17. Mariátegui, *Seven Interpretive Essays*, pp. 187–8.
18. Ernest Gellner, quoted in Anderson, *Imagined Comunities*, p. 15.
19. See Worsley, *The Third World*, p. 130: 'To what extent does this ideological emphasis upon the 'unity' of the nation and the homogeneity of society reflect a real absence of social differentiation in the new societies, and to what extent is it merely another instance of the familiar rhetoric of all nationlists who, from Ficthe onwards, have always appealed to an often spurious solidarity, embracing all classes and conditions of the nation . . . ?'
20. Eric Hobsbawm and Terence Ranger (eds), *The Invention of Tradition* (Cambridge: Cambridge University Press, 1983) p. 7.
21. Anderson, *Imagined Communities*, p. 35.
22. Michael Holquist and Katerina Clark, *Mikhail Bakhtin* (Cambridge, Mass.: Harvard University Press, 1984). Both Holquist and Clark have tried to divorce Bakhtin from the tradition of the Russian school of social critics (Dobrolyubov, Chernyshevsky) and fix him within Russian formalism and a kind of mystical enthusiasm for the complexity and plenitude of the 'utterance', by which Holquist means the principles of 'psychological depth' and 'political pluralism'. To do so, he ignores not only Bakhtin's explicit attempts to revise Russian formalism (to 'socialise' it), but his deliberate

and savage attacks on literary modernism and psychoanalysis. As a whole, Holquist has interpreted Bakhtin's assault on the orthodoxies of fixed language to be veiled attacks on Stalinism; perhaps, but it is just as likely that they were attacks on the belletrism, scientism and obscurantism of Western culture practice. In Tzvetan Todorov, *Mikhail Bakhtin: The Dialogic Principle*, trans. Wlad Godzich (Minneapolis, Minn.: University of Minnesota Press, 1984), we find the critic emphasising 'heteroglossia', and interpreting it (incorrectly) to be a kind of prototype of Julia Kristeva's impersonal 'intertextuality'.

23. Mikhail Bakhtin, 'Epic and Novel', in Michael Holquist and Caryl Emerson (eds), *The Dialogic Imagination*, (Austin, Tx: University of Texas Press, 1981) p. 12.
24. Bakhtin, 'Epic and Novel', p. 13.
25. Hobsbawm and Ranger (eds), *The Invention of Tradition*, p. 5.
26. Anderson, *Imagined Comunities*, p. 19.
27. Regis Debray, 'Marxism and the National Question', *New Left Review*, vol. 105 (September–October 1977) p. 26.
28. Ibid., p. 27 (his emphasis).
29. See 'Populism' chapter in Worsley, *The Third World*, pp. 118–74.
30. Erich Auerbach, *Mimesis: The Representation of Reality in Western Literature* (Princeton, N.J.: Princeton University Press, 1953) p. 491.
31. Bakhtin, 'Epic and Novel', p. 38.
32. King, *The New English Literatures* p. 42.
33. Bakhtin, 'Epic and Novel', p. 30.
34. Todorov, *Mikhail Bakhtin* p. 58.
35. Walter Benjamin, 'The Storyteller: Reflections on the Works of Nikolai Leskov' in *Illuminations* (New York: Schocken Books, 1969) p. 87.
36. Ibid., p. 88 (my emphasis).
37. Ibid., p. 89.
38. Ibid., p. 97.
39. Kedourie, *Nationalism*, p. 54.
40. Hans Kohn, *Nationalism: Its Meaning and History* (New York: D. Van Nostrand, 1965) p. 9.
41. Fascism haunts the studies of Kohn, Kedourie and Hayes especially.
42. According to Eric Hobsbawm, for example, 'The evidence is overwhelming that at this stage [in the nineteenth century] the crux of nationalist movements was not so much state independence as such, but rather the construction of 'viable' states [with the intention of creating] the internal conditions (e.g. a "national-market") and the external conditions for the development of "national economy" through state organization and action. 'Some Reflections on "The Break-up of Britain" ', *New Left Review*, vol. 105 (September–October 1977) pp. 3–23. On the contrary, he continues, 'the characteristic nationalist movement *of our time* is separatist, aiming at the break-up of existing states'. Hobsbawm might have added: not only states, but empires.
43. Kohn, *Nationalism: Its Meaning and History*, p. 89.

44. Ibid., p. 11.
45. Ibid., p. 12.
46. *Many Voices, One World* (the Macbride Commission Report) (London: Kogan Page; New York and Paris: UNESCO, 1980).
47. Herbert Schiller, *National Sovereignty and International Communications* (Norwood, NJ: Ablex Publishers, 1979) p. 1.
48. Edward Said, 'The Mind of Winter: Reflections on Life in Exile', *Harpers Magazine*, vol. 269 (September 1984) p. 50.
49. Harlow, *Resistance Literature*, p. 14.
50. Jeffrey Meyers, *Fiction and the Colonial Experience* (Ipswich, Suffolk: Boydell Press, 1973) p. vii.
51. Terry Eagleton, *Exiles and Emigrés: Studies in Modern Literature* (London: Chatto and Windus, 1970) pp. 9–10.
52. Ibid., p. 18.
53. Frantz Fanon, *The Wretched of the Earth* (New York: Grove Press, 1968) pp. 247–8.
54. Ahmad, 'Jameson's Rhetoric of Otherness', p. 22.
55. For a brief account of this counter-hegemonic aesthetics, see Timothy Brennan, 'Fantasy, Individuality, and the Politics of Liberation', *Polygraph*, vol. 1 (Winter 1987) pp. 89–100. For a longer treatment and overview of many who currently practice it, see Harlow, *Resistance Literature*.
56. Ernesto Gonzalez Bermejo (interviewer), *Cosas de escritores: Gabriel García Márquez, Mario Vargas Llosa y Julio Cortázar* (Montevideo, Uruguay: Biblioteca de marcha, Colección testimonio/9, 1971) p. 58. Translation my own.
57. Mario Vargas Llosa, *The War of the End of the World* (New York: Farrar, Straus and Giroux, 1984) p. 248.

Notes to Chapter 2: Anti-Colonial Liberalism

1. José Carlos Mariátegui, *Seven Interpretive Essays on Peruvian Reality* (Austen, Tx.: University of Texas Press, 1971) p. 226.
2. Tomás Borge Martínez, 'El arte como herejía, in *Hacia una política cultural* (Managua, Nicaragua: Ministerio de Cultura, 1982).
3. Jean Franco, *The Modern Culture of Latin America: Society and the Artist* (Harmondsworth, Middx.: Penguin, 1967).
4. Bharati Mukherjee, *Darkness* (Markham, Ontario: Penguin Books, Canada, 1985) p. 3.
5. Bharati Mukherjee, 'Immigrant Writing: Give Us Your Maximalists', *New York Times Book Review*, 28 August 1988, p. 28.
6. See in this regard Feroza F. Jussawalla, 'Beyond Indianness: the Stylistic Concerns of "Midnight's Children" ', in *Family Quarrels: Towards a Criticism of Indian Writing in English* (New York: Peter Lang, 1985) pp. 103–33; Maria Couto, 'Midnight's Children and Parents: the Search for Indo-British Identity', *Encounter*, vol. 58, no. 2 (February 1982) pp. 61–6; and Robert Towers, Review of *Midnight's Children*, *New York Review of Books*, 24 September 1981, p. 30.

7. Isabel Allende, *The House of the Spirits* (New York: Bantam Books, 1985) p. 335.

8. For some of these arguments, see Aijaz Ahmad, 'Jameson's Rhetoric of Otherness and the "National Allegory" ', *Social Text*, vol. 17 (Fall 1987) pp. 3–25; and Mary Layoun, 'Indigenous Third World Cultural Criticism(s): Against Hegemony or a New Hegemony?', *Critical Exchange*, vol. 21 (Spring 1986) pp. 87–96.

9. Frederic Jameson, 'Third World Literature in the Ear of Multinational Capitalism', *Social Text*, vol. 15 (Fall 1986) pp. 65–88.

10. Mary Layoun, 'The Strategy of Narrative Form', *Critical Exchange*, vol. 22 (Spring 1987) p. 40.

11. For a much fuller treatment of Gramsci's aesthetics and his contributions to Third-World theory, see Timothy Brennan, 'Literary Criticism and the Southern Question', *Cultural Critique*, no. 11 (Winter 1988–9) pp. 87–114.

12. For a developed treatment of this overlapping of nationality and class, see C. L. R. James's account of the mulatto in urban Haiti in *The Black Jacobins: Toussaint L'Ouverture and the San Domingo Revolution* (New York: Vintage, 1963); also A. Sivanandan, 'Race, Class and the State', in *A Different Hunger: Writings on Black Resistance* (London: Pluto Press, 1982) pp. 101–25.

13. See V. G. Kiernan, 'Gramsci and the Other Continents', *New Edinburgh Review* no. 24 (1974) p. 20. As Kiernan correctly points out, Italy's agrarian South was treated as a 'captive market and source of cheap labour'.

14. Ibid., p. 22. Outside of Italy, Gramsci's reputation was given its first boost primarily by the British New Left beginning in the early 1960s, about the time Fanon's work was being published in English. Oddly, Kiernan and Tom Nairn are the only British writers to appreciate Gramsci's awareness of the colonial problem. See also Tom Nairn, 'Antonu su Gobbu', in Anne Showstack Sassoon (ed.), *Approaches to Gramsci* (London: Writers and Readers Publishing Co-operative Society, 1982).

15. See, for example, Sandinista co-founder Tomás Borge's discussions in 'Marginal Notes on the Propaganda of the FSLN [Frente Sandinista de Liberación Nacional]', in Armand Mattlelart (ed.), *Communicating in Popular Nicaragua* (New York and Bagnolet, France: International General, 1986) p. 51. Selected essays and speeches of the FSLN on cultural policy, collected in *Hacia una política cultural* (Managua, Nicaragua: Ministerio de Cultura, 1982) also bears witness to this tendency. See especially, Vice-President Sergio Ramírez's contribution entitled 'The Intellectuals and the Future of the Revolution' (p. 125): 'Gramsci used to point out that the intellectuals, the artists that have always existed in history, have enjoyed a certain autonomy. As if floating in a historical vacuum, they had the possibility of being for themselves alone, isolated from the historical context in whatever type of society you would care to mention.' My translation.

16. Antonio Gramsci, *Los intelectuales y la organización de la cultura*, trans. Raul Sciarreta (Buenos Aires, 1960).

17. Roberto Fernandex Retamar, *Caliban y otros ensayos* (Havana, Cuba: Editor Arte y Literatura, 1979) pp. 80–1.
18. See Armand Mattelart, 'Continuity and Discontinuity in Communications: Points for a Polemic', in Mattelart and Seth Siegelaub (eds), *Communication and Class Struggle*, vol. II (New York and Bagnolet, France: International General, 1983) p. 362.
19. José Luis Velázquez P., *Sociedad civil y dictadura* (San Jose, Costa Rica: Libra libre, 1986).
20. Antonio Gramsci, *Gli Intellecttuali e L'Organizzazione della Cultura* (Turin: Einaudi, 1949) p. 29. All translations my own.
21. Ibid., p. 25.
22. Alberto Flores Galindo, *La Agonía de Mariátegui* (Lima, Peru: Centro de Estudios y Promoción del Desarollo, 1982) pp. 11–12.
23. Mariátegui, *Seven Interpretive Essays* p. 191.
24. Ibid., p. 186.
25. Ibid., pp. 192–3.
26. Ibid., p. 271.
27. Antonio Gramsci, *Quaderni del Carcere*, vol. 3 (Turin: Einaudi 1975), Edizione critica dell'Instituto Gramsci a cura di Valentino Gerrantana, Q 14, item 47, 1705.
28. Wallace Peter Sillanpoa, 'Cultural Theory and Literary Criticism in the Prison Notebooks of Antonio Gramsci', Dissertation, University of Connecticut, 1980, p. 128.
29. Ibid., p. 292.
30. Gramsci, *Quaderni*, vol. 1, Q 5, item 54, 586.
31. Antonio Gramsci, *Note sul Macchiavelli, sulla politica e sullo stato moderno* (Turin: Einaudi, 1974) p. 155.
32. Antonio Gramsci in Pedro Cavalcanti and Paul Piccone (eds), *History, Philosophy, and Culture in the Young Gramsci* (St Louis, Mo.: Telos, 1975) pp. 29–30.
33. Gramsci, *Quaderni*, vol. 2, Q 6, item 29, 708.
34. See Franco, *The Modern Culture of Latin America*, pp. 174–205.
35. Paul Gilroy, *There Ain't No Black in the Union Jack* (London: Hutchinson, 1987) pp. 13, 157.
36. A. Sivanandan, *A Different Hunger: Writings on Black Resistance* (London: Pluto Press, 1982) p. 89.
37. Gilroy, *There Ain't No Black in the Union Jack*, p. 247.
38. Eduardo Galeano, *Open Veins of Latin America* (New York: Monthly Review Press, 1973) p. 267.
39. Derek Walcott, 'The Muse of History', in Edward Baugh (ed.), *Critics on Caribbean Literature* (New York: St Martin's Press, 1979) p. 38.
40. For the first, see, for example, Caryl Phillips's *A State of Independence*, Chinua Achebe's *A Man of the People*, George Lamming's *Of Age and Innocence*; for the second, V. S. Naipaul's *A Bend in the River*, Nadine Gordimer's *July's People*, Manohar Malgonkar's *A Bend in the Ganges*.
41. Basil Davidson, 'On Revolutionary Nationalism: the Legacy of Cabral', *Race and Class*, vol. 27 (Winter 1986) p. 26.
42. Patrick Chabal, *Amílcar Cabral: Revolutionary Leadership and People's*

War (Cambridge and New York: Cambridge University Press, 1983) p. 168.
43. Quoted in ibid., p. 180.
44. Amílcar Cabral, *Unity and Struggle* (New York and London: Monthly Review Press, 1979) p. 147.
45. Chabal, *Amílcar Cabral*, p. 184.
46. Richard C. Onwuanibe, *A Critique of Revolutionary Humanism: Frantz Fanon* (St Louis, Mo.: Warren H. Green, 1983) p. x.
47. Frantz Fanon, *The Wretched of the Earth* (New York: Grove Press, 1968) p. 217. All further references to this work will appear in the text.

Notes to Chapter 3: The Art of Translation

1. George Orwell, *An Age Like This: Collected Essays, Journalism, and Letters*, vol. 1 (New York and London: Harcourt, Brace, Jovanovich, 1968) p. 234.
2. Angel Rama, *Transculturación narrativa en América Latina* (Mexico City: Siglo veintiuno editores, 1982) p. 29. Translations are my own.
3. Jean Franco, 'Beyond Ethnocentrism: Gender, Power, and the Third-World Intelligentsia', in Cary Nelson and Lawrence Grossberg (eds), *Marxism and the Interpretation of Culture* (Urbana and Chicago, Ill.: University of Illinois Press, 1988) p. 509.
4. Rama, *Transculturación narrativa en América Latina*, p. 29.
5. Ibid., p. 38.
6. Salman Rushdie, 'Imaginary Homelands', *London Review of Books*, October 1982, p. 19.
7. Edward Said, 'The Mind of Winter: Reflections on Life in Exile', *Harpers Magazine*, vol. 269 (September 1984) p. 55.
8. The same view is expressed interestingly by Left British culture critic Richard Hoggart when he comments on the artistic value of 'standing at the friction point of two cultures'. Robert Hewison, *In Anger: Culture in the Cold War, 1945–60* (London: Weidenfeld and Nicolson, 1981) p. 171.
9. Salman Rushdie, *Shame* (New York: Vintage/Aventura, 1984) p. 24.
10. Mary Layoun, 'Indigenous Third World Cultural Criticism(s): Against Hegemony or a New Hegemony?', *Critical Exchange*. vol. 21. (Spring 1986) p. 88.
11. Salman Rushdie, *The Jaguar Smile: A Nicaraguan Journey* (New York: Viking, 1987) p. 12.
12. Salman Rushdie, 'Outside the Whale', *Granta*, vol. 11 (1983) p. 136. Also in *American Film*, 10 (January–February 1985) pp. 16–70, 72–3.
13. V. S. Naipaul, *India: A Wounded Civilization* (New York: Knopf, 1972) p. 149.
14. Rushdie, *The Jaguar Smile*, p. 67.
15. *Nova*, Channel 13, New Jersey Public Broadcasting Service, Tuesday 7 January 1986, WGBH/BBC.

16. Rushdie, *The Jaguar Smile*, p. 10.
17. Kathryn Hume, *Fantasy and Mimesis: Responses to Reality in Western Literature* (New York and London: Methuen, 1984) pp. 14, 17.
18. See Rushdie's article 'On Günter Grass' (*Granta*, vol. 15 (1985) p. 180) in which he places *The Tin Drum* among those few books 'that open doors for their readers, doors in the head, doors whose existence they had not previously suspected'.
19. Rushdie does not carefully distinguish among the group of related terms 'fantasy', 'myth', 'fairy tale', 'miracle', 'fable', 'dream', and so on. The terms suggest two interrelated meanings: a departure from fictional realism, and a sense of exasperation, despair and wonder in the face of an authority that is so far outside the moral and intellectual constraints of the observer that its actions are 'unbelievable'.
20. Gabriel García Márquez, 'The Solitude of Latin America', *Granta*, vol. 9 (1983 p. 58).
21. What we've been outlining here as Rushdie's attempt to question fictionality as a means of puncturing social myth is, according to Mabel Morana, a feature of several recent Latin American novels, including *One Hundred Years of Solitude* (*Literatura y Cultura Nacional en Hispanoamérica (1910–1940)*) (Minnesota: Institute for the Study of Ideologies and Literature, 1984) p. 92.
22. Gabriel García Márquez, *El Olor de la Guayaba: Conversaciones con Plinio Apuleyo Mendoza – Gabriel García Márquez* (Bogotá, Colombia: Editorial La Oveja Negra, 1982) p. 36. Translations are my own.
23. García Márquez, 'The Solitude of Latin America', p. 58.
24. García Márquez, *El Olor de la Guayaba*, p. 30.
25. Ibid., p. 31.
26. Ib Johansen, 'The Flight from the Enchanter: Reflections on Salman Rushdie's *Grimus*', *Kunapipi*, vol. VII (1985) p. 25.
27. Oriental Studies Division, New York Public Library.
28. Salman Rushdie, *Grimus* (London: Alfred Knopf, 1975) pp. 261–2. All future references to this book will occur in the text.
29. M. Th. Houtsma, A. J. Wensink, H. A. R. Gibb, W. Heffening and E. Lévi-Provencal (eds), *The Encyclopedia of Islam: A Dictionary of Geography, Ethnography and Biography of the Muhammadan Peoples*, vol. IV (London: Luzac, 1934) p. 685.
30. Tarif Khalidi, *Classical Arab Islam: The Culture and Heritage of the Golden Age* (Princeton, N.J.: Darwin Press, 1985) p. 70.
31. Khalidi, *Classical Arab Islam*, p. 76.
32. Along with Simurg, Eagle and Roc, the Phoenix completes the list of most important mythical birds in a book filled with ornithological symbolism.

Notes to Chapter 4: The National Longing for Form

1. Wilson Harris, *Kas-Kas: Interview with Three Caribbean Writers in Texas* (Austin, Tx.: University of Texas, 1972) p. 48.

Notes

2. V. S. Naipaul, *The Mystic Masseur* (New York: Vintage, 1957, 1984) p. 1.
3. P. Rama Moorthy, 'G. V. Desani: First Impressions', in C. D. Narasimhaiah (ed.), *Indian Literature of the Past Fifty Years (1917–1967)* (Prasaranga: University of Mysore, 1970) p. 208.
4. Rudolph Bader, 'Indian *Tin Drum*', *International Fiction Review*, vol. 11 (Summer 1984) p. 76.
5. Salman Rushdie, '*Midnight's Children* and *Shame*', *Kunapipi*, vol. VII, no. 1 (1985) p. 8.
6. Paul Scott, *The Jewel in the Crown* (London: Readers Union, Heinemann, 1967) p. 236.
7. Raja Rao, *Kanthapura* (New York: New Directions, 1963) p. viii. See also Rushdie himself: 'I thought it must be possible to attempt the creation of a literary form which corresponds to the form of the oral narrative and which, with any luck, will succeed in holding readers, for reasons of its shape . . .' ('*Midnight's Children* and *Shame*', p. 8).
8 Meenakshi Mukherjee, 'The Tractor and the Plough: the Contrasted Visions of Sudhin Ghose and Mulk Raj Anand', in Narasimhaiah, *Indian Literature of the Past Fifty years*, p. 122.
9. Salman Rushdie, *Shame* (New York: Vintage/Aventura, 1984) p. 23.
10. See Rushdie's detailed discussion on the *chamcha* in 'The Empire Writes Back with Vengeance', *The Times*, 3 July 1983 p. 36.
11. Rushdie, *Shame*, p. 92.
12. This dichotomy in its Pakistani guise reappears in the person of Iskander Harappa and Raza Hyder in *Shame*.
13. '[T]hen the day arrived when Aziz threw out the religious tutor. Thumb and forefinger closed around the *maulvi*'s ear. Naseem and her husband leading the stragglebearded wretch to the door in the garden wall . . . . Do you know what that man was teaching your children? He was teaching them to hate, wife. He tells them to hate Hindus and Buddhists and Jains and Sikhs and who knows what other vegetarians', in Salman Rushdie, *Midnight's Children* (New York: Avon, 1980) p. 43.
14. 'Ravana' is a many-headed serpent from Hindu mythology or (alternatively) an evil philosopher-king.
15. Tariq Ali, 'Midnight's Children', *New Left Review*, vol. 136 (November–December 1982) p. 89.
16. Bombay is not only Rushdie's actual birthplace but a living symbol of India's many influences, beginning with its even mix of Hindus and Muslims. As an important port it had a strong British and Portuguese presence; for these same reasons it is a Christian stronghold as well, and also the centre of Zoroastrianism in India.
17. To take only a few examples not already mentioned, Ayi Kwei Armah, *The Beautiful Ones are Not Yet Born* (London: Heinemann, 1969); Ngugi wa Thiong'o, *Petals of Blood* (New York: E. P. Dutton, 1978); George Lamming, *Of Age and Innocence* (London: Michael Joseph, 1960); Caryl Phillips, *A State of Independence* (New York: Farrar, Straus & Giroux, 1986).
18. As a work of postwar British literature, *Midnight's Children* is unusual,

although not unprecedented, in the degree to which it incorporates actual history. This incorporation not only poses interesting formal and thematic questions in and of itself, but does so doubly within the context in which it occurs – namely, as a work of *information* from one race (nationality) to another – as an announcement to England from India. In this sense, the folkloristic panache of Padma can be seen as a cultural message – the inside story of an India the visitor cannot see.

19. The few critics who have written on Rushdie have missed this, seeing in Padma merely the personification of the audience in a general sense: a kind of chorus. See Uma Parameswaran, 'Handcuffed to History: Salman Rushdie's Art', *Ariel*, vol. 14 (October 1983) pp. 34–45.

20. Robin Lewis, 'National Identity and Social Consciousness in Modern Indian Literature', in Anne Paolucci (ed.), *Problems in National Literary Identity and the Writer as Social Critic*, selected papers of the Fourth Annual NDEA Seminar on Foreign Area Studies (New York: Griffon House Publications, 1980) p. 34.

21. Vladimir Propp, *Theory and History of Folklore*, ed. with introduction and notes by Anatoly Liberman, trans. Ariadna Martin and Richard Martin [*et al.*] (Minneapolis, Minn.: University of Minnesota Press, 1984) pp. 4–5. This standard nationalist bias of folklore study is illuminated by comments like the following: 'In the West folklore means the peasant culture of *one* people, most commonly of the researcher's own people. The principle of selection is quantitative and national. . . . [The study of folklore is] the popular-scientific study of one's native country.'

22. Wimal Dissanayake, 'Towards a Decolonized English: South Asian Creativity in Fiction', *World Englishes*, vol. 4, no. 2 (1985) p. 240.

23. Propp, *Theory and History of Folklore*, p. 6.

24. Ibid., p. 8: 'If the reader of a work of literature is a powerless censor and critic devoid of authority, anyone listening to folklore is a potential future performer, who, in turn, consciously or unconsciously will introduce changes into the work.'

25. Margaret and James Stutley, *A Dictionary of Hinduism: Its Mythology, Folklore, and Development, 1500 BC–AD 1500* (London: Routledge and Kegan Paul, 1977) p. 91.

26. Feroza Jussawalla, *Family Quarrels: Towards a Criticism of Indian Writing in English* (New York: Peter Lang, 1985) p. 117.

27. Stanley Wolpert, *A New History of India*, 2nd edn (London: Oxford University Press, 1982) p. 18.

28. Ibid., p. 18.

29. Ibid., p. 82: 'All gods of Hinduism have female counterparts, whose potent earthly "power" or *shakti* was believed to be the active life force.'

30. Wendy O'Flaherty, *Asceticism and Eroticism in the Mythology of Siva* (London: Oxford University Press, 1973) pp. 34, 39.

31. Ibid., p. 132.

32. Ibid., p. 136.

33. Ibid., p. 139.
34. Stutley, *A Dictionary of Hinduism*, p. 92.
35. See Rushdie, *Midnight's Children*, p. 273: 'No never mind *chief*, just think of me as a . . . a big brother, maybe.'
36. If the 'elephantum' clearly stands for Ganeshian style, for Saleem's temporarily-willed poetic output, 'feronia' stands for the appropriate democratic content. Feronia is the Italian patroness of freedman.
37. For an interpretation of these passages along the lines of reader-response criticism, see Keith Wilson, '*Midnight's Children* and Reader Responsibility', *Critical Quarterly*, vol. 26 (Autumn 1984) pp. 23–37.

Notes to Chapter 5: The Artist as Demagogue

1. Victoria Glendinning, 'A Novelist in the Country of the Mind', *The Sunday Times*, 25 October 1981, p. 38.
2. Salman Rushdie, 'Author From Three Countries' (interview), *New York Times Book Review*, 30 November 1983, p. 22. This scenario fits Rushdie's earlier statements to the effect that, after *Shame*, he would no longer write about the Indian subcontinent. For if these two novels systematically represent the subcontinent's two major nations, there would be no reason to write another. Of course, the comment implied what has since come to be – the account of England in *The Satanic Verses*.
3. Stanley Wolpert, *A New History of India*, 2nd edn (London: Oxford University Press, 1982) p. 64.
4. Tariq Ali, *Can Pakistan Survive?: The Death of a State* (Harmondsworth, Middx.: Penguin, 1983) p. 47.
5. Salman Rushdie, 'Dynasty and Democracy (The Idea of India after the death of Miss Gandhi)', *New Republic*, vol. 26 (November 1984) p. 17.
6. Ali Dashti, *In Search of Omar Khayyam*, trans. from Persian by L. P. Elwell-Sutton (New York: Columbia University Press, 1971) p. 74.
7. Thomas W. Lippman, *Understanding Islam: An Introduction to the Moslem World* (New York: Mentor, 1982) p. 152.
8. Wolpert, *A New History of India*, p. 317.
9. Iqbal proclaimed: 'The Muslims of India are the only Indian people who may be described as a nation in the modern sense of the word.' Quoted in Wolpert, *A New History of India*.
10. Aunt Pia at one point says of her late husband, who has killed himself because his realistic filmscripts were never produced, '[H]e died for his hate of melodrama' (*M. C.*, p. 328). In 'Author from Three Countries', Rushdie wrote: 'If you had to choose a form for that part of the world, the form you would choose would be the comic epic' (p. 22).
11. Glendinning, 'A Novelist in the Country of the Mind', p. 38.
12. Benedict Anderson, *Imagined Communities: Reflections on the Origin*

and Spread of Nationlism (London: Verso, and New Left Books, 1983) pp. 46, 19.

13. Rushdie furthers this idea in his contempt for the pious fanatic Maulana Dawood. The 1956 English-language edition of the *Quran* that Rushdie used was translated by N. J. Dawood. In keeping with Rushdie's parodic reversals, Dawood's reserved and scholarly writing suggests a person very different from the fanatic in *Shame* with the same name.

14. There is this typically parabolic passage about Bilquis: 'a woman who was unclothed by change but who wrapped herself in certainties . . . a girl who became a queen, but lost the ability possessed by every beggar woman' (*Shame*, p. 69).

15. The genealogies of Islam are no less daunting than those of Judaism, in part because they contain so many of the same names. Like Judaism, Islam traces its sacred familial lineages back to Abraham, and claims as ancestors many of the same figures we consider 'old Testament' – especially the direct forebears, Hagar and Ishmael. In the words of H. A. R. Gibb, Islam appeared 'not as a new religion, but as a revival of pure Abrahamic monotheism, purified at once of the accretions of Judaism and Christianity and superseding them as the final revelation' (*Mohammedanism: An Historical Survey* (London: Oxford University Press, 1949) p. 47).

16. Interview with the author, Asia Society, New York 17 January 1986.

17. Lippman, *Understanding Islam*, p. 96.

18. With this in mind, for Islamic authorities I have referred mostly to liberal Western scholars and publicist like H. A. R. Gibb, Thomas Lippman and Normon O. Brown – not because they offer more trustworth accounts of Islam, as if objectivity came only from being 'outside' (no one is 'outside'), but because they express more clearly than scholars from Islamic countries the popular view of Islam that Rushdie is manipulating. For a view from the Islamic world itself, a more sensitive and accurate introduction to Islam than any of those above can be found in Tarif Khalidi's recent *Classical Arab Islam: The Culture and Heritage of the Golden Age* (Princeton, N.J.: Darwin Press, 1985).

19. Sir William Muir, *The Coran: Its Composition and Teaching* (London: Wyman, 1878) p. 24. 'The words are almost certainly the actual ones of Mahomet – although we are never sure of the context' (p. 40).

20. Glendinning, 'A Novelist in the Country of the Mind', p. 38. In the interview, however, we learn that the second of these cases was based not on a newspaper article, but on the experience of Rushdie's own sister: 'During the Brixton riots, alone in a compartment of an underground train, [she] was beaten up by a group of white youths. . . . The police at Brixton station declined to take action; an overwhelming feeling of shame made her not press her case.' In the same place he announces that his book would be about 'a girl who suffers excessively from the emotions of shame which unleashes in her a violence of which she could not normally be capable'.

21. Khalidi, *Classical Arab Islam*, p. 75.
22. Edward Said, *Beginnings, Intention and Method* (Baltimore, Md and London: Johns Hopkins University Press, 1975) p. 199.
23. Ibid., p. 199.
24. Ali, *Can Pakistan Survive?*, p. 136.
25. Normon O. Brown, 'The Apocalypse of Islam', *Social Text*, vol. 8 (Winter 1983–4) p. 166.
26. Ibid., pp. 167–8.
27. Similarly, the reference here to old Shakil's 'monologue' is intended to render the monologic quality of *Shame* explicit and thematic. Its 'threes' resolve parodically in a Christian 'three-in-oneness'; its narrator *is* the author; and (once again betraying the influence of García Márquez) it projects in every line the *solitude* of holding power.
28. García Márquez's Holy Book appears in the form of the parchments of Melquíades, with a similar sense of fatedness: 'Aureliano skipped eleven pages so as not to lose time with facts he knew only too well, and he began to decipher the instant he was living, deciphering it as he lived it, prophesying himself in the act of deciphering the last page of the parchments, as if he were looking into a speaking mirror . . . everything written on them was unrepeatable since time immemorial and forever more . . . ' (*One Hundred Years of Solitude* (New York: Vintage, 1972) p. 383).
29. Anthony Barnett, 'Salman Rushdie: A Review Article', *Race and Class*, vol. 26, no. 3 (Winter 1985) p. 97.
30. Jack Zipes, *Breaking the Magic Spell: Radical Theories of Folk and Fairy Tales* (New York: Methuem, 1979).
31. Jack Zipes, 'The Instrumentalization of Fantasy: Fairy Tales and the Mass Media', in Kathleen Woodward (ed.), *The Myths of Information: Technology and Post-industrial Culture* (Madison, Wisconsin: Coda Press, 1980) pp. 96–7.
32. Ibid., p. 100.
33. Eric Leed, ' "Voice" and "Print": Master Symbols in the History of Communication', in Woodward (ed.), *The Myths of Information*, p. 47.
34. Ibid., p. 54.
35. Ibid., pp. 46–7.
36. Zipes, *Breaking the Magic Spell*, p. 10.
37. This image is cited in Peter Worsley, *The Third World* (Chicago, Ill.: University of Chicago Press 1964).
38. Fredric Jameson, 'Postmodernism or the Cultural Logic of Late Capitalism', *New Left Review*, no. 146 (July–August 1984) p. 65; for a criticism of Jameson's view of a monolithic postmodernist world, see Dan Latimer, 'Jameson and Post-modernism', *New Left Review*, vol. 148 (November–December 1984) pp. 116–28. Latimer suggests Jameson overestimates its power because he prefers its style: 'Jameson recommends the conceptualization of a sublime appropriate for individual subjects fixed in some vast network of international business'(p. 123).
39. Rushdie's awareness of the humanistic strain defining his tradition is evident in his review of Vargas Llosa:

Vargas Llosa sets down with appalling and ferocious clarity his vision of the tragic consequences for ordinary people of millenarianism of any kind. . . . The political vision of *The War of the End of the World* is bleak, and it would be possible to take issue with such absolute bleakness. . . . But the greater qualities of this excellent novel are . . . its refusal ever to abandon the human dimensions. ('Peruvian Master', *New Republic*, 8 October 1984, pp. 25–8)

40. The effect of transnational media on the experience of 'belonging' seems such an obvious concern for critics of postmodernism – and one that leads so naturally to the concept of the *nation* – that it is strange that socially-minded critics like Jameson and Foster have not raised it. The issue has perhaps been easier to see in the Third World, especially in connection with the problem of state coercion. See Mabel Moraña, *Literatura y Culturar Nacional en Hispanoamérica (1910–1940)* (Minneapolis, Minn.: Institute for the Study of Ideologies and Literature, 1984) p. 2:

> Así entendido [i.e. national culture] como un esfuerzo de producción y colectivización de la experiencia a través del cual el indivíduo logra representarse como ser social, adquirir memoria de si mismo y projectarse en la comunidad, es obvivo que el nivel cultural requiere para su mantenimiento y desarrollo, mecanismos participativos y de intercomunicación social que el actual regimen político de muchos países latinoamericanos, fundado en la institucionalización de la violencia, no puede permitir.

Translation

> Understood [that is, national culture] as a force of production and collectivised experience in which individuals come to think of themselves as social beings, and in which they become self-conscious and imagine themselves part of a larger community, it is obvious that the cultural level necessary for its maintenance and development requires participatory mechanisms and forms of social intercommunication that the current political order in many Latin American countries, founded on the institutionalisation of violence, cannot allow.

Notes for Chapter 6: Pitting Levity against Gravity

1. Edouard Blissant, *Le discours antillais* (Paris: Editions du Seuil, 1981) p. 265.
2. I thank Syed Hassan for pointing out this reference to me, and for translating from the Urdu. Hassan points out that Iqbal was angrily denounced in the mosque as a *'kafir'* or blasphemer, but

that his reputation suffered very little, and his life was never in danger. Incidentally, it is important to point out that despite the way he has been misused by Jinnah and others, Iqbal was quite clear in opposing the partition of India – a case of literary revision and distortion that is relevant in this context.

3. Aga Shaid Ali, Ibrahim Abu-Lughod, Akeel Bilgrammi, Eqbal Ahmad, Edward W. Said, 'The Satanic Verses', *New York Review of Books*, 16 March 1989, p. 43.

4. Aamir Mufti, 'In the Realm of the Censors', *Voice Literary Supplement*, March 1989, p. 13.

5. Ibid., p. 13. Syed Shahabuddin, an Indian parliamentary opposition leader and head of a Muslim political group called the Babri Masjid Coordinating Committee, was at the centre of the successful attempts in October 1988 to have *The Satanic Verses* banned in India.

6. Aziz Al-Azmeh, 'The Satanic Flame', *New Statesman & Society*, 20 January 1989, p. 17.

7. Salman Rushdie, *The Satanic Verses* (New York: Viking Penguin, 1988) p. 94. All further references to this book will be given in the text.

8. Cited in John Leonard, 'Who Has the Best Tunes?', *The Nation*, 13 March 1989, p. 348.

9. Salman Rushdie, 'The Book Burning', *New York Review of Books*, 2 March 1989, p. 26.

10. Gerald Marzorati, 'Fiction's Embattled Infidel', *New York Times Magazine*, 26 January 1989, p. 45.

11. Salman Rushdie, 'Outside the Whale', *Granta*, no. 11 (1983) p. 125.

12. Salman Rushdie, 'The New Empire within Britain', *New Society*, 9 December 1982, p. 420.

13. Salman Rushdie, 'The Empire Writes Back with a Vengeance', *The Times*, 3 July 1982, p. 8.

14. For an account of the West Indian writers community in Britain in this period, see George Lamming, *The Pleasures of Exile* (London: Michael Joseph, 1960).

15. The range of writers suggested by this short list – all of whom have published their work within the last twenty years – is extensive, and corresponds to the rise of black-run publishing houses such as the *Race Today* Collective, Bogle-L'Ouverture, New Beacon, Creation for Liberation and others. For some idea of the breadth of arts activity among the contemporary black communities, see Kwesi Owusu, *The Struggle for Black Arts in Britain: What We Can Consider Better Than Freedom* (London: Comedia Publishers Group, 1986).

16. A. Sivanandan, 'The Struggle for Black Arts in Britain', *Race and Class*, vol. XXVIII (Summer 1986) p. 77.

17. See, for example, his introduction to Derek Bishton and John Reardon, *Home Front* (London: Jonathan Cape, 1984) and his book jacket endorsements of Peter Fryer, *Staying Power: The History of Black People in Britain* (London and Sydney: Pluto Press, 1984).

18. See Anwar Iqbal, 'I Borrowed My Expressions from the East'

(interview with Rushdie), *The Muslim Magazine*, 18 November 1983, p. 1. Thanks to Syed Hassan for directing me to this poem by Muhammad Iqbal.

19. I thank Ketu Katrak for first pointing this reference out to me, and Suranjan Ganguly for supplying me with the sources to fill in the details.

20. Firoze Rangoonwalla, *A Pictorial History of Indian Cinema* (London: Hamlyn, 1979) p. 24.

21. B. Lewis, Ch. Pellat and J. Schact (eds), *The Encyclopedia of Islam, New Edition* (London: Luzac, 1965) p. 363.

22. Ibid., p. 117.

23. Ibid., p. 286.

24. These lines can be found in Rushdie's manuscript of the novel on p. 32. They were edited out of the text before final publication.

25. Paul Gilroy, *There Ain't No Black in the Union Jack* (London: Hutchinson, 1987) pp. 155–6.

26. Frantz Fanon, *The Wretched of the Earth* (New York: Grove Press, 1963) p. 239.

27. Antonio Gramsci, 'Individual Man and Mass Man', *Antología* (La Habana: Instituto Cubano del Libro, 1973) p. 283.

Select Bibliography

WORKS BY RUSHDIE

Rushdie, Salman, 'After Midnight', *Vanity Fair*, September 1987, pp. 88–94.

———, 'Author from Three Countries' (interview), *New York Times Book Review*, 13 November 1983, pp. 3, 22–3.

———, 'The Book Burning', *The New York Review of Books*, 2 March 1989, p. 26.

———, 'Calvino', *London Review of Books*, 17 September–30 September 1981, pp. 16–17.

———, 'A Dangerous Art Form', *Third World Book Review*, vol. I (1984) pp. 3–5.

———, 'Dynasty and Democracy', *New Republic*, vol. 26 (November 1984) pp. 17–19.

———, 'The Empire Writes Back with a Vengeance', *The Times*, 3 July 1982, p. 8.

———, essay in George Theiner (ed.), *They Shoot Writers Don't They?* (New York: Faber and Faber, 1984).

———, Foreword to Tariq Ali, *An Indian Dynasty: The Story of the Nehru–Gandhi Family* (New York: Putnam, 1985).

———, 'The Free Radio', *Atlantic*, June 1983, pp. 23–5.

———, 'The Golden Bough', *Granta*, vol. 7 (1982) pp. 47–51.

———, *Grimus* (London: Alfred A. Knopf, 1975).

———, 'I Borrowed My Expressions from the East', *The Muslim Magazine* (Islamabad), 18 November 1983, p. 1.

———, 'Imaginary Homelands', *London Review of Books*, October 1982, pp. 18–19.

———, Introduction to Derek Bishton and John Reardon, *Home Front* (London: Jonathan Cape, 1984).

———, *The Jaguar Smile: A Nicaraguan Journey* (New York: Viking, 1987).

———, 'The Location of Brazil', *American Film*, vol. 10 (September 1985) pp. 50–3.

———, *Midnight's Children* (New York: Avon, 1980).

———, '*Midnight's Children* and *Shame*' (lecture/interview at the University of Aarhus, 7 October 1983) *Kunapipi*, vol. VII, no. 1 (1985) pp. 4–6.

———, 'My Book Speaks for Itself', *New York Times*, 17 February 1989, p. 23.

———, 'The New Empire within Britain', *New Society*, 9 December 1982, pp. 34–7.

———, 'On Günter Grass', *Granta*, vol. 15 (985) pp. 180–5.

———, 'On Palestinian Identity: a Conversation with Salman Rushdie' (with Edward Said), *New Left Review*, vol. 160 (November–December 1986) pp. 63–81.

———, 'Outside the Whale', *Granta*, vol. 11 (1983) pp. 123–41; also

in *American Film*, vol. 10 (January–February 1985) pp. 16, 70, 72–3.
——, 'Peruvian Master' (review of *The War of the End of the World*, by Mario Vargas Llosa), *New Republic*, 8 October 1984, pp. 25–8.
——, 'The Press: International Viewpoint', *The Times Literary Supplement*, 21 February 1986, p. 190.
——, 'Prophet's Hair', *Atlantic*, June 1981, pp. 23–9.
——, 'Raggedy Gandhi', *The Movies*, July 1983, p. 14.
——, *The Satanic Verses* (New York and London: Viking/Penguin, 1988).
——, *Shame* (New York: Vintage/Aventura, 1984).
——, 'Song Doesn't Know the Score', *Black Film British Cinema*, ICA Documents 7 (London: Institute of Contemporary Arts, 1988) pp. 16–17.
——, 'Yorick', *Encounter*, vol. LIX (September–October 1982) pp. 3–8.
——, 'Zia Unmourned', *Nation*, 19 September 1988, pp. 188–9.

WORKS ABOUT RUSHDIE

Al-Azmeh, Aziz, 'The Satanic Flame', *New Statesman and Society*, 20 January 1989, pp. 16–17.
Ali, Tariq, 'Midnight's Children', *New Left Review*, vol. 136 (November–December 1982) pp. 87–95.
Allison, Lincoln, 'Race, Reason, and Mr Rushdie', *New Society*, 13 January 1983, pp. 53–4.
Arguello, Xavier, 'The Writer as Tourist' (review of *The Jaguar Smile*), *New Republic*, 29 April 1987, pp. 30–4.
Bader, Rudolf, 'Indian *Tin Drum*', *International Fiction Review*, vol. 11 (Summer 1984) pp. 75–83.
Barnett, Anthony, 'Salman Rushdie: a Review Article', *Race and Class* (Winter 1985) pp. 91–8.
Brennan, Timothy, 'India, Nationalism, and Other Failures', *South Atlantic Quarterly*, vol. 87, no. 1 (Winter 1988) 131–46.
——, '*Shame*'s Holy Book', *Journal of Indian Writing in English*, vol. 16, no. 2 (July 1988) pp. 210–27.
Couto, Maria, 'Midnight's Children and Parents: the Search for Indo–British Identity', *Encounter*, vol. LVIII, no. 2 (February 1982) pp. 61–6.
Cunningham, Valentine, 'Nosing Out the Indian Reality', *The Times Literary Supplement*, 15 May 1981, p. 38.
Dissanayake, Wimal, 'Towards a Decolonized English: South Asian Creativity in Fiction', *World Englishes*, vol. no. 2 (1985) pp. 233–42.
Durix, Jean–Pierre, 'The Artistic Journey in Salman Rushdie's *Shame*', *World Literature Written in English*, Spring 1984, pp. 451–63.
Edgar, David, 'The Migrant's Vision', *New Left Review*, vol. 144 (March–April 1984) pp. 124–8.
Enright, D. J., 'So, and Not So', *New York Review of Books*, 2 March 1989, pp. 25–6.

Glendinning, Victoria, 'A Novelist in the Country of the Mind', *The Sunday Times*, 25 October 1981, p. 38.

Grove, Lloyd, 'Salman Rushdie: Caught Between Two Worlds', *International Herald Tribune*, 27 May 1986, p. 37.

Hoggart, Simon, 'Rushdie to Judgment', *New Society*, 17 February 1983, p. 267.

Hollington, Michael, 'Salman Rushdie's *Shame*', *Meanjin*, September 1984, pp. 403–7.

Hyman, Timothy, 'Back to Bom', *London Magazine*, December 1981–January 1982, p. 23.

——, 'Fairy-tale Agitprop', *London Magazine*, October 1983, p. 40.

Johansen, Ib, 'The Flight from the Enchanter: Reflections on Salman Rushdie's *Grimus*', *Kunapipi*, vol. VII (1985) pp. 53–61.

Jussawalla, Feroza, 'Beyond Indianness: The Stylistic Concerns of "Midnight's Children" ', in *Family Quarrels: Towards a Criticism of Indian Writing in English* (New York: Peter Lang, 1985) pp. 103–33.

Leppard, Dave, 'Round Midnight', *Guardian*, 23 October 1981.

Mars-Jones, Adam, 'A Marriage of Two Minds', *The Times Literary Supplement*, vol. 9 (September 1983) p. 949.

Marzorati, Gerald, 'Fiction's Embattled Infidel', *New York Times Magazine*, 29 January 1989, pp. 24–5, 27, 44–5, 47–8, 100.

Massing, Michael, 'Snap Books', *New Republic*, 4 May 1987, pp. 21–5.

Mojtabai, A. G., 'Magical Mystery Pilgrimage', *New York Times Book Review*, 29 January 1989, pp. 3, 37.

Mufti, Aamir, 'In the Realm of the Censors', *Voice Literary Supplement*, March 1989, p. 13.

Mukherjee, Bharati, 'Prophet and Loss', *Voice Literary Supplement*, March 1989, p. 13.

Nazareth, Peter, 'Salman Rushdie's *Midnight's Children*', *World Literature Written in English*, vol. 21 (Spring 1982) pp. 169–71.

Needham, Anuradha Dingwaney, 'The Politics of Post-Colonial Identity in Salman Rushdie', *The Massachusetts Review*, vol. 29, no. 4 (Winter 1988–1989) pp. 609–24.

Parameswaran, Uma, 'Handcuffed to History: Salman Rushdie's Art', *Ariel*, vol. 14 (October 1983) pp. 34–45.

——, 'Autobiography as History: Saleem Sinai and India in Rushdie's *Midnight's Children*', *Toronto South Asia Review*, vol. I (Summer 1982) pp. 27–34.

Ram, N., ' "My Book Being Put in Jail": Rushdie', *The Hindu*, 10 October 1988, p. 2.

Sangari, Kum Kum, 'The Politics of the Possible', *Cultural Critique*, no. 7 (Fall 1987) pp. 157–86.

Sanghi, Malavika Rajbans, ' "You Fight to Like Where You Live" ' *Indian Express Magazine*, 20 March 1983, p. 1.

Sethi, Sunil, 'After Midnight', *India Today*, 15 April 1983.

——, 'An Indian Scheherazade', *India Today*, 16 May 1981, pp. 126–7.

Special Correspondent, 'Defaming Celebrities, Kings and Premiers', *The Hindu*, 5 August 1984, p. 1.

Towers, Robert, review of *Midnight's Children, New York Review of Books*, 24 September 1981, p. 30.

Watson-Williams, Helen, 'An Antique Land: Salman Rushdie's *Shame'*, *Westerly*, December 1984, pp. 37–45.

West, Richard, 'Rushdie and the Raj', *Spectator*, 7 April 1984, pp. 18–19.

Wilson, Keith, *'Midnight's Children* and Reader Responsibility', *Critical Quarterly*, vol. 26 (Autumn 1984) pp. 23–37.

SELECTED SECONDARY SOURCES

Abdel–Malek, Anouar, *Nation and Revolution* (vol. 2 of *Social Dialectics*) (Albany, N.Y.: State University of New York Press, 1981).

——, and Anisuzzaman (eds), *Culture and Thought: The Transformation of the World* (New York: United Nations University, in association with St Martin's Press, 1983).

Achebe, Chinua, *Morning Yet on Creation Day: Essays* (Garden City, New York: Anchor Press, 1975).

Ahmad, Aijaz, 'Jameson's Rhetoric of Otherness and the "National Allegory"', *Social Text*, vol. 17 (Fall 1987) pp. 3–25.

Ali, Tariq, *Can Pakistan Survive?: The Death of a State* (Harmondsworth, Middx.: Penguin, 1983).

Amin, Samir, *Class and Nation*, trans. Susan Kaplow (New York and London: Monthly Review Press, 1980).

Anand, Mulk Raj, *Roots and Flowers: Two Lectures on the Metamorphoses of Technique and Content in the Indian–English Novel* (Dharwar: Karnatak University, 1972).

Anderson, Benedict, *Imagined Communities: Reflections on the Origin and Spread of Nationalism* (London: Verso and New Left Books, 1983).

Anderson, Perry, 'Components of the National Culture', *New Left Review*, vol. 50 (July–August 1968) pp. 3–73.

Basham, A. L. (ed.), *A Cultural History of India* (Oxford: Clarendon Press, 1975).

Barnett, Lionel D., *Hindu Gods and Heroes* (Delhi: Ess Ess, 1977).

Beck, Lois, and Nikki Keddie (eds), *Women in the Muslim World* (Cambridge, Mass.: Havard University Press, 1979).

Brata, Sasthi, *India: Labyrinths in the Lotus Land* (New York: William Morrow, 1985).

Brennan, Timothy, 'Fantasy, Individuality, and the Politics of Liberation', *Polygraph*, vol. 1 (Winter 1987) pp. 89–100.

Brown, Normon O., 'The Apocalypse of Islam', *Social Text*, vol. 8, (Winter 1983–4) p. 166.

Cabral, Amílcar, *Unity and Struggle* (New York and London: Monthly Review Press, 1979).

Césaire, Aimé, *Discourse on Colonialism*, trans. Joan Pinkham (New York: Monthly Review Press, 1972).

Chaliand, Gerard, *Revolution in the Third World: Myths and Prospects* (New York: Viking Press, 1977).

Clifford, James, and Groege Marcus (eds), *Writing Culture: The Poetics and Politics of Ethnography* (Berkeley, Calif.: University of California Press, 1986).

Coppola, Carlo, 'Politics and the Novel in India: A Perspective', *Contributions to Asian Studies*, vol. 6 (1975) pp. 1–6.

Cultural Industries: A Challenge for the Future of Culture (Fontenoy: UNESCO, 1982).

Dante, Alighieri, 'The Universal Empire', passages from *De Monarchia* taken from *Old South Leaflets*, vol. 5, p. 123 (Boston, Mass.: Directors of the Old South Word, 1902) pp. 1–12.

Dashti, Ali, *In Search of Omar Khayyam*, trans. from Persian by L. P. Elwell-Sutton (New York: Columbia University Press, 1971).

Davis, Horace, *Towards a Marxist Theory of Nationalism* (New York and London: Monthly Review Press, 1978).

Debray, Regis, 'Marxism and the National Question', *New Left Review*, vol. 105 (September–October 1977) pp. 25–41.

Desai, Rashmi, *Indian Immigrants in Britain* (London: Oxford University Press, 1963).

Desani, G. V., *All about H. Hatterr* (New York: Farrar, Straus and Giroux, 1970).

Dhalla, Maneckji Nusservanji, *History of Zoroastrianism* (New York: AMS Press, 1977).

Dombroski, Robert, 'Antonio Gramsci and the Politics of Literature: a Critical Introduction', *Italian Quarterly*, xxv, nos 97 and 98 (Summer 1984; published in January of 1986) pp. 41–55.

Eagleton, Terry, *Exiles and Émigres: Studies in Modern Literature* (London: Chatto and Windus, 1970).

Fanon, Frantz, *Black Skin, White Masks* (New York: Grove Press, 1967).
——, *The Wretched of the Earth* (New York: Grove Press, 1968).

Fitzgerald, Edward, 'The Rubaiyat of Omar Khayyam of Naishapur', in *Norton Anthology of Poetry* (New York: Norton, 1975).

Flores Galindon, Alberto, *La Agonía de Mariátegui* (Lima, Peru: Centro de Estudios y Promoción del Desarrollo, 1982).

Foster, Hal (ed.), *The Anti-Aesthetic: Essays on Postmodern Culture* (Washington: Bay Press, 1983).

Franco, Jean, 'Beyond Ethnocentrism: Gender, Power, and the Third-World Intelligentsia', in Cary Nelson and Lawrence Grossberg (eds), *Marxism and the Interpretation of Culture* (Urbana and Chicago, Ill.: University of Illinois Press, 1988).
——, 'Dependency Theory and Literary History: the Case of Latin America', *Minnesota Review*, vol. 55 (Fall 1975) pp. 65–80.
——, 'The Limits of the Liberal Imagination: *One Hundred Years of Solitude* and *Nostromo*', *Punto de Contacto/Point of Contact*, vol. I (1975) pp. 4–17.
——, *The Modern Culture of Latin America: Society and the Artist* (Harmondsworth, Middx.: Penguin, 1967).

Fryer, Peter, *Staying Power: The History of Black People in Britain* (London and Sydney: Pluto Press, 1984).

García Márquez, Gabriel, *El Olor de la Guayaba, Conversaciones con Plinio Apuleyo Mendoza – Gabriel García Márquez* (Bogotá, Colombia: Editorial La Oveja Negra, 1982).

—, 'The Solitude of Latin America', *Granta*, vol. 9 (1983) pp. 55–61.

Gibb, H. A. R., *Mohammendanism: An Historical Survey* (London: Oxford University Press, 1949).

Gilroy, Paul, *There Ain't No Black on the Union Jack* (London: Hutchinson, 1987).

Gramsci, Antonio, *Antología*, ed. Gaspar Quintana, Selección y notas Manuel Sacrisán (La Habana: Instituto Cubano del Libro, 1973).

—, *Letteratura e vita nazionale* (Genoa: Editori Riuniti, Istituto Gramsci, 1971).

—, *Letters from Prison*, trans. and ed. Lynne Lawner (New York: Harper and Row, 1975).

—, *Quaderni del Carcere* (Turin: Giulio Einaudi editore, 1975), Edizione critica dell'Istituto Gramsci a cura di Valentino Gerrantana.

—, 'Some Aspects of the Southern Question', *The Modern Prince and Other Writings* (New York: International Publishers, 1957).

Grant, James, *Cassell's Illustrated History of India*, vol. 1, part I (New Delhi: Oriental Publishers and Distributors, 1978).

Hacia una Política Cultural, Discursos Eligidos del FSLN (Managua, Nicaragua: Ministerio de Cultura, 1982).

Hall, Stuart, Chas Critcher, Tony Jefferson, John Clarke and Brian Roberts, *Policing the Crisis: Mugging, the State, and Law and Order* (Basingstoke, Hants.: Macmillan, 1978).

Hall, Stuart, 'The Toad in the Garden: Thatcherism among the Theorists', in Cary Nelson and Lawrence Grossberg (eds), *Marxism and the Interpretation of Culture* (Urbana and Chicago, Ill.: University of Illinois Press, 1988).

—, 'The Whites of their Eyes: Racist Ideologies and the Media', in George Bridges and Rosalind Brun (eds), *Silver Linings* (London: Lawrence and Wishart, 1981).

—, and Paddy Whannel, *The Popular Arts* (New York: Pantheon Books 1964).

Harlow, Barbara, *Resistance Literature* (London and New York: Methuen, 1987).

Harris, Wilson, 'Adversarial Contexts and Creativity', *New Left Review*, vol. 154. (November–December 1985).

—, *History, Fable and Myth in the Caribbean and Guianas* (Georgetown, Guyana: The National History and Arts Council, Ministry of Information and Culture, 1970).

—, *Tradition, the Writer, and Society* (London: New Beacon Publications, 1967).

Hayes, Carlton J. H., *The Historical Evolution of Modern Nationalism* (New York: Russell and Russell, 1931).

Hegel, Friedrich Wilhelm, 'Sovereignty *vis-à-vis* Foreign States', in *Philosophy of Right*, trans. T. M. Knox (London, Oxford, New York: Oxford University Press, 1952).

Hewison, Robert, *In Anger: Culture in the Cold War, 1945–60* (London: Weidenfeld and Nicolson, 1981).

Hobsbawm, Eric, 'Some Reflections on "The Break-up of Britain"', *New Left Review*, vol. 105 (September–October 1977) pp. 3–23

——, and Terence Ranger (eds), *The Invention of Tradition* (Cambridge: Cambridge University Press, 1983).

Hume, Kathryn, *Fantasy and Mimesis: Responses to Reality in Western Literature* (New York and London: Methuen, 1984).

Huysen, Andreas, 'Mapping the Postmodern', *New German Critique*, vol. 33 (Fall 1984) pp. 5–52.

Inglis, Fred, *Radical Earnestness: English Social Theory, 1880–1980* (Oxford: Martin Robertson, 1982).

Iyengar, K. R. S., *Indian Writing in English* (Bombay: Asia Publishing House, 1962).

Jameson, Frederic, 'Postmodernism of the Cultural Logic of Late Capitalism', *New Left Review*, vol. 146 (July–August 1984).

——, 'Third-World Literature in the Era of Multinational Capitalism', *Social Text*, vol. 15 (Fall 1986) pp. 65–88.

Jeffrey, Robin (ed.), *Asia – The Winning of Independence* (New York: St Martin's Press, 1981).

Kachru, Braj, *The Indianization of English* (Delhi: Oxford University Press, 1983).

——, *The Other Tongue: English Across Cultures* (Urbana, Ill.: University of Illinois Press, 1982).

——, 'Standards, Codification and Sociolinguistic Realism', in Randolph Quirk and H. G. Widdowson (eds), *English in the World: Teaching and Learning the Language and Literatures* (Cambridge: Cambridge University Press, for the British Council) pp. 11–31.

Keddie, Nikki and Lois Beck (eds), *Women in the Muslim World* (Cambridge, Mass.: Harvard University Press, 1979).

Kedourie, Elie, *Nationalism* (London: Hutchinson, 1960).

Khalidi, Tarif, *Classical Arab Islam: The Culture and Heritage of the Golden Age* (Princeton, N.J.: Darwin Press, 1985).

Kiernan, V. G., 'Gramsci and the Other Continents', *New Edinburgh Review*, no. 24 (1974) p. 20.

——, *The Lords of Human Kind: European Attitudes Towards the Outside World in the Imperial Age* (Harmondsworth, Middx.: Penguin, 1969).

King, Bruce, *The New English Literatures* (London: Macmillan, 1980).

Kipling, Rudyard, 'The Rubaiyat of Omar Kalvin', in *Departmental Ditties and Ballads* and *Barrack Room Ballads* (Garden City and New York: Doubleday Page, 1926).

Kohn, Hans, *A History of Nationalism in the East* (London: George Routledge, 1929).

——, *Nationalism: Its Meaning and History* (New York and Cincinnati, Ohio: D. Van Nostrand, 1965).

——, *The Koran*, trans. with notes by N. J. Dawood (Harmondsworth, Middx.: Penguin, 1974).

Lall, Arthur, *The Emergence of Modern India* (New York: Columbia University Press, 1981).

Lamming, George, *The Pleasures of Exile* (London: Michael Jospeh, 1960).

——, C. L. R. James and Wilson Harris, *Kas-Kas: Interviews with Three Caribbean Writers in Texas*, occasional publication of African and Afro-American Research Institute (Austin, Tx.: University of Texas, 1972).

Layoun, Mary, 'The Strategy of Narrative Form', *Critical Exchange*, vol. 22 (Spring 1987) pp. 37–41.

Lenin, Vladimir Ilych, *Critical Remarks on the National Question* and *The Right of Nations of Self-Determination* (Moscow: Progress Publishers, 1971).

Lewis, Gordon K., *Slavery, Imperialism, and Freedom: Studies in English Radical Thought* (New York and London: Monthly Review Press, 1978).

Lippman, Thomas W., *Understanding Islam: An Introduction to the Moslem World* (New York: Mentor, 1982).

Lukacs, John, Edward Said and Gerald Graff, 'Orwell's Legacy: A Discussion', *Salmagundi*, nos 70–1 (Spring–Summer 1986) pp. 121–9.

Luthi, Max, *The Fairytale as Art Form and Portrait of Man*, trans. Jon Erikson (Bloomington, Ind.: Indiana University Press, 1975).

MacCabe, Colin, 'English Literature in a Global Context', in Randolph Quirk and H. G. Widdowson (eds), *English in the World: Teaching and Learning the Language and Literatures* (Cambridge: Cambridge University Press, for the British Council, 1988) pp. 37–47.

Many Voices, One World, report by the International Commission for the Study of Communication Problems (the MacBride Commission Report) (London: Kogan Page; New York and Paris: UNESCO, 1980).

Mariátegui, José Carlos, *Seven Interpretive Essays on Peruvian Reality*, trans. Majory Urquidi (Austin, Tx. and London: University of Texas Press, 1971).

Marx, Karl, and Frederick Engels, *The First Indian War of Independence, 1857–1859* (Moscow: Progress Publishers, 1959).

——, *On Colonialism* (Moscow: Foreign Languages Publishing House; London: Lawrence and Wishart, 1980).

Mattelart, Armand, and Seth Siegelaub (eds), *Communication and Class Struggle*, vol. II (New York: International General; Bagnolet, France International Mass Media Research Centre, 1983).

Meyers, Jeffrey, *Fiction and the Colonial Experience* (Ipswich, Suffolk: Boydell Press, 1973).

Mohan, Ramesh (ed.), *Indian Writing in English*, papers read at the seminar on Indian English held at the Central Institute of English and Foreign Languages, Hyderabad, July 1972 (Bombay: Orient Longman, 1978).

Moraña, Mabel, *Literatura y Cultura Nacional en Hispanoamérica (1910–1940)* (Minneapolis, Minnesota: Institute for the Study of Ideologies and Literature, 1984).

Mukherjee, Meenakkshi, *The TTwwice Born Fiction: Themes and Techniques of the Indian Novel in English* (New Delhi, London: Heinemann, 1971).

M. K. Naik, 'The Political Novel in Indian Writing in English', *Contributions to Asian Studies*, vol. 6 (1975) pp. 6–16

——, S. K. Desai and G. S. Amur (eds), *Critical Essays on Indian Writing in English* (Dharwar: Karnatak University, 1968).

Naipaul, V. S., *An Area of Darkness* (New York: Macmillan, 1965).

——, *India: A Wounded Civilization* (New York: Knopf, 1972).

Nairn, Tom, *The Break-up of Britain: Crisis and Neo-Nationalism* (London: New Left Books, 1977).

Narasimhaiah, C. D. (ed.), *Indian Literature of the Past Fifty Years (1917–1967)* (Prasaranga: University of Mysore, 1970).
——, *Literary Criticism: European and Indian Traditions* (Prasaranga: University of Mysore, 1965).
Nicholson, Kai, *A Presentation of Social Problems in the Indo-Anglian and Anglo-Indian Novel* (Bombay: Jaico Publishing House, 1972).
Nowell-Smith, Geoffrey, 'Gramsci and the National Popular', *Screen Education*, vol. 22 (Spring 1977) pp. 12–15.
O'Brien, Conor Cruise, Edward Said and John Lukács, 'The Post-Colonial Intellectual: a Discussion', *Salmagundi*, no. 70–1 (Spring–Summer, 1986) pp. 65–82.
O'Flaherty, Wendy, *Asceticism and Eroticism in the Mythology of Siva* (London: Oxford University Press, 1973).
Orwell, George, Introduction to *Talking to India: A Selection of English Language Broadcasts to India* (London: George Allen and Unwin, 1943).
——, *Orwell: The War Broadcasts*, ed. W. J. West (London: Duckworth, 1985).
Owusu, Kwesi, *The Struggle for Black Arts in Britain: What We Can Consider Better than Freedom* (London: Comedia Publishers Group, 1986).
Patel, Vibhuti, 'Women's Liberation in India', *New Left Review*, vol. 153 (September–October 1985) pp. 75–87.
Pratt, Mary Louise, 'Nationalizing Exoticism', *Inscriptions*, vol. 2 (1986) pp. 27–36.
Propp, Vladimir, *Theory and History of Folklore*, ed. with Introduction and Notes by Anatoly Liberman, trans. Ariadna Martin and Richard Martin and several other (Minneapolis, Minn.: University of Minnesota Press, 1984).
Quirk, Randolph, 'The English Language in a Global Context', Quirk and H. G. Widdowson (eds), *English in the World: Teaching and Learning the Language and Literatures* (Cambridge: Cambridge University Press, for the British Council, 1985) pp. 7–11.
Rama, Angel, *Transculturación narrativa an América Latina* (Mexico City: Siglo veintiuno editores, 1982).
Rangoonwalla, Firoze, *A Fictional History of Indian Cinema* (London: Hamlyn, 1979).
Raynal, Abbe, *Philosophical and Political History of the Settlements and Trade of the Europeans in the East and West Indies*, trans. J. O. Justamond (London: A. Strahan and T. Cadell, 1788).
Reddy, G. A., *Indian Writing in English and its Audience* (Bareilly: Parkash Book Depot, 1979).
Said, Edward, 'The Mind of Winter: Reflections on Life in Exile', *Harpers Magazine*, vol. 269 (September 1984) pp. 47–55.
——, *Orientalism* (New York: Vintage, 1979).
——, *The World, the Text, the Critic* (Cambridge, Mass.: Harvard University Press, 1983).
Sarma, Gobinda Prasad, *Nationalism in Indo-Anglian Fiction* (New Delhi: Sterling Publishers, 1978).
Schiller, Herbert, *Communication and Cultural Domination* (White Plains, New York: International Arts and Sciences Press, 1976).

—— (ed.), *National Sovereignty and International Communications* (anthology) (Norwood, NJ: Ablex Publishing, 1979).

Seton-Watson, Hugh, *Nations and States: An Enquiry into the Origins of Nations and the Politics of Nationalism* (Boulder, Col.: Westview Press, 1977).

Sivanandan, A., *A Different Hunger: Writings on Black Resistance* (London: Pluto Press, 1982).

Smith, Vincent A., *The Oxford History of India*, 3rd edn (Oxford: Clarendon Press, 1958).

Sridhar, Kamal K., 'English in a South Indian Urban Context', in *The Other Tongue: English Across Cultures* (Urbana, Ill.: University of Illinois Press, 1982) pp. 141–54.

Stutley, Margaret and James Stutley, *A Dictionary of Hinduism: Its Mythology, Folklore, and Development, 1500 BC–AD 1500* (London: Routledge and Kegan Paul, 1977).

Todorov, Tzvetan, *Mikhail Bakhtin: The Dialogic Principle*, trans. Wlad Godzich (Minneapolis, Minn.: University of Minnesota Press, 1984).

Touré, Sékou, 'A Dialectical Approach to Culture', *Black Scholar*, vol. I (November 1969) pp. 11–27.

Trotsky, Leon, *The Permanent Revolution* and *Results and Prospects* (New York: Pathfinder Press, 1969).

Turner, Bryan S., *Marx and the End of Orientalism* (London: Allen and Unwin, 1978).

Vanaik, Achin, 'The Rajiv Congress in Search of Stability', *New Left Review*, vol. 154 (November–December 1985) pp. 55–83.

Visram, Rozina, *Ayahs, Lascars, and Princes: Indians in Britain, 1700–1947* (London: Pluto Press, 1986).

Williams, Raymond, 'Notes on Marxism in Britain since 1945', *New Left Review*, vol. 100 (November 1976–January 1977).

The Year 2000 (New York: Pantheon Books, 1983).

Wolf, Eric, *Europe and the People without History* (Berkeley, Calif.: University of California Press, 1982).

Wolpert, Stanley, *A New History of India*, 2nd edn (London: Oxford University Press, 1982).

Woodward, Kathleen (ed.), *The Myths of Information: Technology and Postindustrial Culture* (Madison, Wisconsin: Coda Press, 1980).

Worsely, Peter, *The Third World* (Chicago, Ill.: University of Chicago Press, 1964).

The Three Worlds: Culture and World Development (Chicago, Ill.: University of Chicago Press, 1984).

Zipes, Jack, *Breaking the Magic Spell: Radical Theories of Folk and Fairy Tales* (New York: Methuen, 1979).

——, 'The Instrumentalization of Fantasy: Fairy Tales and the Mass Media', in Kathleen Woodward (ed.), *The Myths of Information: Technology and Post-Industrial Culture* (Madison, Wisconsin: Coda Press, 1980).

Index

193